THEREBY HANGS A TALE

THEREBY HANGS A TALE

Stories of Curious Word Origins

by

Charles Earle Funk, Litt.D.

Author of
A HOG ON ICE AND OTHER CURIOUS EXPRESSIONS

HARPER & ROW, PUBLISHERS

New York, Evanston, and London

To

B. M. F.

*Who patiently and often has listened
to many of these tales, this book is
lovingly dedicated.*

PREFACE

THIS book is the outcome of a collection of material that has been slowly accumulating over the past thirty years or so, since the time when, under the guidance of the late Dr. Frank H. Vizetelly, I began to work as his associate in the editorial department of the Funk & Wagnalls New Standard Dictionary. The ancestry of most of the words that we now use glibly or find in books or other current literature, is prosaic. We can trace their lines of descent back to Old English, or Old French, or Latin, or Greek, or other ancient source, but beyond the bare bones supplied by etymologists, which indicate those sources, and the steps by which they became English words, the dictionaries tell us little—for there is little more that can be told. The ancient Roman or Greek, say, who may have been the first to use a word that has strayed on to us, perhaps could have told the story of its origin. It may have been picturesque, based upon some historic episode, like the word *anecdote*; it may have come from a tale in some older language, for the languages that we consider ancient were themselves based upon still more ancient sources, but that story, if any, cannot now be determined. Thus what we know about the origins of the great majority of the words in our present language can be found in an unabridged dictionary or in a work dealing with etymologies, such as that compiled by W. W. Skeat about seventy years ago, or the one more recently prepared by Ernest Weekley.

But there are in our current language a number of fairly common words—some old, some new—which were born, or grew, or acquired their meanings in an unusual manner. They came, as our language has, from all sources—sources of which the dictionaries, for lack of space, can rarely supply more than a clue. These are the tales that I have been collecting and which are offered here. A number of them may be already familiar to some readers, such as the origin of *tantalize*, from the Greek legend of the punishment

vii

meted out to Tantalus by the wrathful Zeus, or *echo*, from the fate of the perfidious nymph of that name. Such tales, though familiar to some, are included here for the benefit of those to whom they may be new. But I have found that few but scholars in the language know how the word *clue*, which was just used, acquired its present meaning; that the Portuguese gave us *coconut* because, to their sailors in the sixteenth century, the nut resembled a *coco*, "a grinning face"; that *sylph* was a coinage of that master charlatan or genius, depending upon the point of view, the sixteenth-century alchemist, Paracelsus; that we owe our terms *chapel* and *chaplain* to the cloak or cape worn by the fourth-century monk, St. Martin; that the name *Easter* was taken from a pagan goddess, and that the names of the days of the week denote dedication to ancient pagan gods.

Whenever it has been possible, the stories are historical; that is, for example, facts in the life of St. Martin are briefly stated to explain why his cloak was venerated; the occasion for the coinage of *sylph* by Paracelsus is summarized; a brief account tells why *magenta* commemorated a battle; short sketches of the invasions of the Vandals and Tatars account for such words as *vandal, tartar,* and *horde*; highly abridged biographies of such persons as the Scottish engineer, John L. McAdam, the Scottish chemist, Charles Macintosh, and others, tell why their names were adopted into the language; an explanation is deduced why the French general, Martinet, became a byword in English, but not in French; the historical circumstances that introduced the word *nepotism* are related, and so on, and so on.

To the best of my knowledge, no similar collection of tales accounting for such a number of English words has yet appeared. The facts have been drawn from numerous sources and have been carefully checked. It would be impossible to list all the authorities that have been consulted during the years through which the material has been collected; they have been numerous, embracing many languages. Murray's *A New English Dictionary on Historical Principles*, usually referred to as the *Oxford English Dictionary*, has been an invaluable aid and has supplied clues to many older references; the various encyclopedias, not only English, but also French, German, and Italian, brought other information to light; considerable source material was obtained from Sir William Smith's *Dic-*

tionary of Greek and Roman Antiquities, checked against later findings, which sometimes gave occasion for variant stories; the files of the British *Notes & Queries,* as well as the American *Notes & Queries,* were frequently consulted, as well as a number of volumes dealing with medieval life and customs. With few exceptions, the stories as written are entirely my own, and those exceptions have been duly accredited to their authors. I am indebted to Robert (Bob) Burns for the account, by letter, of his creation of the term *bazooka;* to Mr. R. W. Henderson, also by letter, for his findings on the word *tennis,* and to Mr. H. L. Mencken, and his publisher, for permission to reprint his conclusions, in which I concur, on the origin of *yankee.*

Sometimes, because of the relationship existing between some of our words, it has seemed advisable to group several words together to avoid repetition. Thus, for example, *augur* and *inaugurate* are related, and a common story suffices for each; so are *money* and *mint, eliminate* and *preliminary,* and various others. Similarly, though in different manner, is there relationship between such divergent words as *grotesque* and *antic, matinee* and *noon, monster* and *prodigy, foreign* and *denizen,* and others. These also have usually been grouped into common stories. Hence, although the book is alphabetical in general arrangement and no index is therefore essential for the main list of words, an index is provided at the end of the book to show under what heading other words may be found. Thus: *augur,* see *inaugurate; mint,* see *money; grotesque,* see *antic,* and so on. The index also includes the names of the persons, mythological characters, and places directly associated with a word-story, as well as those persons to whom the author is indebted for material. Thus: *David,* see under *Abigail; Mencken, H. L.,* see under *Yankee; Theseus,* see under *clue,* etc.

Rarely, in this work, has an attempt been made to follow the various alterations in the form of a word from its ancient source. Although that has sometimes been done for the purpose of clarification, such lines of development have been left generally to etymologists. It may be well, however, to review with extreme brevity the general outlines of the main sources of our language for the benefit of those to whom the subject is new. With few exceptions, our commonest words—the prepositions, the pronouns, the conjunctions, the auxiliary verbs (do, may, can, have, be, etc., and their derivatives), and the common objects pertaining to domestic and agricultural life—have descended to us from the period known as Old English, sometimes referred to as Anglo-Saxon. Such words are usually of Teutonic origin, surviving from the early centuries of the Christian Era when England was conquered, overrun, and settled, its earlier occupants wiped out, by Angle, Saxon, and Danish invaders from regions now embraced by Germany and Denmark. The language introduced by these invaders, intermixed with each other and absorbing some of the older tongue, became standard speech until the eleventh century. It was chiefly a spoken language and there were few scholars to preserve its integrity. Consequently, through the centuries, the forms of the original words often became greatly altered and corrupted in common speech. Spelling in this period was usually phonetic, according to the values placed upon the alphabet that was then in use.

In the year 1066, William, duke of Normandy, with a well-armed force of sixty thousand followers, entered England, defeated Harold II, the Saxon king, at Hastings, seized the throne and became the lord of the country. During the next two centuries, the English, or Saxons as they were called, were reduced almost to servitude by their conquerors. Norman-French became the language spoken by all except the common folk, and even they were driven to become somewhat familiar with it to understand the speech of their masters. All royal proclamations and the proceedings of all law courts were also in that language. Thus, through that period, many Old French words were grafted upon the language. And again, through the general illiteracy of the people, these in turn were corrupted in the common speech of a folk unaccustomed to French speech—like the French *naperon*, being first *a napron*, and then further corrupted to *an apron*.

But Old French was itself, to a considerable extent, an outgrowth of Latin. That is, just as William the Conqueror imposed his language upon the people of England, so, in the days of the emperors of Rome, had Latin been imposed upon the people of the conquered country that later became France. But it was largely the Latin of the Roman soldier quartered upon the country—a debased Latin—that became further corrupted when adopted into the native speech.

Many of our words thus trace back through Old French to a former Latin source.

Preceding the flood of Old French after the Norman Conquest by several centuries, and continuing steadily side by side through it and until at least the sixteenth century, our language was being enriched through another channel. That increment came through the form of Latin that we call Low or Medieval Latin and Late Latin, used by the fathers of the Christian Church and by the later priests and monks in their devotions and intercourse with one another. It was a development from classical Latin and formed a language common to all Europe, enabling the clergy to travel anywhere. It was also used in the church services of England. Hence, though some of the words became incorporated into our language without much change, others were sadly misunderstood by the illiterate listeners and were altered into strange meanings. Thus, for example, we have *patter* from *pater noster*, *dirge* from the funeral chant with the opening word, *dirige*, direct, *anthem* from *antiphon*, and so on.

This stage in the development of the language, in which Old French and Medieval Latin were mingled with the corrupted remnants of Old English, is referred to as Middle English. The works of Geoffrey Chaucer furnish an example of its later form. Spelling was, in a measure, phonetic, employing the Roman alphabet. But the sounds of words were often unlike those we now give to the same words, thus accounting for many of our modern spellings, such as *thought*, *eight*, *once*. There were no rules to guide one in spelling; each man spelled according to the way words sounded to him. Hence, any uniformity that may have existed was accidental.

Finally, without considering here the immense number of words that we have constantly borrowed from every language with which English-speaking people have been in contact, we owe a large volume of our words to the period that we call Modern English, beginning, roughly, with the sixteenth century. Scholarship, previously limited largely to the clergy, was opened to all, and the study of classical learning became a fetish. Writers and thinkers sprang up from every walk of life, and did not hesitate to cull their words from the Latin of Cicero, or Horace, or Ovid, or Seneca. Many also went to the Greek of Æschylus, or Plato, or Plutarch to derive their words. It is thus chiefly through these writers and their unceasing stream of successors that the great bulk of words derived directly from Latin and Greek ancestry and meanings have entered our language. From this practice also has descended our present custom of looking to one or another of those languages for the formation of new words, especially those of scientific nature.

At the beginning of this last period, the old dialectal pronunciations continued to influence the spellings of the older language. Many of those pronunciations, in fact, were carried along in cultured speech until the seventeenth century or later, and continued in the common speech for at least another hundred years. With the advance of learning, our spelling, though continuously subjected to fads and mistaken notions, has gradually assumed a certain degree of uniformity. Because it still retains many of the sixteenth-century forms, however, it cannot be called phonetic. But it is highly probable that the unwieldy forms that we have inherited will disappear one by one in course of time, as the people find it more convenient to drop them.

CHARLES EARLE FUNK

September, 1949

THEREBY HANGS A TALE

abet

The so-called sport of bear-baiting was widely known among the Teutonic countries a thousand years ago, but it became nowhere more popular than in England, especially after the fourteenth century. For the pleasure of the spectators, a bear, freshly caught and starved enough to make it vicious, was fastened to a stake by a short chain or, it might be, was turned loose in a small arena. Then dogs were set upon it, fresh dogs being supplied if the first were maimed or killed. In the end, of course, after perhaps hours of sport, one of the dogs would succeed in seizing the exhausted bear by the throat and worry it to death. The man or boy who urged his dog to attack was said to *abet* it, using a contracted Old French word— *abeter*, meaning to bait, or hound on. The early French, in turn, had taken a Norse word, *beita*, which meant to cause to bite. So, though we now use *abet* in speaking of persons—chiefly of persons who encourage others in wrongful deeds—the word traces back to an Old Norse command to a dog, an order to attack, equivalent, perhaps, to the modern "Sic 'em!"

abeyance

When anything is in *abeyance* now we mean that it is in a state of inaction, that the matter, whatever it was, is dormant, although some action is expected to occur eventually. It was that expectancy that gave us the word, for it came as a law term, after the Norman Conquest, from the Old French *abeance*, a state of expectancy. The term referred especially to the condition of a property or title while, after the death of the former possessor, often by foul means in those days, his successor could be determined from among various claimants. The Old French word was derived from the verb *beer* (modern *bayer*), to gape, to expect, perhaps because of the gaping expectancy with which the settlement of an estate was awaited either by the rightful heir or by a hopeful usurper, none too certain that his claim would pass scrutiny.

abhor

When the hair stands up from fright or dread, we have the literal meaning of *abhor*. The Latin source of our verb was *abhorreo*, from *ab*, away from, and *horreo*, to stand on end, to bristle. Thus the literal meaning was to shrink back from with horror, but, though the verb still expresses great repugnance, it no longer conveys the notion of shuddering dread or fear that its use indicated to the Romans.

abigail

We must turn to the Bible to see why this feminine proper name started to become a synonym for servant. In the First Book of Samuel, the twenty-fifth chapter tells how David, in return for past favors, made a peaceful request to the wealthy Nabal for food for his followers. Nabal rejected the request and David was about to take by force what had been denied. But *Abigail*, Nabal's wife, heard of the affair. She learned, first, that the request was reasonable, then taking more food with her than had been requested, she went to David to turn away his wrath. She was just in time. Her abject apologies for the churlishness of her husband fill the next eight verses of the chapter; in them, to show her great humility, she refers to herself six times as David's "handmaid." The association of name and occupation was further fixed in men's minds by the dramatists, Beaumont and Fletcher. When writing the play, *The Scornful Lady*, in 1609, they gave the name *Abigail* to the very spirited lady's maid who had one of the leading parts. This character, or the actress who played the part, made so great an impression on the audiences that the later writers, Congreve, Swift, Fielding, Smollett, and others began to use the name as that of any lady's maid.

abominable

The Romans were intensely superstitious. Any chance event or chance remark that occurred on the eve of an undertaking was carefully examined to determine whether it might indicate good luck or bad luck. Thus Cicero tells us that Crassus, when about to embark upon his ill-fated expedition against the Parthians, should have turned back. At the harbor, a man selling dried figs from Caunus, gave the cry, "Cauneas!" to signify the source of his wares. This to the Romans sounded like "*Cave ne eas*," meaning, "Beware of going," which Crassus should have taken to be a sign of bad luck, an evil omen. Crassus had not heeded the warning, however, and was treacherously slain by the Parthians. Any such omen as that was considered to have been a clear portent of doom, amply warning one to avoid whatever undertaking he had in mind. For that reason it was described as *abominabilis*, from *ab*, away from, and *omen*. The early sense of the term, "direful, inspiring dread, ominous," came through association of ideas to mean "loathsome, disgusting," because it was usually loathsome things that were taken as omens of evil.

abound, abundant

When things are in such profusion as to be like the waves of the sea overflowing the land, we may properly say that they *abound*. Literally, that is what the word means. It comes to us from the Latin, *abundo*, to overflow, from *ab*, from, and *unda*, wave, billow, surge. Our words *abundant* and *abundance* have the same poetic source.

aboveboard

Card-playing has been known in Europe since about the middle of the thirteenth century, but it is not known how soon thereafter the players discovered ways to cheat their opponents. But by the late sixteenth century, at least, the players had learned that cheating was more difficult, more easily detected, if the cards around the table were all kept in open sight—literally, "above the board." This expression was used so frequently among card-players that it became contracted in the early seventeenth century to *aboveboard*.

academy

Helen, who later became noted as the owner of the "face that launched a thousand ships," was the fabled Grecian queen whose abduction by Paris brought on the Trojan War described by Homer almost three thousand years ago. As a little girl in Sparta her beauty was even then so remarkable that, according to legend, the Athenian prince, Theseus, was so affected by it when he saw her dancing that he seized and hid her, intending to hold her until she was old enough to become his wife. But her mother, Leda, sent her sons, the twins Castor and Pollux, to find their sister. When they reached Athens, the story goes, they found someone who could help them, an Athenian named Academus. It was through his assistance that Helen was recovered and returned to Sparta. The Spartans were so grateful, according to one account, that they purchased a grove on the outskirts of Athens and presented it to their benefactor. In later years, this spot became a public garden, known as the Grove of Academus.

About the year 387 B.C., the Athenian philosopher, Plato, took up his residence upon a plot of ground that he owned, which directly adjoined this grove. It then became his habit, when the young men of Athens came to pursue their studies under him, to walk and talk with them along the paths of this peaceful spot. Plato continued this mode of instruction during the rest of his life, or for about forty years, as he was about eighty when he died, so it is not surprising that among the Athenians the school that he conducted was called the *Academia*, after the name of the grove. And when he died, it was found that he had made arrangements, according to the customs of that day, for his own estate to be converted into a religious foundation sacred to the Muses, for in that way his school could be perpetuated as an institution of learning. Thus, through Plato's chance use of a grove that had been the legendary property of an obscure Athenian countryman, we have obtained our word *academy*.

accost

The early sense was nautical, so much so that it was often written *accoast*, as if the meaning were "to lie along the coast of." The original meaning was not far from that, because the word was derived from the Latin prefix *ad*, to, plus *costa*, which, though actually meaning "rib," was extended to "side." So the nautical meaning was "to lie alongside," almost, as it were, rib to rib. Later the meaning became less exact, "to approach for the purpose of addressing," and now we use it most frequently just in the sense of "to address."

acre

The Old English word was *æcer*. In the Middle Ages, however, it was adapted to the Latin of the period and became *acra*, which gave rise to our present spelling. The word originally meant unoccupied country, whether field or woodland. But through increased interest in agriculture, the meaning became limited to land that could be cultivated. And by the time of the Norman Conquest, the extent of that land had become limited to the area that a yoke of oxen could plow in one day. Through the course of the next two centuries that method of measurement was seen to be unfair, the land allotted to a tenant depended not only upon the condition of his oxen, but upon the kind and condition of the soil to be plowed. A good yoke of oxen on level ground and rich light soil could plow twice as much as an ill-conditioned yoke on hilly, stony ground. In the reign of Edward I, therefore, the acre was fixed as a piece of land 40 rods in length by four rods in width. (A rod measures 16½ feet.) The practical farmer of those days took this to be thirty-two furrows of the plow, a furlong in length. But it has been many centuries since the acre was necessarily rectangular; now it may be of any shape, though its area is still fixed at 160 square rods or 4,840 square yards, as in the days of King Edward. (See also FURLONG.)

acrobat

From time immemorial, perhaps as proof of our relationship with the ape, man has amused himself by performing feats of daring upon ropes—ropes hanging from trees or high structures, or ropes tautly or loosely stretched high between two trees or other supports. In ancient Greece, skill in such feats became highly developed, though, like most paid entertainers of that era, the reputation of the performers was not above suspicion. Any such performer was known as an *acrobat*, one who walks aloft, from Greek *akros*, aloft, and *batos*, climbing or walking. (The full Greek term, *akrobatos*, is translated by some to mean walking on tiptoe.) Today we would call such a man a rope-walker or rope-dancer. But, although all the performers were classed as acrobats, among themselves or other

well-informed persons they were separated into their several skills.
The *neurobat* was at the top of the profession; considered among
them as the true *acrobat*, for, as the name signified—*neuron*, sinew
—this aerial dancer exercised his skill upon tautly stretched cords
the thickness of catgut. So slender was the cord that, from a slight
distance, he appeared to be dancing lightly upon air, sometimes
playing the flute as he danced. The *schœnobat*—from *schoinion*,
rope twisted of rushes—performed upon a thick rope, suspended
from aloft, climbing it to dizzy heights, as a sailor does, tumbling
about it held by a foot or knee, and showing his great strength and
agility.

admiral

Abu-Bekr, the first successor to Mahomet, who died in A.D. 632,
had been his faithful follower for many years. Upon taking the
new title, *Caliph*, or "successor," he relinquished his former title,
"The Faithful." This latter title was then taken by Omar, the man
appointed to succeed him, who announced himself to be "Commander of the Faithful," or *Amir-al-muninin*. The title, "Commander," or *Amir* became increasingly popular after that. The
Caliph himself was *Amir-al-Umara*, "Ruler of Rulers"; the minister
of finance became *Amir-al-Ahgal*, and finally there came *Amir-al-
Alam*, "Commander of Banners," and *Amir-al-Hajj*, "Commander
of Caravans to Mecca."

Christian writers of the period naturally assumed that *Amir-al*
was a single word, *amiral*. Later English writers then assumed that
this word beginning with "am" was just another queer foreign way
of spelling Latin words that began with "adm." But, though they
now changed the spelling of the Moslem expression to *admiral*,
they retained the original meaning, ruler, or prince, or commander.
Italy, France, and Spain, however, began to follow the Saracen lead
with a "Commander of the Sea" (*Amir-al-Bahr*). England also, not
to be outdone, appointed such an officer for the British fleet in the
late fourteenth century, and gave him the title *Admiral*. Thus when
we say "Admiral Smith," we are using an Arabic expression which,
if the literal meaning were observed, would be "Commander of the
Smith," *Amir-al-Smith*.

afraid

Scarcely known nowadays, except in stories laid in olden times, is the verb *affray*. Its ancient meaning was "to startle out of one's rest," as by a clap of thunder or other sharp noise. That is, one who was *affrayed* was one who was alarmed. From alarm to fright was a natural development in meaning, so *affrayed*, in the sense of "frightened," had come to be common usage in the fourteenth century. Thanks to lack of uniform spelling before the eighteenth century, it has come down to us in the form *afraid*.

agony (antagonist)

Although we have since extended the meaning of this word to include intense physical suffering, such as we experience when in great pain, its original meaning in English referred to intense mental suffering or anguish, specifically that experienced by Christ in the Garden of Gethsemane, for it was in the English translation of the Bible in the fourteenth century that our word first appeared. This meaning was taken from the Greek *agonia*, but the way in which the Greek word developed that meaning is peculiar.

As far back as the days of Homer, *agon* denoted an assembly, a meeting of the people, usually for the discussion of public affairs. Hence, as time went by, any meeting of the Grecian people for any purpose came to be called an *agon*, especially one of the meetings devoted to games or contests. These contests might be athletic, such as the Olympic games, comprising foot races, wrestling, jumping, throwing the discus and the spear, or they might be musical, or for poetic competition, or for other competition in which one man or group might vie with another. From the place of the assembly, the *agon*, any such contest was an *agonia*.

Each *agonia* was, of course, a struggle between competitors, whether a physical combat between wrestlers or a mental combat between two dramatists. It was from the mental struggles of the latter group that *agonia* acquired its figurative sense of mental anguish, thus giving rise to our term, *agony*.

Incidentally, since it is derived from the same source, it might be noted that one of the rivals in the Greek *agonia* was an *agonistes*.

His opponent was therefore called an *antagonistes*, from *anti*, against, thus giving us the word *antagonist*.

aisle

One wonders how we acquired such a curiously formed word. By way of answer, we shouldn't have it. The spelling is the result of confusion; its present common meaning—a passageway, as in a church or theater—arose from still another confusion. The English word was originally *ele*, borrowed from the French in the fourteenth century; and that, in turn, came from the Latin *ala*, a wing, the original meaning of the word. It applied to the part on either side of the nave of a church, usually separated from the nave by a row of columns. But, as with many other words, *ele* had many spellings during the fifteenth and sixteenth centuries, of which *ile* was the most common. But *ile* was also the common spelling for a body of land surrounded by water; so when the latter word was given the spelling *isle* in the seventeenth century, the term relating to church architecture followed suit and also became *isle*. Changes in the French spelling of *ele* were taking place as well, and the French term had become *aile* in the meantime. English writers of the eighteenth century, in desperation, unwilling to have their readers think they were writing of "islands" in a church, threw the French and English spellings together into our present anomaly, *aisle*.

The French *aile*, however, had become confused through the centuries with *allée*, alley. So along with the union of *isle* and *aile* into *aisle*, the English word acquired, as well, an additional meaning, "passageway," and it is this meaning that has become the more common.

alarm

The Norman-French military call when, for example, a sentinel spied an enemy force approaching, was *"As armes! as armes!"* That summons was introduced into England where it was used for a while, but eventually it was translated into the equivalent English, "at arms!" which became the modern "to arms!" Similar calls were employed at the same period elsewhere in Europe. That used in Italian armies was *"all' arme!* (to arms!)" This became the popular call among other armies; but in every case the words that were called soon became the name of the cry or the name of any kind of signal to indicate danger. Italian *all' arme!* (to arms!) became *allarme*, French *alarme*, and English *alarm*, meaning "a warning sound," and lost its strictly military use. The word *alarum* arose from mispronunciation of *alarm*, for the same reason that causes many people to sound "film" as if it were spelled "fillum."

alcohol

From very early times the women of Oriental countries, desiring to enhance their beauty, have stained their eyelids with a very fine dark powder. This they call *koh'l*. The cosmetic is usually obtained from antimony. English writers of the sixteenth and seventeenth centuries in describing this cosmetic, thinking the definite article to be part of the word (*al-koh'l*), wrote it as *alcohol*. Early chemists then took this name and applied it to any extremely fine powder, so fine that one could not feel the separate grains. Thus, as one example, powdered sulfur was known as "*alcohol* of sulfur," a name that it retained into the nineteenth century. In the next step, the notion of similarly complete refinement began to require the name *alcohol* for liquids which seemed to have reached the superlative of refining. Such, in the late seventeenth century, seemed to have been attained by a wine which chemists and distillers spoke of as "*alcohol* of wine," and the term *alcohol* has since applied to liquids partly or wholly of the composition of that wine.

alert

Literally, *alert* means "on the watchtower." It came from an Italian military expression of the sixteenth century, *all' erta*, in which *all'* is a common contraction of *alla*, on. The original phrase was *stare all' erta*, "to stand on the watchtower." As conditions changed, the phrase merely meant "to stand watch." Ultimately, with the omission of the verb, it came into English in the seventeenth century further contracted to *alert*, and with its meaning altered to signify "on watch; vigilant."

alimony, aliment

Someone has said that *alimony* is no more than a telescoping of "all the money." It may seem so to a man who has little left after his former wife has received the monthly allowance awarded to her. Actually, however, the Latin *alimonia* was just a new-fangled spelling, two thousand years ago, of the older *alimentum*. Both of them, in those days, had the same meaning—nourishment, sustenance, provisions. From the first has come *alimony*, from the other, *aliment*. Thus the real intent of the word *alimony* is an allowance that will provide *aliment*, or a means of living.

alkali

Like our mathematics, we owe much of the early study of chemistry to Arabic scholars of the so-called Dark Ages. Thus the word *alkali* is but a transliteration of the Arabic *al-qaliy*, which means "the ashes of saltwort." Saltwort is a marine plant used in the production of sodium carbonate, formerly called soda ash. As chemists learned that other salts than sodium carbonate possessed some properties in common with it, *alkali* became a term common for all.

alligator

English writers of the sixteenth century correctly called this American creature a *lagarto*, for that was the Spanish name for this huge saurian—"lizard." But because Spaniards, like Arabs, are accustomed to put the definite article *al* before a noun—*al lagarto*, the lizard—careless English writers assumed that this was a single word—*allagarto*. This became further corrupted in the seventeenth century to *allegator*, and the present spelling became established in the early eighteenth century.

alone

One who is *alone* is distinctly "one," not two or more. And that was the original intent and use of the word. It was formed from *all one*, wholly one, and was used as two words until the fourteenth century. In those days and until about the end of the seventeenth century the word *one* was pronounced just as we pronounce "own" today. This pronunciation survives in "only." (See also ATONE.)

amazon

Before the days of the Trojan War, according to the legendary tales of Homer, there was a tribe of fierce warriors living near the Caucasus Mountains. They were ruled by a queen, it was said, and they had waged war against other tribes in Asia Minor and had even invaded Greece. But the peculiar thing about this tribe was that all its members were women; there were no men among them. Once each year they met a neighboring tribe of men, but any boys that might be born from such a union were either killed or sent over the hills to their fathers. The girls were kept and were trained for warfare and the hardships of military life. These strange women were called *Amazons*, a name that the Greeks believed came from the two words, *a*, without, and *mazos*, breast, because, as Homer explained, in order that they might be more skilled in the use of bow and arrow, the right breast of each woman had been removed. Many paintings and some statuary of this warlike race have been preserved which, though they do not support the explanation that was given for the origin of the name, do show that the Greek artists believed the Amazons to have been large and powerful women of noble proportions. It is in this sense in which *amazon* is now used. The large river in South America received its name from the Spanish explorer, Orellana, who, in his first descent of the river in 1541, was attacked by a tribe of natives, among whom the women fought alongside the men. He thought them to be another tribe similar to that known by ancient Greeks, and gave them the name *Amazon*.

ambiguous

In the Latin language, it was the custom to do about as we do today; that is, to give a verb a particular meaning by using a preposition along with it. Thus, with our verb "to walk," we may say "to walk in," meaning "to enter"; "to walk up," meaning "to ascend"; "to walk down," meaning "to descend," and so on. The Romans, however, placed their prepositions before the verb, and usually combined the two words into one. The preposition *ambi*, which means "around" or "roundabout," was one of those usually combined. And when combined it was often shortened into *amb*, or into *am*, or even changed into *amp*. Our English word *ambiguous*, from the Latin *ambiguus*, was thus originally formed from the Latin verb *ambigo*, which came from the two Latin words *ambi*, roundabout, and *ago*, to drive. So the verb meant to drive roundabout, or in a wavering or uncertain manner—as a charioteer might drive if he weren't certain of the road or if the way were indistinct. At a time when there were few roads it was a common experience to wander hesitantly about the countryside when seeking a strange place, so the verb came to denote any kind of wandering or uncertain moving, and it is thus that *ambiguous* acquired the meaning "uncertain, vague."

ambition

Roman candidates for public office who wore a white toga (see CANDIDATE) were not content simply to be seen whenever they happened to be outdoors. They knew that if they wanted many of the voters to notice their glistening white togas they would have to go about from place to place where the voters were, talking with them—canvassing for votes, as we would say. Now the Latin word for "to go about, to move round," was *ambio*, from *ambi*, about, and *eo*, go. In time this verb acquired the extended meaning, "to go about for the purpose of soliciting votes." Thus the noun *ambitio*, from which our noun *ambition* was formed, formerly meaning "a going about," now denoted "a soliciting of office; a canvassing for votes"; and a person who was *ambitiosus*—*ambitious* is our word— was one who went about with the obvious intent of courting favor, seeking by his manner to obtain votes.

What had been originally a harmless practice of walking about to exhibit one's white toga generally, began to acquire a sinister meaning; an *ambitious* person was suspected, and was often guilty, of using underhand methods to obtain votes. In fact, so definite did the practice become and so identified in the Roman mind with *ambitio*, that the word *ambitus* was coined to designate bribery by office-seekers. In 181 B.C., the first of many laws was enacted against it. But when *ambition* and *ambitious* came into our language, through French, back in the fourteenth century, men were usually appointed to public office by kings. The words then lost the flavor of political crookedness; the chief meaning of each, as today, implied no more than eager desire for advancement or power.

ambulance

Until late in the eighteenth century any soldier wounded in battle was likely to lie where he fell until nightfall or until the battle was over. Even then his chance of surgical attention was slim unless a comrade carried him to the rear, for surgeons did not reach the battlefield until the next day. But toward the end of that century there was introduced into the French army a rather crude system for bringing quicker aid to the wounded. A vehicle, equipped to carry the injured, and furnished with bandages, tourniquets, and the like to stop the flow of blood, moved behind the lines to pick up and transport the wounded to the hospitals. Such a vehicle was called *hôpital ambulant*, traveling hospital, from the Latin *ambulo*, travel, walk, move. They had been devised at the instigation of a young surgeon, Dominique Jean Larrey, later created baron by Napoleon in appreciation of his services. For a time the vehicles were called *ambulances volantes*, literally "flying travelers." The name was shortened in England to the present *ambulance*, literally, thus, "a traveler."

amethyst

Among the many superstitions of the ancient Greeks was one concerning the wearing of a certain rare stone. To be effective, this stone had to be clear and very like the wine of the grape in color; that is, a clear purple or bluish violet. The possessor or wearer of such a stone, it was believed, would not become intoxicated, no matter how much wine he might drink. So the Greeks named this precious charm against intoxication, *amethystos*, not drunken, from the negative prefix *a*, and *methy*, wine. It is in dim remembrance of the ancient belief that this stone, the *amethyst*, has been favored by men, worn in a ring or as a watch fob.

ampersand

Back in the Middle Ages, when only a few people could write, and those usually priests, most of the writing was in Latin. But in those days, just as with us now, one of the words that occurred very frequently was "and." The Latin word for "and" is *et*. In part because of the script then used, and in part because of frequent use, this Latin word came to be generally written "*&*." Later, English began to replace Latin, and the character which we generally see now (&) began to replace the older one.

Now, when children were learning the alphabet in those early days, they were taught to distinguish between the letter "a" and the word "a"—that is, to see that in "a boy," "a" is a word. So the word was described as "*a per se*," in which the Latin *per se* means "by itself." Sometimes it was written "*a-per-se*," sometimes, "*A-per-se-A*"; the meaning was, "*a* taken by itself makes the word *a*." The pronoun "I" was also so distinguished—"*I-per-se-I*." And at the very end of the alphabet, after the letter "z" in their "A-B-C books," the children were taught to recognize the common character "&." This, in similar manner, they called, "*and-per-se-and*." That is, the old monks who first taught them said, "*and-per-se-and*," but children's ears in those days were no more acute than in these, so it was repeated as *ampassy-and*, *ampussy-and*, and even as *amsiam*. The least corrupt of the forms, however, came down to us as *ampersand*, which is now recognized as the name of the character, &.

anecdote

Justinian, emperor of the Byzantine Empire from A.D. 527 to 565, was one of the few really great emperors of that division of the old Roman Empire. He is noted especially for the framing of the legal code, since known as the Justinian Code. Among the attendants at his court was the historian, Procopius, who, when he had completed a history of the wars waged during the reign of his emperor, wrote also an account of the many structures erected by his master. Now Justinian, though professedly a Christian monarch, indulged in or permitted many of the vices and excesses common to Oriental courts of the period, and Procopius had an observant eye and a satiric pen. He knew the inside lives of the persons of the court, and he was moved to indulge his satire and to write brief accounts of some of the incidents he had observed concerning the emperor, his wife, Theodora, and other eminent persons. Some of his tales were witty and pleasant, but most of them were indecent or absurd. Possibly he did not intend that the tales should ever be published, because he gave them the title, *Anecdota*, a Greek word meaning "unpublished, kept secret." The manuscript was published, however, and the term thereafter meant a brief true story about someone or some event. Early *anecdotes*, like those of Procopius, related to persons or events connected with court life, but the term is now used for any short story assumed to be fact.

anthem

Originally this was the same word and had the same meaning as *antiphon*, a response, sung or chanted. Introduced into Christian worship, the Greek *antiphon*, in the speech of the priests, became Old English *antefne*. Then and for many centuries thereafter it referred to a composition for two voices or two choirs sung or chanted alternately. The Old English word gradually altered to the present *anthem*. Later, when the meaning of *anthem* was extended to embrace sacred music generally, whether for solo, duet, or choral singing, the Greek term *antiphon* was reintroduced to provide for the original meaning.

antic (grotesque)

Back in the early sixteenth century, some Italian archeologists, in Rome, were digging about in the ruins of the huge structure now known to be the Baths erected by the emperor Titus. Unexpectedly running across some chambers that had long been buried, they found that the walls were covered with paintings. These paintings were of a strange composition, hitherto unknown among the painters of the Christian Era. They showed fantastic representations of human, animal, and floral forms, curiously intermixed and compounded— heads of beasts upon the bodies of men; centaurs, satyrs, tritons, as well as shapes and fancies designed by the artist about such figures; flowers and vines of unknown kinds, impossibly supported figures seated among them. Because these paintings were ascribed to the ancients, the Italians described them as *antica*, antique. In the spelling of England at that time this became *antike*, *anticke*, *antick*, and finally *antic*. Hence, though first pertaining to the ancient and comic type of decorative art, the meaning gradually became also synonymous with ludicrous, and referred especially to an absurd gesture, pose, or trick that excited laughter, such as those shown in the ancient Roman paintings. The Italian name for these curious paintings, however, and for the equally fantastic sculptured forms sometimes found, was *grottesca*, a name formed from *grotte*, the grottoes or excavations in which the curious figures were discovered. This Italian term was later borrowed by French scholars in the form *grotesque*, and the French name ultimately reached England, though not until a century later than *antic*.

antimacassar (tidy)

Our ancestors were just as vain as we are, and, like ourselves, were always searching for ways to make the hair more attractive. Early in the nineteenth century a new unguent for the hair was produced which, its makers vowed, possessed marvelous properties. This oil, they said, came from the Dutch East Indies, from a district named Macassar on the Island of Celebes. Lord Byron, in 1819, referred to this preparation in *Don Juan*:

> In virtues nothing earthly could surpass her,
> Save thine "incomparable oil," Macassar.

The preparation retained its popularity for a long period, but housewives found it to be a source of serious annoyance. The oil left its stain upon the back of their brocaded chairs, and could not be removed. They could do nothing more than cover the spot with a cloth until the chair could be reupholstered; but as use of the grease persisted and they could not constantly have chairs recovered they had to seek ways to prevent the damage. They solved this by a lace or crocheted piece of fancy-work hung over or pinned to the back of the chair. It protected the chair and could be easily removed and washed when soiled. Because of its purpose it was called an *antimacassar*, from *anti*, against, plus *Macassar*. It was also less pretentiously called a "tidy," for it was intended to keep the chair tidy. Both names have been extended to include similar coverings for chair-arms.

apron (adder, auger, umpire, orange)

Strangely enough, even as recently as the fifteenth and sixteenth centuries, our ancestors were accustomed to speak of this protective garment as "napron." The word was adapted from the French *naperon*; in modern French, *napperon*, now meaning "napkin." But our forefathers were careless, even as we are, and "*a napron*" became slurred in speech into "*an apron*," and so it remained. Other similar corruptions were "*an adder*" (snake) from "*a nadder*"; "*an auger*" from "*a nauger*"; "*an eft*," formerly spelt *ewt*, from "*a newt*," though both forms have survived, and *"an umpire"* from *"a num-pire,"* taken from the Old French *non*, not, and *per*, peer. Our word *orange* was adapted from the Italian *arancia*, which itself had suffered a like alteration from *"una narancia."*

arena

The amphitheaters of ancient Rome were structures that resembled in many respects the stadiums in many of the colleges and cities of the United States. The structures, both ancient and modern, were erected so that spectators could easily see and enjoy the contests in the large open spaces which they surrounded. But the great difference lies in the nature of the contests. In the stadium a contestant is injured only by accident; but in the amphitheater the crowds of spectators expected to see bloodshed—gladiators fighting one another to death with swords or other weapons, or infuriated wild animals turned loose upon poorly armed or defenseless human victims. Therefore, because the hard-packed ground of the old amphitheaters would not soak up the quantities of blood spilled upon it in a contest, it was always liberally covered with sand. And it was this sand by which the place of combat became known, for *arena* is the Latin word for "sand."

arrant (errant)

We use it now to mean downright, out-and-out, unmitigated; as, an *arrant* coward, an *arrant* scoundrel. But it was formerly just another spelling of "errant," and it meant wandering, vagabond, nomad. Thus a "knight errant," in the Age of Chivalry, was a knight, usually young, who roamed the countryside, seeking an opportunity to win an accolade through good deeds. In similar style a bandit or highwayman five or six centuries ago was termed an *"arrant* thief," meaning one who wandered over the countryside, holding up persons whom he might encounter.

arrive

If we were to use this word only with regard to its source and original sense we would use it exclusively when the destination was reached by water. That was the usual application until about four centuries ago. The source was the Latin *ad*, to, and *ripa*, land or shore. Its meaning was "to come to the shore; to reach land."

assassin

Late in the eleventh century, Hassan ben Sabbah, forced from his studies in Cairo, returned to his home in Persia. He then acquired a mountain fortress in the southern part of the country, and made it the seat of a new religious organization. Though the principles were mainly those of one of the leading sects of Mohammedanism, he determined that the head of the organization itself should be an absolute ruler. During the two centuries in which it flourished, the new sect wielded great power, not only throughout Persia, but also in all of Asia Minor, because of the terror it inspired. The hereditary title of its chieftain was Sheik-al-Jebal, known among the European Crusaders as "the Old Man of the Mountains," a name that caused the bravest among them to tremble.

The lowest order and the most numerous of its members was a body of young men known as the *Fedahvis*, "the Devoted Ones." The most absolute obedience was required of them, even, if ordered, to embrace death without question or hesitation. And it was this group that caused the terror in which the sect was held, for it was the duty of its members to kill any person whom the chieftain might designate. That person would be killed. If the first youth were slain in the attempt, another, or another, or another would fulfil the order. The score of murder in Persia, Syria, and Arabia was high during those centuries.

But before these young men were sent out on their tasks, they were induced to partake liberally of hashish. This is the Oriental equivalent of marihuana, but is more powerful. The young votaries, under the stupefying influence and ecstatic effect of this drug, were not only utterly fearless, but eager for the bliss of Paradise. In the Arabic language, they were *hashashin*, or, "eaters of hashish." Travelers from Europe understood the word to be *assassin*.

assets

When a person dies the immediate concern of his heir or the executor of his estate is to determine whether he left sufficient property to pay his debts and legacies. In England, after the days of William the Conqueror, this was known by the Anglo-French legal term, *aver assetz*, from *aver*, to have, and *assetz*, sufficient, hence "to have sufficient (to meet the claims)." In the French of today this would be *avoir assez*. Thus *assets*, stripped of meanings that it has acquired through the years, rightfully means nothing more than "sufficient."

atlas

One of the oldest of the Grecian myths tells of the struggle for supremacy between Zeus and the Titans, the sons and grandsons of Uranus and Gæa. The leader of the Titans was the powerful Atlas. And when the Titans were overcome, Atlas, in punishment, was obliged thereafter to bear the weight of the heavens upon his shoulders throughout all eternity. (Later legends say that he was transformed into a mountain, which bore the heavens upon its peak. This legend accounts for the name of the Atlas Mountains in north-west Africa.) Ancient artists, in picturing the scene, showed the heavens as a huge globe of tremendous weight that Atlas supported. A copy of one of these pictures was used in the sixteenth century by the Flemish geographer, Mercator, as a frontispiece to his first collection of maps. Such a picture was deemed so happy a selection for a volume of maps that similar ones were carried by all succeeding map makers. Thus through constant association of the Greek hero with a volume of maps, the book itself began to be known by his name.

atone

Nowadays when we are in full agreement or have a fellow-feeling with another, we say that we see eye to eye, or that we are hand in glove with him. Back in the thirteenth century and for the next several hundred years, the saying was to be *at one*, or to set *at one* with the other. The expression was so commonly employed, especially in sermons—"to set *at one* with God"—that by the fifteenth century, it was frequently written as a solid word, "*atone*." (The word "one" was pronounced in those days as we pronounce "own.") The change in meaning of the solid word was gradual. Thus, when Shakespeare wrote, in Richard II, "Since we cannot *atone* you," he meant, "Since we cannot set you at one." From this notion of reconciliation came the idea of expiation; that is, to become reconciled with another by making amends for a fault, or by settling differences. The noun *atonement* developed in similar manner from *at onement*, the condition of being *at one*. (See also ALONE.)

atropine

Three goddesses were in control of all human destinies, according to ancient Greek belief. They determined when a man should be born, what his activities should be during his life, and when and under what circumstances he should die. These three beautiful sisters were known, therefore, as the goddesses of Fate, or the Three Fates. Clotho, the first of the sisters, controlled the time and place of birth; Lachesis laid out the course of life, and Atropos, the dark-haired one of the three, cut the thread of life. Thus, because Atropos had in her power all the agencies which might cause man to die, according to this ancient thought, the name of this goddess was fancifully given by botanists to one of the genera of deadly plants of the nightshade family, the poisonous *Atropa*. And chemists in their turn have still further commemorated the death-disposing goddess by the name *atropine* given to the poisonous drug extracted from this plant.

auburn

Strangely enough, when this first came into the language, after the Norman Conquest, it was used as a perfect description of the color of the flaxen hair of the Saxons, a yellowish hue. The Old French spelling was *alborne* or *auborne*. But after being taken into English the spelling began to vary, taking a number of different forms. Thus in the seventeenth century it moved from *abron* to *abroun* and *abrown*, and because of this latter spelling the meaning of the word shifted into that which we still give it, a reddish brown. Our present spelling, however, is a compromise of the eighteenth century.

August (July)

In the name of this month we still commemorate the first emperor of the Roman Empire, more than nineteen hundred years after his death. His real name was Caius Octavianus, which was also his father's name. His mother, Julia, was the sister of Julius Caesar, the great Roman general. The young Octavianus, better known as

Octavius, was but nineteen when the news of the murder of Caesar reached him in Spain in 44 B.C. Upon returning to Italy immediately thereafter he learned that his late uncle, who had always treated him as a son, had previously adopted him secretly and had willed him his entire property. Octavius then took as his official name, Caius Julius Caesar Octavianus. Trained both in the science of war and the art of statesmanship by his uncle, he became immensely popular with the army and with the people, his successes in the field increasing his popularity at home. Egypt fell before his armies in the year 30 B.C., and both the Roman senate and people vied with each other to heap additional honors upon the young general. Already a consul for the fifth successive year, he became the actual ruler of the Roman Empire in 29 B.C. and, two years later, was declared *Augustus* by the senate, a title equivalent to that of "imperial majesty." As a further honor, because the fifth month of the year (see JANUARY), previously called *Quinctilis*, had been renamed *Julius* (*July*) in honor of Julius Caesar, the senate decreed that the sixth month, previously *Sextilis*, should be renamed *Augustus* (*August*). And, so that the two months would be of equal length, a day was taken from the last month of the year, February, and added to the sixth month. Octavius Augustus, the name by which he is known in history, ruled his vast empire wisely until his death at the age of seventy-five in the year A.D. 14.

auspice

Ancient peoples held the firm belief that future events and the purposes of their gods were revealed by certain signs. These signs, however, could be understood only by the very devout, especially trained to observe and to interpret. Different nations had different beliefs in the way these signs were delivered, but among the forerunners of the Roman people, and by the Romans also, the signs or omens were thought to come through the birds, which, flying in the heavens, could readily be guided by the gods on high. Hence, among the ancient Latin peoples, certain men were appointed to watch the flights of birds, to determine what kind of birds they were, to note the quarter of the sky in which they appeared and the direction of their flight, and, in some instances, to listen to their songs and to observe the food which they ate. Such a man was called an *auspex*, a word derived from the Latin *avis*, bird, and *specio*, to see. (In later times the *auspex* was replaced by the *augur*. See IN-AUGURATE.) The services of the auspex were called upon when anything of importance was under consideration. It was his function to say whether the signs were or were not favorable. That function was termed an *auspicium*, a term that was later applied to the prophetic token itself, to the omen or sign. This latter meaning was retained in the English *auspice*, but with a favorable sense especially. Thus when we use the phrase, "under the auspices of," we mean that our undertaking is under the benevolent protection or patronage of the named person or body. And when we say that such and such a moment, or occasion or event is *auspicious*, we express belief in its success, as if the gods were approving the undertaking.

babbitt

When still a young man, Isaac Babbitt produced the first of several inventions by which he became famous. He had been apprenticed as a youth to a goldsmith in Taunton, Massachusetts, where he was born, and it was in this employment that he acquired an interest in metallurgy. Hence, in 1824, when he was but twenty-five years old, he turned out the first Britannia ware that was produced in the United States. This metal is an alloy of copper, tin, and antimony; its successful production led the young man to further investigations with the same three substances, with the result that, in 1839, he produced a metal which, when used for machine bearings, was found to be far better than anything yet discovered at that time for reducing friction. Mr. Babbitt received a grant from Congress for this invention, which is still widely used in mechanical operations and still carries the name *babbitt* or *babbitt metal*. There are also many housewives who are familiar with the soap, *Babbitt soap*, that he manufactured. (Isaac *Babbitt* did not furnish the model for the fictitious character, George Follansbee *Babbitt*, described by Sinclair Lewis in his novel, *Babbitt*. The latter name has also taken its place in the language as a descriptive term for a type of American businessman, ambitious and smugly satisfied with the outward show of prosperity, but totally lacking in culture and refinement.)

babel

Every Sunday School scholar knows that we got this word from the high tower which the descendants of Noah started to erect, "whose top may reach unto heaven." The name of the tower and of the city which was also being built was *Babel*. But the Lord, according to the eleventh chapter of Genesis, did not approve of the presumption of these men, and brought their purpose all to nought by causing each to speak in a tongue unknown to any of the others. No one could understand anyone else. Probably, as we do to this day on like occasions, each thereupon shouted the louder. Hence, any such confusion of voices we refer to as *babel*.

baffle

Little is known of its source, but *baffle*, in the sixteenth century, was thought to be a Scottish term. We use it now when we mean "to flabbergast, confuse, frustrate, foil"; but in those days it meant "to disgrace publicly." It seems to have referred especially to the manner in which a knight who had forsworn his oath was held up to ridicule and ignominy. For, in the earliest record, we are told that the Scots would "baffull" such a man. This, says the account, was done by painting a picture of him, in which he was shown hung up by the heels. Edmund Spenser describes it in *Faerie Queene*:

> He by the heels him hung upon a tree
> And bafful'd so, that all which passed by
> The picture of his punishment might see.

bailiwick

A *wick*, in olden times, was a village—from the Latin, *vicus*, village. (It survives now chiefly in place names, often as *wich*, as in Warwick, Greenwich, Norwich.) And the bailie, whom we now call *bailiff*, was the administrative officer. Thus a *bailiwick* was actually the district over which a bailiff had jurisdiction. We use the term figuratively now to mean also any place that one regards as one's own.

baize

Back in the sixteenth century, during the period when Spain had given the cruel Duke of Alva complete authority over the Netherlands, more than 100,000 Dutch Protestants were forced to flee the country. Many of them went across the channel to England, and of these, many were weavers. Textile weaving had long been a staple industry in England, but these Dutch weavers, as well as similar emigrants who fled from France, were welcomed because they introduced a number of fabrics that had not previously been made in England. Among these was a woolen fabric, light and fine in texture and, originally, of chestnut color. Because of its color, this material was known among the foreign weavers by its French name, *bai*, though more commonly under the plural form, *bais*. English spelling was most erratic in those days, so the French *bais* became *bays* (often with a second plural *bayses*), *bayes*, *baies*, *bayze*, and *baize*. This last artificial form has persisted, but the material, of any color nowadays, would not now be recognized by the early Dutch weavers.

Bakelite

Leo Hendrik Baekeland was born in Belgium in 1863, studied and taught chemistry in his native land, but then, at the age of twenty-six, emigrated to the United States. There, for the rest of his life—he died in 1944—he engaged in industrial research. His earliest invention was the photographic paper, "Velox." But the invention for which he was best known is a plastic, valuable as a nonconductor of electricity and as a heat resistant. This was given the registered name *Bakelite*, formed from the name of its inventor.

ballot

Originally, this meant "little ball," contracted from the Italian *ballotta*. It may be easy to recall this original meaning if we remember that, formerly, the method of voting was through the use of a small ball—white or black, according as one voted affirmatively or negatively—dropped secretly into a receptacle. The method, still used in some organizations, is extremely old. In ancient Athens it was employed by the judges, or dicasts, in giving their verdicts, except that small shells or beans or balls of metal or stone, variously colored or marked, were used as the ballots. From the frequent use of beans in Athenian elections, a politician was sometimes humorously called a "bean-eater."

baluster (banister)

Probably because they could be turned out more easily on a lathe, the short upright columns for supporting a handrail were made, in the Middle Ages, in circular section and a doubly curved outline, a narrow neck above, swelling into a pear-shaped bulge below. These columns strongly resembled the shape of the flower of the wild pomegranate. The Italian name of this flower, taken from the Latin and thence from the Greek, is *balaustra*, and this then became the Italian name of the column. French architects adopted the column because of its beauty, but spelled the name *balustre*, which, in turn, became *baluster* in English. Thanks to careless speech and to indifferent hearing, the form *banister* began to be used shortly after the new word *baluster* was introduced. The corrupted term has been frowned upon and condemned by purists ever since, but it has taken a firm position in the language and is now more commonly used than *baluster*.

balloon

Back in the late 1500's and early 1600's the young men of England had a game of football that seems to have borne some resemblance to the later game of rugby. The player might either kick the ball or strike it with his arm or hand, though the inflated ball was so large and so heavy that the players were obliged to wear a bracer of wood strapped to the arm and hand to prevent injury. Both the game and the ball with which it was played were named *balloon*, a name derived from the French *ballon*, meaning a large ball. The next step in the history of the word came in the early 1630's. Some unknown genius discovered a way to stuff pyrotechnics into a cardboard ball which, shot from a mortar, made a wonderful display of fireworks when the ball was high in the sky. This was also a large ball, and so, naturally, was called *balloon*. But a far larger ball was devised by the Montgolfier brothers of France in 1783. This was a huge bag which, when filled with hot air, ascended above the earth. This too, obviously, was called *balloon*. It was the forerunner of that which we now know by the name.

bandanna

When Portuguese explorers in India, back in the sixteenth century, began to learn about the various beautiful cloths produced in the country, they saw that one owed its interesting appearance to the curious manner in which it was prepared for dyeing. The cloth was tightly knotted before it was dipped into the dye, and thus some portions of the cloth retained the original color. The Hindus called this method of dyeing, *bāndhnu*, a word that, coming through the Portuguese, has given us the English *bandanna*. The original material in India was silk. The process was later applied to cotton, and chemical means have been substituted to obtain the former effect produced by knots.

bankrupt

From time immemorial there have been money-changers. These were men who, for a premium, calculated the value of currency received by a merchant dealing with foreign countries and exchanged it for domestic money. Their business was conducted in some public place, such as the market place in Athens, the forum in Rome, or the temple in Jerusalem. There they set up a small table or bench for the convenience of their customers. In later times, as in the cities of Florence and Venice, which were the chief trading centers of the Middle Ages, such a table or bench had the name *banca*, the source of "bank," for these money-changers corresponded in some degree with our modern bankers.

Although the principal occupation was changing money, these men sometimes took money from wealthy patrons which, with their own, they lent to others at a profit—a rate of interest that would be considered usury now. But there was always a risk involved in such a loan—the borrower might lose his life, his goods, and his ship through some disaster. A succession of such misfortunes could cause the failure of the banker, unable to repay his own creditors. The laws of ancient Rome, though perhaps never exercised, permitted creditors actually to divide the body of a debtor into parts proportionate to their claims. However, the penalty was less severe in the Middle Ages. The creditors of such a banker or his fellows in the market place merely broke up his table or bench, thus showing that he was no longer in business. This, in Florence, was designated *banca rotta*, broken bench. Italian bankers of the sixteenth and seventeenth centuries carried this expression of business failure into England, but the Italian *rotta* gradually gave way to the Latin word for broken—*ruptus*—and *banca rotta*, altered to *banca rupta*, became corrupted to our present term, *bankrupt*.

barbarous

To the ancient Greeks the sound made by two foreigners talking together was as if they said "bar-bar-bar-bar" to each other. So they called any unintelligible speech, *barbaros*, and applied it to any language that was not Greek. Later on, the Romans borrowed the word, changing it to *barbarus*, and had it apply to any language that was neither Roman nor Greek. The sense then became extended to embrace anything of any nature that was foreign to either Greece or Rome. That included the people. So great was the feeling of superiority among Greeks and Romans that they considered customs which differed from their own and all foreign persons to be necessarily crude, uncultured, and uncivilized. Although *barbarous*, which we in turn have borrowed, still retains this latter meaning, we no longer apply it indiscriminately to all foreign ways and persons.

barbecue

The Spaniards, when they took possession of Haiti shortly after its discovery by Columbus, saw many customs among the natives which were strange to them. Among those for which they could readily see the reason was an elevated framework upon which to sleep. This was a protection against marauding beasts. A similar framework, with a fire beneath, was used for drying or smoking fish and meat. The natives, as nearly as the Spaniards could understand, had a general name for such an elevated framework, regardless of its use. They called it *barbacoa*. Thus when the Spaniards themselves roasted meat upon a spit over an outdoor fire, they fell into the habit of using the native name, calling the frame upon which the meat was roasted, *barbacoa*. The name was carried to various Spanish colonies, and was thus introduced into the colonies of North America, slightly corrupted into *barbecue*. (See also BUCCANEER.)

Barmecide

This occurs usually in the expression "Barmecide feast" or "Barmecide banquet." It comes from the "Story of the Barber's Sixth Brother" in *Arabian Nights*. A poor man who had been without food for several days, it relates, begged for bread at the door of the rich Persian noble, Barmecide. To his amazement he was invited to the table. Servants brought in golden platter after golden platter, and his host urged him to help himself bountifully. But there was nothing upon any of the platters, though the beggar, entering into the spirit of the jest, pretended to pile his plate full and to eat heartily. Finally the wine jug was brought. It, too, was empty, though the beggar pretended to fill his goblet frequently and to become quite drunk. Then, seeming to be intoxicated, he boxed his host heartily on the ears. This and the good nature of the poor man so delighted Barmecide that a real banquet was brought upon the table. Hence, in modern literature, a *Barmecide* is one who offers an unreal or disappointing benefit, and a *Barmecide feast* is either nothing at all or a meal that leaves much to the imagination.

barnacle

It was firmly believed by our ancestors, even so recently as in Shakespeare's time, that the goose which we still call *barnacle goose* came out of the shell of a nut or tiny gourd growing upon certain trees along the seashore. Some thought that the immature birds were attached to the trees by their bills, but the more general belief was that the birds did not develop until the nuts fell into the sea, where they became small shellfish and attached themselves to any floating object until the birds were ready for flight. That is to say, the small shellfish or *barnacle* which we find attached over the face of a rock in the sea or upon the bottom of a ship, or the like, was formerly believed to have begun its life as the nut of a tree and to be itself capable of developing into a kind of goose. The legend developed because the breeding habits of the barnacle goose were long unknown. Always some fable was invented, in olden times, which would account for the unknown.

basilisk

Although we apply this name now to a South American lizard, which grows to a length of about two feet, this harmless animal only faintly resembles the fabulous reptile that terrified the people of medieval and ancient times. The name was originally Greek, *basiliskos*, little king, from *basil*, a crown, because the monster was said to have a spot on its head that resembled a crown. (The South American basilisk has a crest which it can erect.) The mythical *basilisk* came, it was believed, from an egg laid by a cock; it lived in the deserts of Africa; its hissing was so powerful that all other serpents fled from it; its breath was fatal and so fiery as to kill off all vegetation. The very sight of it, according to some writers, was enough to kill a man. (See also COCKATRICE.)

batiste

Among the weavers of Kameric, the oid Flemish name of Cambrai, was one who was able to produce upon his loom a linen fabric that was even softer and finer than that produced by any of his neighbors. Nothing is known of this man beyond his name, Jean Baptiste. But English merchants, having already given the name "cambric" to the general products of Kameric, needed a name for the newer and finer material which they began to import in the seventeenth century. Therefore, they decided to call it by the name of the weaver and, indifferent to French spelling, wrote it *batiste*. The material was originally of linen, but the name is now often applied to sheer cotton or silk fabrics, and to thin, lightweight wool.

battering-ram

Long before the days of Alexander the Great some military genius hit upon a scheme for entering the walls of an opposing city. He ordered a group of his soldiers to take a long log and swing it repeatedly against a vulnerable spot in the wall. In later improvements, the beam, sometimes eighty, a hundred, or even a hundred and twenty feet in length, was hung by chains from a frame under a protective canopy and operated by a hundred or more men. No wall could be built in those ancient times, according to one chronicler, that could withstand such battering if long continued. To protect the head of the beam and to make its blows more effective, it was at first shod with iron. The machine was already called a *ram* (Latin, *aries*), in allusion to the butting propensities of the male sheep. Hence, to make the allusion even more fitting, the ancient artisans fashioned the head into the form of a ram's head. The Roman military machine remained in use among European armies until the invention of gunpowder. Its English name, *ram* or *battering-ram*, is no more than a translation of the name used in the days of Caesar.

bazooka

Bob Burns, radio humorist, in a letter to the author, says that he coined this term to fit the alleged musical instrument that he has made familiar to radio listeners. His explanation follows:

I started taking mandolin and trombone lessons when I was six years old in Van Buren, Arkansas. When I was eight, I started playing the mandolin in the school string orchestra, and when I was nine, I was playing the slide trombone with Frank MacClain's "Van Buren Queen City Silvertone Cornet Band." In 1905 our string band was practicing in back of Hayman's Plumbing Shop in Van Buren, and while we were playing "Over the Waves" waltz, I broke a string on the mandolin. With nothing else to do, I picked up a piece of gas pipe, inch and a half in diameter and about twenty inches long. And when I blew in one end, I was very much surprised to get a bass note. Then, kidlike, I rolled up a piece of music and stuck it in the other end of the gas pipe and found that sliding it out and in like a trombone, I could get about three "fuzzy" bass notes. The laughter that I got encouraged me to have a tin tube made that I could hold on to and slide back and forth inside the inch-and-a-half gas pipe. Later on I soldered a funnel on the end of the tin tube and a wire attached to the funnel to give me a little longer reach.

No doubt you have heard the expression, "He blows his bazoo too much." In Arkansas that is said of a "windy" guy who talks too much. Inasmuch as the bazooka is played by the mouth, it's noisy and takes a lot of wind. It just seemed like "bazoo" fitted in pretty well as part of the name. The affix "ka" rounded it out and made it sound like the name of a musical instrument—like balalaika and harmonica.

Mr. Burns adds that the proudest moment of his life was when he learned that the rocket gun, used by American soldiers in World War II, had been named *bazooka* after his instrument. According to a letter from the Ordnance Department, he says, when the new gun was being demonstrated in the presence of General Somervell a captain in the group of officers gave the gun a surprised look and said, "That damn' thing looks just like Bob Burns' bazooka." There was general laughter, in which General Somervell joined, and from then on the gun became known as a *bazooka*.

bedlam

Back in the time when Henry VIII was king of England, that is, back in the first half of the sixteenth century, there stood in London a structure known as the Hospital of St. Mary of Bethlehem. It had been erected three hundred years earlier, in 1247, as a priory for the sisters and brethren of the religious order of the Star of Bethlehem. One of its functions was to serve as a place of rest and entertainment for visiting dignitaries of the Order, for that is what the word "hospital" indicated in those days. But sick people were also sometimes received at such places, and by the year 1400 the Hospital of St. Mary of Bethlehem was one of the few places in Europe where insane persons were occasionally cared for.

In 1536, after Henry VIII had brought about a severance of the Church of England from the Roman Catholic Church, he ordered that most of the monasteries in England should be dissolved. He had little better reason for this act than to display his power. The religious order of the Star of Bethlehem was among those affected, so the Hospital of St. Mary of Bethlehem passed into the possession of the corporation of London. It was then entirely converted into an asylum for the insane, with fifty or sixty lunatics confined in it.

In those days, it must be remembered, insane persons were treated more like animals than like human beings. If violent, they were chained to the wall, and, as recorded by Samuel Pepys and others, they were often exhibited to visitors and made sport of, like wild beasts in a cage. And the confusion and din created by these wild, crazed people must have been indescribable.

Now, the name of the hospital had long previously been shortened to "Bethlehem." People in those days were even more careless in their speech, however, than those of today, so "Bethlehem" had been further contracted to "Bethlem," and this in turn was commonly pronounced and often spelled "Bedlam." Thus *Bedlam*

became the common name for the hospital after it was converted
into an insane asylum. From that time to this, therefore, anything
that compares with the din and confusion in that ancient madhouse
is described as *bedlam.*

beggar

Because proof is lacking, the dictionaries play safe by saying that
this is probably just a derivative of *beg,* which in turn may have
come from an unusual Old English term, *bedecian.* But some
scholars flout that theory; they believe that *beggar* was first in the
language, with the verb, *beg,* derived from it, and that neither
term was in use before the thirteenth century. They explain the
origin thus: About the year 1180, a priest of Liège, Lambert le
Bègue, founded a religious sisterhood, the members of which, from
his name, were known as *Beguines.* They devoted themselves to a
religious life and to chastity, but were permitted to leave the order
for marriage. At a subsequent date, probably in the early thirteenth
century, a similar order for men became established. These members
were called *Beghards.* But the organization of the brotherhood was
very loosely drawn; it was possible for thieves and mendicants to
go about the country, professing to be Beghards, and even before
the end of the thirteenth century the order was held in low repute
and its members persecuted. But the name was already attached to
such men, whether religious or not, who lived by asking for and
receiving alms, to mendicants. Thus, it is explained, the *Beghards*
of the Low Countries became, by natural phonetic spelling, the
beggars of England.

belfry

While besieging a fortified place, in the early Middle Ages, German
soldiery sometimes protected themselves under the shelter of a
movable wooden tower. This protection they called a *bergfrid,*
literally, shelter shed. The device was soon borrowed by the armies
of other countries, and the soldiers probably thought that they
were still using its German name. But by the time it reached England, in the early fourteenth century, the name was spoken and
written *berfrey.* Within another hundred years this had become
belfroy and *belfrey,* winding up as *belfry.* The name resulted from

mispronunciation, for there was then no association with bells. Along with altered name, the structure began to acquire a different military use and to become a formidable mechanism of offense. It was made of sufficient height to enable archers, sheltered by its roof, to overlook the fortified place under siege and fire directly at persons within. But when gunpowder replaced arrows, these cumbersome wooden towers were no longer of use in military operations. Probably at first, then, because there was no other use for them, it was found that they did serve as excellent watchtowers, when hauled within the walls of a city. A watchman stationed within could sound an alarm upon the approach of danger. For such purposes these towers were then provided with bells. Ultimately, as we know, the towers were attached to church buildings, sometimes erected to great heights; the bells, except at rare times of great public peril or celebration, serve only to summon the populace to worship or to announce the passing time.

berserk

In Norse mythology there was a famous, furious fighter who scorned the use of heavy mail, entering battle without armor. His only protection was the skin of a bear fastened over one shoulder. From this he became known as *Berserk*, or "Bear Shirt." It was said of him that he could assume the form of a wild beast, and that neither iron nor fire could harm him, for he fought with the fury of a beast of the forest and his foes were unable to touch him. Each of his twelve sons, in turn, also carried the name *Berserk*, and each was as furious a fighter as the father. From these Norse heroes, it came to be that any person so inflamed with the fury of fighting as to be equally dangerous to friend and foe, as was that legendary family when engaged in battle, was called *berserk* or *berserker*.

bessemer

Henry Bessemer, though of English birth, was the son of a French artist, and was dependent almost entirely upon himself for his education. Metallurgy was his chief interest, and while still a young man he invented a highly successful machine to replace the former cumbersome hand method of reducing gold and bronze to powders. Later, he became interested in the metallurgy of steel. In the preceding century great strides had been taken in steel making, after the introduction of the first blast furnace in 1714, the latest, in 1830, being the employment of the hot blast. Even so, the output of steel was slow, the English production being only about fifty thousand tons a year. In 1856 Bessemer, then forty-three years old, revolutionized the industry. Basically it was through the use of molten pig iron in his converter, through which a blast of air was forced. The process has since been greatly improved, but after its introduction the English output of steel per year was tripled. *Bessemer*, for whom both process and product have since been named, was knighted for his services in 1879.

Bible

Though our word traces back to the Greek *biblia*, little books, the Greek word was itself derived from *byblos*, which was the name for the particular kind of papyrus from which ancient books were made. Such books, of course, were not bound into pages, but were long rolls or scrolls of paper, each scroll containing an entire book, closely written. Probably during the third century of the Christian Era it became customary among the Church Fathers to speak reverently of the Holy Books as *ta biblia*, the books. In such fashion *biblia* came to refer especially to the collection of books sacred to Christians. The term was early anglicized to *Bible*.

bigot

The origin of this word has been greatly disputed. About all that is certainly known is that it was used in France, before the beginning of the thirteenth century, as an opprobrious name for the Normans. Some scholars believe that the French borrowed it from the old Teutonic oath, "*bi got.*" They quote a legend circulated in the twelfth century that when Charles the Simple, in 911, granted the lands of Normandy to Rolf, which that wily Norse chieftain had already seized, Rolf refused to perform the usual courtly act of kissing the royal foot with the indignant words, "*Ne se, bi got* (No, by God!)" The saying became historic, they believe, and was later applied by the French to anyone obstinately set in his opinions, beliefs, or mode of life.

billingsgate

The gates in the old walled city of London were known by the names of those who had constructed them. Thus the one below London Bridge has been known as *Billingsgate* since time immemorial, probably so called from a man named Billings, although a map of 1658 ascribes it to "Belen, ye 23th Brittish Kinge." A pier was built alongside this gate in 1558 as a landing place for provisions and, later, as an open market for fish. In each instance, the shops or stalls were conducted by women, wives of the sailors or fishermen. Through the coarse tongues of these viragos the place became noted for its vituperative language—"the rhetoric of *Billingsgate*," as one wag described it.

blackguard

Four or five centuries ago it was not so easy as it is today to move from one's winter residence to his place in the country for the summer and to make the reverse move in the fall. Today, the very wealthy may have a retinue of servants at each place, and the actual change of residence may be accomplished by automobile or airplane with little inconvenience in a matter of a few hours. But in the sixteenth century even the king was compelled to shift his entire retinue—and the retinue of the royal house or of any of the noble houses ran into large numbers. The more important members went before on horseback. Huge springless wagons carried the linens and the multitudinous boxes of raiment. Bringing up the rear were the unsightly but necessary men and women of the kitchen, the lowest menials of the household, the scullions and knaves who performed the needful dirty work of the smoky kitchen; they, with their black and sooty pots and pans, had one large wagon to themselves, or rode on mules or traveled on foot, loaded with their clattering greasy implements. In playful allusion to the appearance and most unmilitary equipment of these tailenders, they were called "the black guard." In later years, whether or not these kitchen menials were drawn from or became loafers and criminals, the name became attached to that class, and still later, as at present, *blackguard* came to denote a low, vicious person, addicted to or ready for crime.

blackmail

Farmers and small landholders along the border counties of England and Scotland, until roughly a century and a half ago, lived in constant dread of being raided by robbers and outlaws in that poorly protected area. Some of them, however, escaped those depredations by paying a regular tribute to the principal robber chieftain of the neighborhood in exchange for protection. Such tribute was called *blackmail*. "Mail" in Scotland, has long been the term for rent. And rent, according to the terms of a lease, might be paid in cattle or grain, or in silver. If paid in silver, white in color, the rent was known as "white mail"; if in cattle for grain or the like, it was *"black mail."* It was the latter which was demanded by robber chieftains, who had their men and horses to feed. Consequently, *blackmail* came to be known along the Scottish border as the tribute the landholders were forced to surrender.

blarney

Blarney Castle, in County Cork, Ireland, was built about 1446 by Cormac McCarthy. Its name was derived from that of a little village nearby. When Queen Elizabeth appointed Sir George Carew Lord President of Munster, something over a hundred years later, it became his duty to obtain, by peaceful means if possible, the surrender of all the castles and strongholds in the region to the crown. However, the owner of Blarney Castle, descendant of its builder, was unwilling to agree to this plan, but did not wish to appear wholly rebellious. So, by blandishment, it is said, he kept putting off the actual surrender, using vast powers of persuasion to delay the event from month to month. The repeated postponement finally became a joking matter among the associates of the Lord President, and *blarney* became a byword for soft speech, cajolement, or persuasive words to gain an end. (Sometimes this legend is attributed to an earlier period and to the original builder of the castle.) To commemorate the achievement, it is said that a certain stone set high up on the wall of the castle, accessible only with great difficulty, has such potency that if one can succeed in kissing it, he too will become gifted with all the soft speech and per-

suasiveness that served the lord of the castle in such good stead
centuries ago.

blatherskite

During the Revolutionary War the American soldiers, gathered about
their campfires, of course sang all those songs that any of them
could recall. Among the favorites was the Scottish song, *Maggie
Lawder*, one verse of which ran:

> O wha wadna be in love wi bonny Maggie Lawder,
> A piper met her gaun to Fife, and speir'd what
>   was't they ca'd her;
> Right scornfully she answer'd him,
>   Begone ye hallen shaker,
> Jog on your gate, ye bladderskate,
>   My name is Maggie Lawder.

Bladder skate is the Scottish name for a skate that is able to inflate
itself. Thus it became a fitting term for a person who is full of
empty vainglorious talk. The song dropped out of memory in the
years after the war, but the term, altered to *blatherskite*, stayed in
the language.

blizzard

Nobody knows when or how this American word originated. Its
earliest occurrence in print was in 1829, but it may have been well
known in frontier speech long before that. According to the collection, *Americanisms*, published by Schele de Vere in 1871, the usual
western meaning was a stunning blow, as by the fist. But in 1870,
as recorded after extensive research by Allen Walker Read, in the
February, 1928, issue of *American Speech*, an obscure editor of an
obscure newspaper in Iowa, in telling his readers some of the effects
of an unusually severe snowstorm, accompanied with high wind and
intense cold, mentioned it each time as a *blizzard*. The storm had
occurred on March 14, 1870, and was of such severity that it was
long known locally as "the great *blizzard*." The editor of that small
paper continued to use *blizzard* in referring to similar storms in
subsequent years; other newspapers in the state began to adopt it,
and when much of the country experienced a succession of heavy
snowstorms and gales in the winter of 1880-81, *blizzard* had become

so widely known as to be employed, not only in mid-West papers, but also in those of New York and Canada.

bloomers

This article of feminine attire, as someone has said, was named after a woman who "did not invent it, was not the first to wear it, and protested against its being called by her name." She was Amelia Jenks Bloomer, wife of Dexter C. Bloomer, of Seneca Falls, New York, whom she married in 1840. Her husband was the proprietor and editor of a small magazine, in which she became interested. But in 1849 she started a small journal of her own, *The Lily*, chiefly devoted to temperance, woman's suffrage, and dress reform. None of these notions originated with Mrs. Bloomer, however. They had long been advocated by others. In fact it was through the well-known suffragist, Elizabeth Cady Stanton, that she first learned of the garment that was to bear her name. Mrs. Stanton, who was also living in Seneca Falls at that time, was visited in 1850 by her cousin, Mrs. Elizabeth Smith Miller, daughter of the very wealthy philanthropist and abolitionist, Gerrit Smith. It was Mrs. Miller's costume, of her own designing, which Mrs. Bloomer described as "sanitary attire" in the February, 1851, issue of *The Lily*. Later, Mrs. Bloomer herself adopted the costume and appeared in it upon the lecture platform. Today, it would seem extremely modest, but in that day of multiple heavy skirts, dragging on the ground, it was daring. These skirts, in Mrs. Miller's costume, were replaced by a single short skirt over long loose trousers which were gathered round the ankles—very similar to the bathing dress seen at our beaches in the early twentieth century. Although Mrs. Bloomer constantly denied credit for the garment, the public persistence in giving it her name introduced *bloomers* into the language.

bluestocking

About 1750 some of the ladies in the upper circles of London society got thoroughly tired of the empty life which they led, with its constant card-playing and incessant idle chatter every evening of the week at one house or another. So, under the leadership of Lady Mary Montagu, they decided upon a different kind of social diversion. Lady Mary, herself an author, had been an intimate friend of Joseph Addison and Alexander Pope, and was well known among the literary men of the later day. The ladies, then, meeting at the houses of one another, filled their salons with the eminent and the aspiring men of letters. Sumptuous evening dress was not a requisite at these affairs; in fact, to put at ease those who could not afford costly raiment, the ladies themselves dressed simply. Because of this simplicity, the group was held in ridicule by the social circle which they had deserted. And when it was observed that one of the regular attendants of the literary evenings, Mr. Benjamin Stillingfleet, habitually wore his ordinary blue worsted stockings, instead of the black silk stockings usual among gentlemen at an evening affair, merriment was unbounded. "The Bluestocking Club," the set was promptly dubbed by some wit, said to have been Admiral Edward Boscowan, and the ladies were thenceforth *bluestockings*. The epithet was subsequently applied to any lady of literary bent.

blurb

In 1907 the gifted humorist, Gelett Burgess, added to his list of whimsical writings with the small book, *Are You a Bromide?* The book was such a success that the dictionaries were obliged, not only to add in their pages a new definition of "bromide," but also, as a by-product, to add a new word to their lists. The word was *blurb*. The story of its creation was told by Burgess' publisher, B. W. Huebsch, in the summer, 1937, issue of the publication, *Colophon*. Mr. Huebsch wrote, in part:

It is the custom of publishers to present copies of a conspicuous current book to booksellers attending the annual dinner of their trade association, and as this little book was in its heyday when the meeting took place I gave it to 500 guests. These copies were differentiated from the regular edition by the addition of a comic bookplate drawn by the author and by a special jacket which he devised. It was the common practise to print the picture of a damsel—languishing, heroic, or coquettish—anyhow, a damsel, on the jacket of every novel, so Burgess lifted from a Lydia Pinkham or tooth-powder advertisement the portrait of a sickly sweet young woman, painted in some gleaming teeth, and otherwise enhanced her pulchritude, and placed her in the center of the jacket. His accompanying text was some nonsense about "Miss Belinda *Blurb*," and thus the term supplied a real need and became a fixture in our language.

bogus

The origin of this American term has not yet been traced. According to a letter to the editor of the *Oxford English Dictionary*, in the earliest appearance of the word in an Ohio newspaper, it was applied to a kind of mechanism used in making counterfeit coins. The date given to that paper was 1827. Whether *bogus* was used earlier than that, and in what sense, is not known. But thereafter it acquired general use in the United States as a substitute for counterfeit, sham, false, spurious.

bombast

Probably the use of cotton for padding started when men wore armor during the Middle Ages. A chunk of soft cotton where a hard metal joint chafed the skin would relieve the pain. But in the sixteenth century such cotton padding began to be used for another purpose, to stuff into the linings of the large doublets which the men of the court wore. In England this was done in servile flattery of Henry VIII, who was naturally very broad across the shoulders and chest. Such padding was known by the French word for "padding," *bombace* or *bombase* (from a Late Latin word *bombax*, cotton). The thing padded was at first said to be *bombast*, past tense of the verb *bombase*, to pad. But then *bombast* gradually replaced *bombace* as the name of the padding itself. It was not long before this word of fashion came to be applied to any kind of talk which could be recognized as nothing more than padding, the sense in which *bombast* is known today.

It is sometimes said that the word came from the real name of the fifteenth-century German physician, Theophrastus Bombast von Hohenheim, who is best known under his assumed name, Paracelsus. This physician was actually several centuries in advance of his time, so far as his theories and practice were concerned. But he was also a great talker, especially about himself. For these reasons he was held to be a quack and a charlatan by all the medical practitioners of his own and later generations. Because of his arrogance and vanity, it is possible that his own name, Bombast, was used by his enemies to hold him up to ridicule. But the identity of the name is actually nothing more than coincidence.

bonfire

We know very little of pagan times in England. A number of early customs have survived which originated, undoubtedly, before Christianity was introduced, but in the absence of written records the sources of some of those customs cannot be determined. Thus we know that annually upon a given day in midsummer all the bones that had been collected throughout the year, especially the bones of cattle and sheep, were gathered up and burned in a huge outdoor fire. Whatever its pagan significance, the custom continued to be observed generally throughout England. By the sixteenth century, however, the celebration had been transferred to the eve of St. John's Day (June 24) in order to give it a Christian significance. Such literal "bone-fires" were made in certain parts of Scotland until about the nineteenth century. But the name *bone-fire*, later corrupted to *bonfire*, was also applied in the literal sense after the sixteenth century to any funeral pyre upon which a corpse was cremated. And the term was further used then for a fire heaped about a heretic, condemned to be burned at the stake. Probably from early times, however, other things than bones were consumed in these ceremonial fires. At least there is written record that by the sixteenth century *bone-fire* or *bonfire* had also become a term for any large fire in the open air.

book

In Rome, the inner bark of certain trees furnished the material that was used for paper. This inner bark was called *liber*, a word that furnishes us the root of "library." In England, and other Gothic countries, it was the inner, thin bark of the beech tree which the scribes used. The word for this tree was, in Old English, *boc*; so the name of the writings upon the bark came to be known by the same word, which, after many centuries, became *book*.

boulevard

There came a time, in the city of Paris, when the walls of the city were no longer useful. The ramparts were broad, but when gunpowder came into military operations they were of little value for defense. So the ramparts fell into disrepair, until some engineer, seeing that they encircled the city and were broad and flat, thought that a wonderful promenade could be made of this abandoned structure. The Parisians called this promenade *le boulevard*. There was then only one. English visitors took it to be a fashionable name for "path," or, because of its width, for a wide road. Thus the French term *boulevard* came to signify, especially in America, a broad highway which, in the aspirations of its namer, has greater social distinction than "avenue" or "street." Paris is now full of boulevards, though rightly there should, perhaps, be no more than one, because the actual meaning of the French term is "bulwark, rampart."

bowdlerize

Now and then someone comes along who, just like the heroes of mythological times, does something that causes his name to be perpetuated. Sometimes his action is altogether innocent, with no thought that it will bring him lasting glory; sometimes his name becomes noted because the action was held to be especially ridiculous or arbitrary. Thus, back in 1818, the Scottish physician, Dr. Thomas Bowdler, had no other thought than the favor he was conferring upon conscientious British families when, at great pains, he brought out a new edition of the works of William Shakespeare. The value of this edition, he thought, lay in the fact that he had so edited it that all "words and expressions are omitted which cannot with propriety be read aloud in a family." But it is a risky business for a publisher to decide how the works of a famous writer may be improved, and Dr. Bowdler found himself being held up to ridicule. From his name, *bowdlerize* became a symbol for the arbitrary expurgation of words from famous literary works.

boycott

By 1879 the effects of the land laws had driven the people of Ireland to a state of desperation. Most of the land was held by absentee landlords and, through several years of crop failures, tenants unable to pay their rents were being evicted. Home rule had long been demanded from the British Parliament. Now, in that year, under the leadership of Charles Stewart Parnell, a National Land League was organized with an aim to force Parliament into the passage of bills that would, at least, ameliorate existing conditions. Parliament was slow to act. In September of 1880, speaking before a gathering of tenants, Parnell advocated that anyone who took over the land from which a tenant had been evicted should be punished "by isolating him from his kind as if he was a leper of old." This policy was accepted and its scope immediately enlarged. In County Mayo occurred the most notable test. The tenants upon the estates of the earl of Erne, unable to pay the rents charged to them, set up a lower scale which, if accepted, they felt that they could pay. The manager of the estates, however, Captain Charles Cunningham Boycott, would not accept those figures. In retaliation, the tenants applied the measures advocated by Parnell, but with more intense force. Not only did they refuse to gather the crops, but they forced his servants to leave him, tore down his fences so that cattle might enter, intercepted his mail and his food supplies, hooted him in the streets, hung him in effigy, and even threatened his life. He was but the first to be subjected to such treatment; others received it soon after. But the intimidation practiced against Captain Boycott became so famous that within two months the newspapers of England were using his name to identify any such practices. The term *boycott* became not only a new word in our own language, but was speedily adopted in the French, German, Russian, and Dutch languages.

braille

Though not born blind, Louis Braille, born in 1809, lost his eyesight when he was only three years old. When he was nine he was left a homeless waif and was taken to the Paris Institute for the Blind. Here he developed great talent in scientific studies and in music, becoming an instructor for the blind when he was nineteen. At the age of twenty he developed a marked improvement in the so-called "point system" for the printing and writing of raised characters for the use of the blind. It is this system, modified through the experience of time, which, known by his name, is chiefly used in correspondence with blind persons, and in books and music prepared for them.

bribe

Where it came from, no one knows; but in France, six hundred years ago, *bribe* was the alms or the food that one gave to a beggar. When the word reached England it meant, as Chaucer used it, to steal or extort, as well as the thing stolen or extorted. But in the sixteenth century that which was extorted was ironically regarded as a voluntary offering by the person from whom it was taken as an inducement to act in the interests of the giver. The irony thus suggested in the word *bribe* at that time has now been lost. In our present use it has a sinister sound. The giver of the *bribe* expects or demands something in return; the taker, however reluctant, upon his acceptance agrees to the terms, whatever they may be.

broker

We think of a broker these days chiefly as one who, acting for another, buys and sells stocks and bonds for a commission, though there are, of course, other kinds of brokers; as cotton brokers, tea brokers, insurance brokers, and by no means least, pawnbrokers. The last differs from the others in that he advances money upon security, for a premium, rather than acting as an agent who handles the money of others. But *broker* comes from precisely the same Anglo-French source as our word *broach*, and the broker of old was actually a broacher of casks, a tapster, one who drew off wine to sell it at retail to his customers. It was through such retail sales that the term gradually changed its meaning, for it then became applied to any retail dealer, to one who bought either new or secondhand commodities to sell over again. From that its meaning became further extended to the senses in which we use it today.

buccaneer

Explorers from Spain, Portugal, and France of the sixteenth century found many strange customs among the people whom they encountered along the coasts of South America and on the islands of the Caribbean. Some of these they were able to adopt to their own advantage. One of the latter was a simple method for drying or smoking meat. In this, four posts were set in the ground, with a wooden grating or grid for the meat set over the top, at sufficient height to be above the flames of a fire beneath. It was, no doubt, similar to the structure which the natives of Haiti called *barbacoa* (see BARBECUE). French explorers then picked up the name, perhaps from the natives along other shores, as *boucan.* The device was easy to build and convenient to use. So French navigators, hunters, and explorers took to it quickly. Those who used it called themselves *boucaniers.* But when French pirates began to replace the earlier navigators in the seventeenth century, *boucanier*—which had already become *buccaneer* in English—was the innocent name which they adopted for themselves. It was through these *buccaneers,* sea rovers, or pirates, that western Haiti was wrested from Spanish control in 1697.

budget

When this first came into use back in the fifteenth century, it meant a little wallet or purse, from the French *bouge,* purse, or *bouget,* little purse. The diminutive sense died out, and *budget,* the anglicized word, was used for a purse of any size, especially for a purse made of leather. It is a trait of our language, however, that the name of a container is often transferred to the thing contained, so *budget* shortly acquired another meaning also—the contents of a bag or wallet, including whatever papers it might contain. Thus, in the eighteenth century, when the English Chancellor of the Exchequer "opened his *budget,*" as the Parliamentary phrase became, he was in effect opening his wallet or bag to extract papers pertaining to the public finance. And when, in our own family circles, we make up our *budget* for the year, we are really examining the family purse to see how much it will receive during the year and how much of that we can spend.

bug, bugbear, bugaboo (bogy)

The people of Cornwall and Wales, seven or eight hundred years ago used to frighten their children with tales of fearful hobgoblins or specters. We don't know what those ancient tales were nor how they described those imaginary creatures which became very real beings to the children. The Welsh term for specter is *bwg.* The English in telling about the Welsh specter called it *bug,* for the original meaning of that word was "specter" or "ghost." The word hasn't been used in that sense for several centuries, however, except in *bugbear* and *bugaboo*, but became another term for "beetle," some varieties of which resemble a hideous specter. In *bugbear*, the thought may have been a ghostly bear of very frightening appearance, but the concluding syllables of *bugaboo* were apparently meaningless, possibly resulting from nothing more than alliteration. *Bogy*, or *bogey*, which now has the original meaning of *bug*, was probably a dialectal form of the older word.

bugle

In Roman days the forerunner of this musical instrument was originally made from a horn. It was not, however, made from any horned creature, but from one particular kind. That was a bullock, a young bull. The Latin name for such an animal was *buculus*. The name later became *bugle* in French and English, and was long retained as the term for a bullock. In all that period the musical instrument made from its horn was properly called a *bugle-horn*. The name was often shortened to *bugle*, and when that term for a bullock fell into disuse, the musical instrument took full possession of the name. It has been many centuries, however, since the instrument was actually made from the horn of a bullock. Even in Roman times metal was often used for the purpose.

bulldozer

After the American War between the States and the abolition of slavery, there was a natural tendency for the newly enfranchised Negroes of the South to vote for the political party represented by their emancipator, Abe Lincoln. Southern whites objected. Violence and threats of violence sprang up toward the eve of all elections, continuing for many years. In Louisiana especially, the terrible bullwhack, bullwalloper, or bullwhip, as it was variously called, was employed to intimidate the Negro voters. This was a long, heavy, leather lash, fixed to a short wooden handle, and used chiefly by Texan drovers to keep strings of cattle from straying off the road. An expert could lay open the flesh of a bull's hide at a distance of twenty feet. It is a matter of dispute whether the whites were the first to threaten refractory Negroes with "a dose of the bull," or whether Republican Negroes, spurred on by northern carpetbaggers, used the threat against such of their own brethren as were suspected of an intent to vote Democratic; but in either case the victim was first warned and then flogged, "given the *bulldose*," as it was called. The term was spelled both *bulldose* and *bulldoze*. From it was developed *bulldozer*, a bully, one who wields the *bulldose*, who intimidates through superior power or strength. Thus, because of its great power, the mechanical *bulldozer* of today inherited the name.

buncombe, bunkum, bunk

Back in 1820 the petition of the residents of the Territory of Missouri for admission into the Union as a state came before the Sixteenth Congress. Immediately the question of slavery came into discussion, for even then, forty years before the Civil War, there was strong feeling among the northern states against any further extension of slaveholding rights. Debate became furious and bitter, with representatives from the southern states supporting the cause of the many slave-owners in the Territory. Finally a compromise was reached—the historical "Missouri Compromise." It provided that, although Missouri should be admitted as a slave state, slavery would thereafter be prohibited north of 36° 30'. Before a vote could be taken, Representative Felix Walker, from Buncombe County, North Carolina, took the floor and asked permission to speak. He then proceeded to deliver a long oration. It did not have much bearing on the question before the House; in fact, it did not have much bearing upon anything. The weary members began to take up the cry of "Question," but the representative calmly continued his address until it finally came to an end. When he was asked to what purpose he had taken up the time of the House, he replied, it is said, that his constituents expected him to make a speech of some sort in the Congress, that he had carefully prepared one, that this seemed as good a time as any to deliver it, and that he was not speaking so much for Congress, "he was only talking for Buncombe." *Buncombe*, later frequently spelled *bunkum* and contracted eventually to *bunk*, was first, then, any political claptrap or political expedient that was expected to win the favor of one's electors. The term was eagerly seized by the press of the United States and later, of England as a fitting term for such measures. We have since broadened it to include any kind of empty talk or humbuggery believed to be for effect only.

burke

In England and Scotland an intense interest in the study of anatomy had been aroused among young medical students in the last half of the eighteenth century through the researches of Dr. John Hunter. Such study, however, was badly cramped by the laws of the period. For, according to law, none but the bodies of persons executed for murder could be placed upon the dissecting table. Plenty of persons were being executed in those days, but the number executed for murder was comparatively low. There was thus greater demand for bodies than there was a legal supply. In consequence, a new profession sprang up—grave-robbing, or, as it was called, body-snatching. The men who supplied bodies by such means came to be called "resurrection men" or "resurrectionists." Despite the risk, for detection might result in heavy fines and deportation, the grave-robbers found their profession highly lucrative. At the peak of the demand they received as high as £14 for a single body. Students of anatomy did not ask questions as to the source of supply.

In 1827, two Irishmen living in Edinburgh, William Burke and William Hare, happened upon an easier way to obtain corpses than grave-robbing. Hare was running a lodging house, in which Burke had a room. One of the other tenants, an old army pensioner, died, but instead of having him buried, Burke suggested that they sell his body to an anatomist. This was done so readily and for so handsome a price—£7, 10s—that they contrived a scheme for supplying other bodies. Successively, then, they enticed various obscure travelers into Hare's lodging house. It was not difficult to ply them with drink and then suffocate them, being careful to leave no marks. The bodies brought from £8 to £14, and it was subsequently estimated that fifteen victims were thus disposed of. The police eventually became suspicious and the two men were brought to trial. Hare turned king's evidence, but Burke was found guilty and hanged in 1829. The crimes brought such notoriety that even to this day a strangler is said to *burke* his victim, and *burking* has become a synonym for strangling. Partly as a result of these crimes the laws were greatly modified, so that anatomists did not have to resort to illegal methods for pursuing their studies.

bus, (omnibus)

In the spring of 1662 a new conveyance appeared upon the streets of Paris. They were large coaches or *carosses* with places for eight passengers and, under decree of Louis XIV, they were authorized to run upon fixed schedules, whether filled or empty, to extreme parts of the city. Their great virtue was in the low cost of transportation, five sous per person. This made it possible for persons in modest circumstances to ride; the cost of carriage hire at that time might come to thirty or forty times such a fare. However, though expressly designed for the conveyance of infirm and needy persons, it was not long before the coaches catered almost exclusively to the wealthy or to those well able to provide themselves with other transportation. But Dame Fashion is notoriously fickle; it became unfashionable to ride in these coaches, and the socially elect abandoned them to the common herd. They, in turn, would now have nothing to do with the cast-offs of society, and the enterprise failed.

Nevertheless, these coaches, running upon regular schedules over established routes and at fixed low fares, were the forerunners of a system of passenger transportation which has become universal. A century and a half passed after the initial failure, when, again in Paris, larger coaches with places for fifteen to eighteen persons appeared upon the streets in 1827. These bore the inscription along the sides, *Entreprise générale des Omnibus.* The venture became successful immediately, for the word *omnibus*—a Latin term meaning "for all"—was assurance that anyone who could pay the fare was acceptable as a passenger. Two years later, when a similar system of transportation was introduced into London, its promoter, Mr. George Shillibeer, wisely adopted the name already generally used in France and called his larger coach, drawn by three horses and carrying twenty-two passengers, an *omnibus*. Within three years Londoners had familiarly lopped off the first two syllables and, in speech and writing, said that they were traveling by *bus,* the term now ordinarily employed.

butcher (buck)

The *butcher* of today may rarely see a living cow, sheep, or hog, or may never be called upon actually to slaughter anything larger than a turkey or goose. Most of the killing and dressing of animals destined for food is now done in large packing houses, and the word *butcher* is often applied to one who merely handles portions of the dressed carcass. But, unlike the tradesman to whom the term was anciently applied, he deals with meat of all edible kinds. The early *butcher* of France and Italy, slaughtered and sold only goat's meat, according to the name of his occupation. For the name is the Old French *bochier*, one who deals in goat's meat, from *boc*, whence our word *buck*, a "he-goat."

cab, cabriolet (hansom, taxi)

It would seem awkward to say, "Call a cabriolet," rather than "Call a cab," but *cab* is merely a contraction of *cabriolet*, just as *taxicab* is a doubled contraction of *taximeter cabriolet* further shortened to *taxi*. The original cabriolet, or *cabriole*, as it was also called, was built in France in the latter part of the eighteenth century. It was a light two-wheeled affair drawn by a single horse, and had a large hood, usually of leather, and a leather apron to protect the legs of the one or two passengers from the mud of the roads. The springs which supported the body of the vehicle were probably designed for the heavier chaise of the period, for, in combination with the uneven roads of that day and the trotting of the horse, imparted through the shafts, the springs gave the light carriage an elastic bounding motion which reminded someone of the capering of a young goat. In French, *cabri* means a kid, and *cabriole* describes its frolicsome leaps, both from the Latin *caper*, a goat. So *cabriole*, sometimes *cabriolet*, became the descriptive name of the vehicle. In England, where the vehicle was introduced in the early years of the nineteenth century, its more common name, *cabriolet*, was shortened to *cab* within twenty-five years; *cabriolet* became obsolescent and was not revived until an automobile with a similar type of body received the name in the early twentieth century. The *hansom cab*, or, in shortened form, *hansom*, which has all but disappeared from our streets, was so named for its inventor, Joseph Aloysius Hansom, who died in 1882. The first appearance of this improved vehicle was in 1834; its twofold popularity came from its greater safety, provided by a low-hung body, and the privacy afforded to the passengers, for the driver's seat was upon a dickey behind the cab.

cabal

There has long been a popular notion that this word was formed from the initials of the name of five of the members of the English ministry who were particularly given to intrigue during the reign of Charles II, especially during the period from 1667 to 1673. There were indeed five such men, and because of them the word *cabal* did acquire additional prominence. Their names were Clifford, Ashley, Buckingham, Arlington, and Lauderdale. But the word did not arise from their initials; it had been in the language before their time. These five men were not the only ministers who met for secret intrigues, in fact, and they were not likely to meet often with such a purpose. Two of them usually met with one cabal or set of connivers and the other three with another. These five, nevertheless, were those who signed the infamous and secret Treaty of Alliance with France in 1672, without sanction of Parliament, and thereby plunged the nation into war with Holland in defiance of existing treaties.

Cabal actually comes, however, from *cabbala*, sometimes written *cabala*. This was the name used by the Jews for their traditional and occult interpretation of the Old Testament. Thus the word came to apply to anything that was hidden or secret. In English use it became contracted to *cabal* and came to mean a secret or conspiratorial intrigue.

cabbage

The ordinary cabbage which grows in the garden fittingly comes from the Old French word *caboche*, meaning a head, derived from the Latin *caput*, a head. But we use *cabbage* also when we mean "to steal," and this has nothing to do with a head. The origin of the word in this sense isn't positively known, but it is interesting to know that back in the seventeenth century, when it first appeared, it referred to the small pieces of leftover cloth that a tailor appropriated after making a garment. He *cabbaged* them, though they belonged to his patron. The poet, Robert Herrick, spelled the word either *carbage* or *garbage* as the fancy struck him. One place in his *Hesperides*, he wrote:

> Pieces, patches, ropes of haire,
> In-laid *garbage* ev'rywhere.

But in another, these lines appear:

> . . . His credit cannot get
> The inward *carbage* for his clothes as yet.

cad, caddie

A dishonorable word from an honorable source, it is little more than a hundred years old, and came, in roundabout manner, to its present form and meaning from the French word *cadet*. Back in the sixteenth century, and at present, a cadet was a younger son, or younger brother, of the head of a family, and this remained the chief sense of the word when it was taken into English use in the early seventeenth century. Then, in both England and France, cadet became also applied to any such younger son who entered into the military profession, one of the few professions that a young gentleman could enter, in those days, without loss of social standing. (In democratic United States, where brains are more honored than family, cadet applies to any military, naval, or aeronautical student undergoing training to become an officer.) Those young men had no commissions and received no pay. They were dependent upon their families, and, as a result, were usually hard up, probably willing to accept chance employment by an officer.

That may or may not be true, but English *cadet* was usually pronounced and often spelled *caddie* in those days. This at first retained its earlier meaning, but eventually came to be applied to any young fellow on the lookout for chance employment—ultimately, to carry a golfer's clubs. Such fellows, around Oxford University, came to be familiarly designated as *cads*. And thus, because a man who hangs around awaiting a chance job is likely to be ill-bred and vulgar, the term *cad* came to have a meaning opposite to that of its origin.

cadre

It may help, in recalling the military usage, to remember that, although this came originally from the Latin *quadrum*, a four-

53

sided thing, it came to us from the French, in which language a *cadre* was a picture frame or a framework. Thus a military *cadre* is the framework or skeleton organization of officers and men upon which a complete unit may be built.

cajole

We cannot do more than speculate about this word. It was borrowed from the French *cajoler* in the seventeenth century, but it is not certainly known how it originated. Its French meaning, at the time, was to babble or chatter, like a jay or magpie in a cage. That may have been a slang or secondary meaning, because the word was also used as we now use it, to wheedle, or coax by flattery or false pretenses. Perhaps the strident tones of the jay and magpie reminded some French joker of the shrill voice of his querulous wife, demanding that he do some favor for her. He may have ironically termed it *cajolery*, in likeness to the insistent chatter of a jay.

cake

Outside of Scotland, the original sense of this word applied to something edible occurs chiefly in combination, as pan*cake*, hoe*cake*, fish*cake*. That is, back in the days of Chaucer (and still among the Scots), a cake was distinguished from a loaf by its appearance and the manner of its baking. The cake was flattened and, usually, small and round or oval in shape, was generally baked hard, ordinarily being turned over in the process. In Scotland, such cakes have long been made of oaten flour, and the predilection of the people for these oatcakes caused the country to be banteringly nicknamed the "land of Cakes." But English cooks began to experiment, adding other ingredients, such as sugar, spices, raisins, or the like, to their batter, and did not always bake it hard or turn it over while baking. In fact, except by its rounded and flattened shape, it did not greatly resemble the cake of old. This modified and more tasty concoction is what we in America understand by the word today.

calculate (abacus)

The *abax* of ancient Greece, used as a counting board, was found to meet fully the needs also of later Roman mathematicians, who changed its name to *abacus*, a name that we still employ. Wooden beads, or the like, strung upon wires, are used on modern boards. But in ancient times the board was divided by partitions into the number of compartments that might be wanted, and small pebbles were used for the counters, such pebbles being moved from compartment to compartment as the reckoning might require. The Latin name for a pebble was *calculus*. One who *calculates* is, therefore, one who, in ancient times, moved pebbles about upon an abacus for a mathematical reckoning.

calico

Nowadays in America this applies to a printed cotton cloth of plain weave, though in England it is unprinted. But originally, back in the sixteenth century, the name applied to cotton cloth of various kinds which might be stained, dyed, printed, or plain, for it then referred to any of the various cloths that were imported into England from the seaport city of *Calicut*, India, from which it got its name.

caliph

After the death of Mahomet in 632, the question immediately arose among his loyal adherents who should serve as his representative. The leading spirit among them was Omar who, as a young man, had opposed the Prophet, but who later was to be one of his ablest supporters. Omar decided, however, that the honor should first be bestowed upon the man who had been Mahomet's sole companion in the flight from Mecca (the Hegira) and who subsequently became his father-in-law. This was Abu-Bekr, long known as "the faithful." Abu-Bekr thus became the first "successor," a word that, in Arabic, is rendered *khalifah* and which in English became *caliph*. (See also ADMIRAL.)

calliope

Among the Muses, honored by the Greeks as goddesses of poetry and song, the ninth was the silver-toned *Calliope*. Her name was derived from the two Greek words, *kallos*, beauty, and *ops*, voice, and she was assumed to preside over the arts of eloquence and epic poetry. About a hundred years ago, however, an inventive genius by the name of Lax took the older steam organ and made some improvements upon it—possibly making its whistles louder and shriller. This new and strident musical device he graced with the name of the goddess, calling it a *calliope*. Mounted upon a circus wagon, as it usually was, its blatant tones could be heard a mile or more. In later construction its tones have been softened and made more pleasing.

calumet

While the English were doing little more than talk about the colonies they hoped to establish in North America, Frenchmen were busily engaged in exploring the vast reaches that stretched along either side of the great St. Lawrence River, making friends with the tribes of Indians whom they met, observing their customs, and building up a large trade in furs. Wherever they went they found one unchanging custom: after being convinced that the mission was peaceful, the chieftains, in solemn conclave, would pass a lighted pipe of tobacco from one to another and to their guests as a supreme proof of hospitality. Each took a few brief puffs of smoke from it. Acceptance of the pipe was a sign of friendship; refusal was a grievous affront. Because the practice of smoking was new or as yet unknown to the early French explorers, these pipes were of great interest. The bowl was often made of an easily carved red stone, later found to have come from a region in South Dakota near Big Stone Lake. But it was the stem of the ceremonial pipe that was chiefly honored. This was of reed or of slender hollowed wood, highly decorated with the quills of an eagle or of the porcupine, and often further ornamented with beads made of shell. These stems, usually about two and a half feet in length, reminded the French of the reed upon which the shepherds of their own country evoked soft music. Such a reed, in Norman speech, was called a *calumet*, and it was thus that *calumet* became the name of the American Indian ceremonial pipe.

cambric

Weaving in France and the Low Countries, was the chief industry of the Middle Ages. Each town prided itself upon the nature and quality of its products, vying with one another. Astute buyers, just as in parts of Persia, India, and China, were able to recognize the textiles of one community from those of another. Thus, a little Flemish village (now in northeastern France) was noted for the fine, white linen fabric woven upon its looms. The material was admirably adapted for the making of luxurious shirts, ruffs, neckbands, and when introduced into England in the early sixteenth century, king and courtiers demanded its use by their tailors. It was then the English custom to call an importation by the name of the place from which it came; hence, merchants gave this cloth the name *cambric*, for that is how the Flemish name sounded in their ears, though the Flemish spelling was *Kameric*. (This village is now the town of Cambrai, and the fabric is more often of cotton than of linen. See also BATISTE.)

camellia

A humble Moravian Jesuit is honored by the name of this beautifully flowered plant. He was George Joseph Kamel, who was born in 1661 and died in 1706. He took the name Camellus, a Latinized form of his name, after his entry into the religious order of his choice, and was sent on missionary work to the Philippine Islands. There he found a fascinating interest in the plants and animals of the islands, and wrote extensive accounts of them. Among the plants was a beautiful flowering member of the tea family, previously unreported. So when Linnæus, the eminent Swedish naturalist of the eighteenth century, was obliged to find names for many of the formerly unknown plants of the world, he chose the word *camellia* for that first reported by the priest, Cammellus.

camera

So long ago that no one can say when, it was discovered that if one were in a room shuttered so as to be quite dark, except for the light entering a small hole, say, in the shutter, an image of any object in the sunshine and directly facing that hole would be projected in reverse position upon the opposite wall of the room. This phenomenon was apparently known to Aristotle, and down through the later centuries. It seems to have been known to Roger Bacon in the thirteenth century and to Leonardo da Vinci in the fifteenth. In the latter part of the fifteenth century several experimenters found ways to show the image in a natural position by the use of a mirror to reflect the rays, or by inserting a small lens in the aperture through which the rays passed. But it was not until the early seventeenth century, when the German astronomer, Johannes Kepler, was finding practical use for the plaything in his observations on the size of the sun and moon, that it acquired a name. He called it *camera obscura*, literally, "dark chamber." The later British physicist, Robert Boyle, found that it was not necessary to darken an entire room, but that a small box, fitted with a lens at one end, would serve the purpose admirably. Paper stretched across the opposite end received the image. The *camera obscura*, or *camera* as it was then sometimes called, made little advance during the next hundred years or so, except by an occasional use of additional lenses or a reflecting mirror. In 1802, however, Thomas Wedgwood announced to the British Royal Institution that he had been able to find "a method of copying paintings upon glass and of making profiles by the agency of light upon nitrate of silver." From that time the *camera obscura* became the *camera* that we know today.

camouflage

Slang can rarely be traced with any certainty, and this, prior to World War I, was Parisian slang. It was the smoke blown into a person's eyes, in fun or seriously, to blind him from observing what was going on around him. Thus, in reverse, it was a kind of smoke screen. And, in World War I, it may have been that the term was first applied to a smoke screen, a screen of smoke emitted by a vessel to conceal its movements from an enemy or to make difficult the determination of the distance between them. But it was found that a ship painted in varicolored designs was likely to escape detection entirely, and thus *camouflage* came to embrace any kind of disguise. It is probable that the word came from an earlier French military term, *camouflet*. This was applied to a kind of bomb which was discharged, by countermining, within the mine of an enemy. It was filled with a powder which, when discharged, would emit dense fumes that would asphyxiate the enemy's mine crew.

canard

The French have an old saying, *vendre un canard à moitié*, literally, to half-sell a duck, for *canard* means "duck." But, so the explanation goes, one cannot half-sell anything, let alone a duck flying in the sky, and when one says that he has half-sold a duck, he is, of course, trying to make a fool of the person to whom he is talking. Thus, more than three centuries ago, one who related false stories or circulated false reports became known, in France, as one who delivered ducks, or, that is, uttered *canards*.

canary

A few years after the death of Julius Caesar, or about 40 B.C., the chieftain of an extensive region in northwest Africa, then called Mauritania, set out upon a sea journey of exploration. On clear days, about sixty miles off the coast of the southern stretches of his country, the peaks of small islands could be seen. Juba, the Mauritanian chieftain, determined to explore those islands. An account of his explorations was preserved by Pliny the Elder. The islands are believed to have been known long before this time, however, for somewhere to the west of the "Pillars of Hercules"—by which ancient mariners meant the Strait of Gibraltar—lay the mythological "Fortunate Islands," or "Isles of the Blest." By old Greek legend, this was the abode of such mortals as had been saved from death by the gods. The climate was idyllic and food was abundant. These are thought to have been the same islands seen and explored by Juba. One of the islands, Juba found, had its peaks—which were above eleven thousand feet in elevation—covered with snow. To this he gave the Latin name, "*Nivaria*," or "The Snowy Island." But the impressive feature of another of the larger islands was the multitude of large dogs which roamed over it. For that reason he named it *Canaria*, or "The Island of Dogs," from *canis*, dog. This last name was kept by later explorers and colonists—becoming *Canary* in English—and was the name by which the entire archipelago was known. Spain took possession of the islands in the fifteenth century, but it was another hundred years before the most widely known of the products of the islands, the songbird, was domesticated and carried to all parts of Europe. We call the bird a *canary*; the dogs from which the name originated have long been extinct.

cancel

The learned monks of the Middle Ages, and perhaps the less learned scribes who copied their writings, were just as likely to find errors in the things they wrote as we of today find in our own. But they had no erasers, and parchment was too precious to risk the removal of ink with a knife, so they merely crossed out the matter in which an error had occurred by drawing lines obliquely across it. To the monks such criss-cross lines looked like lattices, so they called them *cancelli*, the Latin word for lattices. This gave rise to the French verb *canceler*, modified into the English *cancel*.

candidate, candid, candor

The Latin source, *candidatus*, originally meant "clothed in white." But the whiteness indicated by this word differed from ordinary white, for which the Romans used *albus*, because it meant a glistening or shining whiteness, the whiteness of newly fallen snow in brilliant sunshine; hence, spotless purity, stainlessness.

Now it was the custom in ancient Rome, from three or four centuries before the days of Cæsar until a similar period after his death, that a man who aspired to one of the high offices—consul, edile, pretor, tribune—should declare his intent to seek that office and should make public appearance clad in a pure white toga, one in which the natural whiteness of the cloth was intensified by applications of chalk rubbed into its fabric. By implication, that man publicly declared that his character was as pure as the stainless snow; that, through this array, the voters might be assured that he sought public office with none but the highest of motives, and that he was the soul of honor and integrity.

From the color of the robe traditionally worn upon such occasions, the name *candidatus* became transferred to the person seeking office. Our English derivative, *candidate*, no longer carries the implication of stainless purity that its source conveyed, although office seekers and their adherents often try to give us such an impression. The English word is comparatively recent; it is not recorded until a dozen years or so after the death of Shakespeare in 1616; he knew neither this word nor the related words, *candor* and *candid*, in which honesty, frankness, and fairness are still implicit.

cannibal

Christopher Columbus, when he landed in Cuba, inquired of the natives how they were named. In their dialect they said that they were *Canibales,* or people of *Caniba.* Because Columbus thought that he was in Asia, however, he took this to mean that the people were subjects of the Great Khan, or Great Can, as the name was sometimes spelled. Actually, however, *Caniba* was no more than a dialectal form of *Caribe,* and the Cuban natives were Caribs. Later explorers used either name, *Canibales* or *Caribes,* in referring to any of the people of the West Indies. They learned also that all of these people were very fierce. Some were known to be eaters of human flesh, so within less than a century after the voyages of Columbus all Europeans, hearing the name *Canibales,* promptly associated it with man-eaters, or anthropophagi, until at last that became its accepted meaning. The change in English spelling to *cannibal* took place in the seventeenth century.

canopy

The Greeks were bothered by mosquitos, just as we are—and so were the Egyptians before them. So, taking the idea from Egypt, the Greeks draped a mosquito curtain about their couches at night to have some unmolested sleep. From *konops,* mosquito, the Grecian name for such a protected bed was *konopeion.* Romans, who found similar beds afforded great relief from the pesky insects breeding along the Tiber, borrowed its Greek name also and called it *canopeum.* Thus *canopy,* by which we now mean almost anything in the way of an overhead covering, was originally a mosquito-protected bed.

canter

In 1170, Thomas à Becket was murdered near the altar of the Cathedral of Canterbury, of which he was archbishop. He had defied King Henry II and was slain when he refused to retract. But Becket was canonized two years later and the anniversary of his death, December 29, was set by the pope as his feast day. His bones, however, remained in the crypt in which they had been hastily interred for a period of fifty years. Then, in 1220, King Henry III had them placed in a splendid shrine in the cathedral. For the next three hundred years this shrine became an object of peculiar veneration among English people and, as related in Chaucer's *Canterbury Tales,* the aim of countless pilgrimages. These pilgrimages were as often for a summer excursion as for actual piety, but they served for a leisurely journey along roads and to a place where well-kept inns and pleasant companionship could be found. Many of the pilgrims rode, but in the pleasant summer weather no one was in a hurry, and the usual pace was a leisurely amble. This became so common a sight to farmers and others along the roads leading to Canterbury that the style of riding became spoken of as a *Canterbury pace*, or, depending upon the speaker, a *Canterbury trot*, or *rack*, or *gallop*. Eventually it became customary to call it just a *Canterbury*. Even this shortened form was ultimately found to be too long, and thus the name of the leisurely pace became further abridged to *canter* some two hundred years ago.

canvas, canvass

Strangely enough, *canvas* and *canvass* sprang from the same source, the Latin word, *cannabis*, hemp. In fact, they were identical words. It is only within the past century or so that we have been using different spellings to indicate their different meanings. *Canvas* was originally made of hemp, which accounts for its name. It has always been of various weights or thicknesses, depending upon the purpose for which it was needed. Thus, five or six centuries ago, it was sometimes woven sufficiently fine to be used as a bolting cloth, that is, for sifting flour after it was milled. From that use of the cloth, the word *canvas* came to be used as a verb, meaning to sift, examine, or scrutinize. Then it was not long before it began to be used in a figurative sense, as in speaking of the need for examining or sounding out voters and discussing the qualifications of a candidate. Thus we find that by the middle of the sixteenth century, it had passed to the next step, meaning to solicit support for a certain cause, or to solicit votes. Then, because both meanings were just as commonly spelled one way as the other, it was decided that the textile should be spelled *canvas* and that the term pertaining to scrutiny should be *canvass*.

caper, caprice, capricious

Men, women, and children will stand for hours watching the antics of goats enclosed in a pasture. The goats will nibble the grass contentedly and soberly, until suddenly, as if pricked with a thorn, one or another will bound away for a short distance, perhaps prance a bit, or playfully butt another, and then with the utmost composure fall to nibbling grass again. The young kids indulge more frequently in these sudden outbursts of exuberance and are, therefore, more amusing to watch, but the antics of the older ones are more unexpected. Now the Latin word for goat is *capra*. Thus, from the unaccountable leaps upward, forward, or sideward of these animals has come our word *caper*. And when, through a quirk of the mind, one indulges in something unexpected, we call such an action a *caprice*, and one is *capricious* when, through whim, he turns from one thing to another. (See also CAB.)

cardigan

The Crimean War, 1854 to 1856, with England and France fighting against Russia, might have left little impression upon the people of the United States, except for two notable features connected with it. It was the great suffering of the British soldiers in battle and during the terrific winter of 1854-55 in Crimea that enabled Florence Nightingale to overcome opposition and establish well-equipped hospitals, staffed with women trained in nursing, as a part of the military unit. And it was the Crimean War that furnished the incident, in 1854, which was made famous through Tennyson's *Charge of the Light Brigade*. The leader of this charge and the first man to reach the strongly intrenched Russian guns was James Thomas Brudenell, 7th Earl of Cardigan, who was an English major general at that time. Whether the charge was a tactical mistake or not was a matter of debate for many years, but no one questioned the heroism of Lord Cardigan and his prompt obedience of orders, though two-thirds of his brigade were left on the battlefield. He became the hero of the hour. It is not known how many things may have been named in his honor, but the only one bearing his name that has survived is the knitted woolen jacket, still referred to as a *cardigan*.

carnival

The real meaning is "the putting away of flesh (as food)," for it comes, through Italian, from the Latin *carnem*, flesh, and *levare*, to put away. Originally it pertained to the day preceding the beginning of Lent, to the last day when, for a period of forty days, one would again be permitted to eat meat, to the French *Mardi gras* and to the English *"Shrove Tuesday."* This was, therefore, a day of feasting and revelry. In some countries, especially during the Middle Ages, the period of riotous amusement began on the previous Sunday and extended through Tuesday, some places it lasted a week, and in England a general period of festivity and entertainment began the day after "Twelfth Day," January 6, and lasted through Shrove Tuesday. But, three and a half centuries ago, *carnival* began to be used as a term to denote any period or occasion for gay festivity, revelry, or riotous sport, and the modern affair rarely has any connection now with the Lenten period or abstinence from meat.

carol

In the Middle Ages, a *carol* was not a song, but a dance—one probably performed by a ring of men and women, or boys and girls, holding hands and dancing round to the music of a lute. The poetic thought has been expressed that Stonehenge, that mystical circle of stone monoliths in southern England, was originally a group of gay maidens who, dancing a carol on Sunday, were turned to stone for breaking the Sabbath day. It is thought that the word *carol* is related to the Latin *chorus* and Greek *choros,* each of which denoted a band of dancers.

carousel

In Italy, during the late Middle Ages, when jousts and tournaments and feats of archery had given way by a century or more to the more deadly and impersonal bombard and cannon, the courtiers made up a pageant to commemorate the olden days. Grouped into sets of four, each set distinguished by similar old-time costume, and mounted upon gaily caparisoned horses, they engaged in harmless and picturesque tournaments, mainly exhibiting equestrian skill. Such a pageant was called a *carosello.* When introduced into France, in the early seventeenth century, the Italian name was altered to *carrousel,* from which the English term was derived. Other features were added to the pageantry in France, the most popular being to run with a lance at the pasteboard head of a Turk or Moor. The *carousel* of the United States, which we usually call "merry-go-round," retains the gaily caparisoned galloping horses, though they are now of wood and move mechanically up and down on steel posts, and the Turk's head at which they charged is replaced by an arm containing, now and then, a brass ring that permits the lucky young "knight" to mount his trusty steed for a free second joust.

carpet

This was not always a floor covering. In fact, back in the thirteenth century, it merely designated a rather thick, wooly cloth which, in certain religious orders, was used as a garment. However, it was more commonly used as a cover for beds or as a tablecloth. It was the latter use that gave rise to the expression, "on the *carpet*," meaning under consideration at the council table. But some fine lady of the fifteenth century discovered that these thick bedspreads were an excellent protection under foot against the chill of a cold stone floor. Her modified use soon became general, and the earlier use of a *carpet* for a bedcover or tablecloth is all but forgotten.

cartridge

Back in the sixteenth century, when pistols, like the small cannons or curtalls, were loaded through the bore, the powder and shot were poured first into little paper cornucopias, to be ready for use. Because these were identical in shape, though not in size, with the paper horns which grocers used for the goods which they sold at retail, the French gave the military cornucopia the same name, *cartouche*. Both the device and its name were borrowed by the English army. Then English soldiers began giving their own versions of the pronunciation of the word, calling it *cartage, cartalage, cartrage,* and, later, *cartredge* and *cartridge,* among a variety of other forms. For no good reason, the form *cartridge* was adopted by the majority of writers in the eighteenth century, and became the accepted spelling.

caterpillar

Pilare is the Latin for "to grow hair" and gives an adjective *pilosus,* meaning "hairy." From this and their own word *chat,* a cat, the French formed *chatepelose,* "hairy cat," which may be compared to "woolly bear," the common name by which English children refer to the same fuzzy creature, the *caterpillar*. The French word, *chate-*

pelose, was in due course taken into English; but the significance of the latter part of the word was not recognized. It was actually confused with the stem of the old English word "to pill," meaning "to strip or plunder," the idea being that the caterpillar strips the bark off trees. This is the reason why the spelling of the word has departed so far from the French form.

caucus

A group of men, meeting in Boston in colonial Massachusetts for political purposes, called themselves the *"Caucus* Club." Very little is known about this Club beyond a statement made by the historian, William Gordon. Gordon had lived in Massachusetts for sixteen years, returned to England in 1786, and then wrote a four-volume *History of the Rise and Independence of the United States.* In part, his statement reads:

More than fifty years ago Mr. Samuel Adams's father and twenty others, one or two from the north end of town, where all the ship-business is carried on, used to meet, make a caucus, and lay their plans for introducing certain persons into places of trust and power. . . . By acting in concert, together with a careful and extensive distribution of ballots, they generally carried the elections to their own mind. In like manner it was that Mr. Samuel Adams first became a representative from Boston.

Mr. William Adams, father of Samuel Adams, died in 1747, and it thus seems probable that the Club existed ten or more years before that date, as Mr. Gordon implies.

If Mr. Gordon was correct in his spelling of the name of the Club, as our leading dictionaries believe, the name seems to have been taken from the Algonquian term, *caucawasu*, which means advisor, or counselor. This derivation, however, is doubted by some scholars. They point out that Mr. Gordon, an Englishman, might have heard the name of the Club incorrectly; they argue, on the basis that some of the members were "from the north end of town, where all the ship-business is carried on," that the name might have been, "Calkers' Club," that is, a club composed of those whose profession it was to calk ships. And in the *Dictionary of American English* another theory is advanced. It is brought forth that in 1745, at least, one section of Boston was known as "West Corcus"; hence, presumably, another section was "Corcus." Thus the Club may have been named from a geographical region, the "Corcus Club." And more recently, according to H. L. Mencken in *The American Language: Supplement I*, Dr. L. C. Barret, in 1943, announced the discovery of some papers which John Pickering, the philologist, received from a correspondent, later than 1816 undoubtedly, in which it was alleged that the word *caucus* was derived from the "initials of six men, viz.: Cooper (Wm.), Adams, Urann (Joyce, Jr.), Coulson, Urann, Symmes." Mr. Mencken points out, however, that at least one of the persons named could not have been more than twelve or fourteen years old in 1736 when, presumably, the Club was already active.

chancellor

The term from which this word was derived originally applied to an individual whose duties were no more onerous than to stand at the railing of a court, back in the days of the Roman Empire, to protect the court from the press of the people. He was just an usher. His title came from the place where he stood, at the railing or latticework. *Cancelli* was the name of that railing, hence the usher was known as *cancellarius*. At the breakup of the Roman Empire, the functionary represented by the title became of great importance in the Roman-German Empire and the kingdoms of the West. In England—where the title was first *canceler*, and ultimately became *chancellor*, through French influence—it became the title of the highest judicial officer of the crown.

chaperon

As a part of their costume, French nobles of the late Middle Ages wore a kind of hood, not unlike the hood that is a part of the academic gown of today. It somewhat resembled the mantle, *chape*, worn by priests and others of that period, and for that reason the hood was called a *chaperon*, little mantle. In England, when Edward III founded the Order of the Garter, in 1349, the *chaperon* was a part of the full-dress costume worn by the members. Except by these members, however, this hood was not worn by men after the fifteenth century. It was then taken up by ladies, especially by those of the court. Ultimately, but not before the eighteenth century, the term acquired its present general sense, which has thus been explained: "When used metaphorically (it) means that the experienced married woman shelters the youthful *débutante* as a hood shelters the face."

chapel, chaplain

In the early part of the fourth century a young soldier in the army of the Eastern Roman Empire became converted to Christianity. His name was Martin. It is said that, while a soldier, young Martin passed a beggar shivering in his rags one bitterly cold day. Moved with compassion, the soldier took his own cloak and, with his sword, cut it in half. Keeping half for himself, he wrapped the other about the poor beggar. Some years after his discharge from the army he founded a monastery in Gaul, with the aid and advice of the great St. Hilary, over which he presided until 371. Then, with reluctance, he agreed to leave his peaceful monastery to become Bishop of Tours. There he was credited with many cures of the sick and with many miracles. So great became his fame for saintliness and miracles that he was again obliged to take refuge in a nearby monastery, where he died in A.D. 400. A later biographer listed more than two hundred miracles wrought by him after death. But St. Martin of Tours, as he was subsequently known, became the patron saint of France. The Frankish kings preserved his cloak, or *cappella*, as a sacred relic, bearing it before them in battle, and keeping it otherwise within a holy sanctuary. This sanctuary thus became known as a *cappella*, and those under whose charge the cloak was placed were known as *cappellani*. These terms became *chapele* and *chapelain* in Old French, and thus yielded the English *chapel* and *chaplain*.

chapter

Even in its Latin form, *capitulum*, the extended meaning among Romans was "a division of a book," and this remained a familiar usage in the Christian Era, especially with reference to a division of one of the books of the Bible. But in the days of Saint Augustine, in the fourth century A.D., a custom was introduced which led to a further extension in the meaning of *capitulum*—and the much later English word *chapter* formed through French corruption of *capitulum*. That custom, established in monasteries, was the reading of one of the chapters of the Bible to the assembled canons or monks of the establishment. Later a chapter from the Rules of the Order was sometimes substituted. Thus through this custom it became the familiar practice to refer to the assemblage which met for the reading as a *capitulum* or *chapter*. And from this usage arose the further development in which *chapter* referred also to the members of one branch of a monastic order, the members of one house, or, later, of one branch of a fraternal order of whatever nature.

charity

Saint Jerome, who translated the New Testament into Latin in the fourth century, sought to avoid the use of the ordinary Latin word for "love," *amor*, because of the distinctly worldly associations attached to that word. It did not agree with his interpretation of *agape*, in the original Greek, which denotes more nearly brotherly love or the deep affection between close friends. So he substituted, wherever the Greek text would naturally have required *amor*, one or another rather colorless word, one of them being *caritas*. Its meaning is "dearness," but, being colorless, it was capable of taking the color of its biblical surroundings and thus came to mean, specifically, Christian love of one's neighbor, and especially of the poor. The English word *charity*, derived from it, perhaps owes its sense particularly to the great passage in I Corinthians, chapter 13, which begins: "Though I speak with the tongues of men and of angels, and have not *charity*, I am become as sounding brass, or a tinkling cymbal."

chattel (cattle)

Under the feudal system, one's "capital" consisted in what was considered to be his personal property, that is, in such possessions that could be moved, whatever the form of those possessions. To an English peasant of the Middle Ages, such possessions were largely restricted to his livestock, to the oxen, cows, sheep, that the tenant on an estate might have. These were his "capital"; they were his chief and principal holdings, as the Latin word *capitale* implies. But Latin was a stumbling block to the common man, and *capitale* was a difficult word for him to master. It became corrupted in ordinary speech to *catel*, or to a dozen other spellings having similar sound, and finally wound up as our present word, *cattle*. In France, similar difficulty was found with the Latin *capitale*. Eventually, in French speech of medieval times, it became *chatel*, and this term found its way into England after the Norman invasion. Its meaning was at first the same as the English *catel*, movable property of any sort, including goods and money, as well as livestock. Hence, in due season, *cattle* meant only "livestock" to the common Saxon serf, who had no other possessions, while the aristocratic Norman-French *chattel* became the legal term for all personal property, including such livestock as the Norman conquerors might possess.

chauffeur

In the struggle between the Vendeans and the Republicans in France from 1793 to 1795, a band of brigands sprang up, pillaging and firing the countryside. They entered such houses as they suspected of holding treasure, demanding that the owner turn over his gold and silver to them. Their chief leader was one called *Schinder-hannes* or *Jean l'Ecorcheur*, "Jack the Scorcher," who introduced ways of enforcing their demands. If a householder refused or was thought to have concealed some of his valuables, he would be bound to a chair and his feet thrust into the fire on the hearth. For that reason these brigands became known as *chauffeurs*, firemen, from the French verb *chauffer*, to heat, to stoke. Later, after the introduction of steamships, locomotives, and so on, the term was more honorably applied to stokers and firemen. The name was logically transferred to the mechanic employed to tend an automobile (later its driver) because the early automobile, which operated by steam, required a stoker.

chauvinism

Nicolas Chauvin was one of Napoleon's soldiers, wounded seventeen times, it is said, in the cause of his emperor. He retired with a pension of two hundred francs a year—and for the rest of his life talked to all who would listen of nothing else but the glory, majesty, and generalship of Napoleon and the greatness of France. He became a laughingstock in his village, but it is likely that he would have remained unknown to the rest of France had it not happened that the two dramatists, Charles Théodore and Jean Hippolyte Cogniard, brothers, heard of him and his boasts. They used Chauvin as a character in their first successful comedy, *La cocarde tricolore*, produced in 1831. In the play they represented him as an almost idolatrous worshiper of Napoleon, which was literally true. Because of the popularity of the play, the name then appealed to the popular fancy, and *chauvinisme* (*chauvinism* in English) was coined to typify this kind of extreme hero worship or national adoration.

check, checkmate, chess, checkers, (exchequer)

Chess is an exceedingly old game. No one knows how old, but it appears to have been played in Hindustan in remote times, and was probably taken from there to Persia where the Arabs acquired a knowledge of it. The Arabs then introduced the game into Spain in the eighth century. Thence it spread into all Europe. The main piece in the game is the king. The Arabs, taking the name of this piece from the Persians, called it *shah*, and when the king had been maneuvered by an opposing player into a position from which it could not be extricated, thus ending the game, they said, "*Shah mat* (The king is dead)." In Old Spanish this became *xaque mate*; in Old French *eschec mat*, and this in turn produced the Middle English *chek mate*, coming down to us as *checkmate*. And when a player notified his opponent that his king was exposed, the Arabian *shah*, through the same process, became the English *check*. (All other uses of our word *check* and of the British *cheque* have been extensions of this original sense.) When the game had reached France it became known by the Old French name, *eschès*, a plural of *eschec*. And when this term reached England the first syllable was dropped, like many other similar words of French origin. Thus was produced the name by which we know the game, *chess*. So, if we go back to original sources, "chess" is another word for "kings."

The game of *checkers* (British *chequers*) was originally a modification of chess, and its name came from the same source. (In England, the game is preferably known as "draughts.") And the *Court of Exchequer*, an English department of government connected with the public revenue, is believed to have taken its name in the twelfth century from the square table which was laid out into square spaces, like that of a chessboard, for convenience in making calculations in the system of accountancy then in use.

chevaux-de-frise

During the long struggle for Dutch independence from Spanish rule, in the latter part of the seventeenth century, the people of the Low Countries were greatly handicapped by a lack of adequate cavalry or, especially, by lack of protection against cavalry charges. They might, to some extent, flood their lands by opening dikes, but that often hampered their own movements on foot more than it impeded the opposing cavalry. In this dilemma, some Friesian military engineer devised a kind of movable abatis which, when rolled into position, could be linked with others of like construction with heavy chains. The device consisted of a log or heavy beam, some twelve or more feet in length, with sharply pointed stakes or steel tipped lances mounted radially about its sides, each stake about six feet or so in length. A series of these devices chained together thus provided an effective barrier. Because they were first used as substitutes for the cavalry that the Dutch did not have, they were known by the French name, *chevaux-de-frise*, or, literally, "horses of Friesland," each unit being a *cheval-de-frise*.

chivalry, chevalier (cavalry, cavalier)

When William the Conqueror sailed from Normandy with 60,000 men to bring England under his subjection, he took with him many mounted men, their horses, and their armor. These men were knights, for it was then not likely that any lesser man than a knight had the means to own a horse and its caparison. In the literal sense, that mounted knight was a *chevalier*. That is, from the French word *cheval*, meaning horse, he was a rider. Thence, because a knight had taken an oath to bear himself with bravery and honor and to be at all times courteous and gallant, *chevalier* became an equivalent of a knight, or a term for a man of knightly deportment.

A body of *chevaliers*, in William's day, was *chevalerie*, literally a collection of mounted men. This became *chivalry*, in English. Then, because "the *chivalry*," or group of mounted knights, was composed of *chevaliers*, the term *chivalry* came to denote the conduct or the ideals of those upon whom it depended.

The Age of Chivalry passed before the invention of gunpowder, but then, in the seventeenth century, came the military need for greater numbers of mounted horsemen than those gallant gentlemen of earlier times could have supplied. This later body took its name also from the Latin *caballarius*, horseman, which had been the source of French *chevalier*, but came instead through Italian *cavalleria* into all of western Europe. It was readily accepted in England in the form *cavalry*. *Cavalier* had already come from Spain (Old Spanish *cavallero*), from the same Latin source, to denote a gay and courtly military equestrian. It was applied ironically to the partisans of Charles I, both military and political, by their Parliamentary opponents during England's Civil War, because those who followed the king in his fight against Parliament, were held to be nothing but riffraff, far removed from courtliness.

clerk

We do not now necessarily impute scholarship to the person whom we call a *clerk*, but such was the original significance of the word and is still assumed to be the case in many instances of its use. The term was originally a slurred pronunciation of *cleric*, and it designated a clergyman, one who was ordained to the ministry of the Christian Church. Scholarship, in medieval times, was rarely found outside of the religious orders, so the *cleric* or *clergy* was called upon for most of the secretarial work of the period. Gradually, as learning became more general, the early significance faded, except in certain long-established legal and clerical titles.

climate

Contrary to general impression, the fact that the earth is a sphere was accepted by Greek geographers more than two thousand years ago. Their writings and theories, however, were denounced as heresy and contrary to biblical interpretation by the Christian Church of the fourth century A.D., and thus remained sealed books for more than a thousand years. An earlier Greek belief, before the spherical shape was advanced, was that the earth sloped from the equator to the north. (The Greeks knew nothing of the southern hemisphere.) The slope at the equator, they thought, was slight, but it became steadily steeper toward the north. Thus, for geographical purposes, they conceived the earth to consist of seven equal broad belts, parallel with the equator, each belt having its own degree of slope. The Greek word for "slope" being *klima*, the successive belts were referred to as first *klima*, second *klima*, and so on northward. Cities and other places were thus said to be in such and such a *klima*. With increased learning and the discovery that the earth was a globe, other methods of geographical location became essential. It had long been known that the farther one went toward the north, the longer the summer daylight lasted. So a new method was worked out on that basis. Daring navigators were sent out into the Atlantic Ocean, and expeditions were made southward along the coast of Africa probably to the Gulf of Guinea, and northward probably to the northern tip of the British Isles. These navigators were to determine, among other things, the length of the longest day of the year. From these data Greek mathematicians worked out a new series of *klima*, as they continued to call the belts, based on half-hourly differences in the longest day of the year. Thus the first belt or *klima* or *climate* (to give the term its English form, derived through Latin) ranged from the equator, where the longest day was twelve hours, to a line parallel with it where the longest day was twelve hours and thirty minutes. This first *climate* was eight degrees and twenty-five minutes in width. Each belt or *climate* became progressively narrower. Thus the tenth *climate*, along the British coast, ranging from a longest day of 16 hours to 16 hours, 30 minutes, embraced a belt less than three degrees wide. The half-hourly *climates*, as worked out by the Greeks, extended to the Arctic Circle, and were 24 in number. In those days, then, "a change of climate," had the expression been used, would have meant nothing more than a change of latitude, that is, to a place nearer to or farther from the equator. But observations began to reveal that there was a direct relationship between distance from the equator and average atmospheric conditions, such as temperature, humidity, etc. These differences then began to be embraced in the term *climate* Hence, when time belts gave place to more accurate means for determining location, *climate* was retained in the language with the extended meaning in which we now use it.

cloak, clock

It may seem odd to combine these words, but they are closely related. The *clock* got its name from the bell that sounded its hours; the *cloak* from its resemblance, in the early Middle Ages, to the shape of a bell, to its form when hung over the shoulders. Both words descend from a common Medieval Latin word, *cloca* or *clocca*, which was probably formed by early Christian priests from an earlier Celtic or Teutonic source. The Dutch *klok*, the Norwegian *klokka*, the the German *glocke*, and the Welsh *cloch*, each meaning "bell," all bespeak a common source. But it must be remembered that early bells showed little resemblance to the church bells of today. They were little larger than our modern hand bells, and, made up from thin plates of hammered iron, riveted into quadrangular shape, they looked something like the modern cowbell and were about the same size.

clue (clew)

Several thousand years ago, the large island of Crete, in the eastern Mediterranean, was at the height of its glory. Explorations show that its culture, about two thousand years before Christ, must have rivaled that of Egypt at its best and was far more advanced than that attained in Greece for many centuries. But among the legends of ancient Greece that have come down to us, one of the most interesting, possibly based upon an actual form of animal worship in early Crete, is the slaying of the Minotaur by the Greek hero, Theseus. Minos, legendary king of Crete, had offended one of the gods. In retribution, his wife became captivated by a sacred bull and gave birth to a creature of ferocious appetite that had the head of a bull and the body of a man. This creature was given the name "Minotaur." Because of its ferocity, Minos had it confined in a vast labyrinth of so intricate a design that any person entering was unable to find his way out. Here, the Minotaur, roaming at will, was fed upon criminals who were thrust within the maze. But, every ninth year, its fare was supplemented by a tribute of seven youths and seven maidens exacted by Minos from Attica on account of the murder of his son in that country. When the time for the third of these mournful tributes approached, Theseus, son of the Athenian king, offered himself as one of the victims, believing that he could slay the monster and thus free Athens from the terrible tribute. This he was able to do; but he and his companions would have wandered hopelessly within the labyrinth, except for the aid given by Ariadne, daughter of Minos. She had fallen in love with Theseus and secretly gave him a ball of yarn, one end of which, when he entered the labyrinth, he tied to the portal; then, unrolling it as he went, he and the others were able to follow it back to the entrance and make their escape after the Minotaur was slain.

Now, in the time of the English poet, Geoffrey Chaucer, a ball of yarn was called a *clew*, a word still used with that meaning in Scotland and parts of England. And it was this word that Chaucer used when, in his *Legends of Good Women*, he told the tale of Ariadne:

> By a clewe of twyn as he hath gon
> The same weye he may returne a-non
> ffolwynge alwey the thred as he hath come.

This episode and the popularity of Chaucer introduced among other writers a figurative use of "clew of thread" as an expression for any guidance through a perplexity or difficulty. Later, when the spelling of *clew* changed to *clue*, in conformity with that which changed "blew" to "blue" and "trew" to "true," the newly formed *clue* came to have as its prevailing sense the idea based upon the legendary tale of Theseus—that which serves as a guidance to the solution of a problem or mystery. The older spelling is still sometimes used in this sense, but is generally retained for certain other meanings of nautical nature.

coach

In a little town in Hungary, back in the fifteenth century, there lived an obscure carriage builder, destined to make his village known throughout Christendom, though his own name is unrecorded. Possibly the king, Ladislaus Posthumus, or his successor, Matthias Corvinus, for the date is uncertain, wished something more elaborate or larger than the usual state carriage for his personal use while traveling. Or maybe the carriage builder had dreams and wished to offer something new in carriages. Whatever the cause, he built a heavier and larger vehicle which, over the unpaved roads of those days, provided greater comfort to the passenger than was found in the earlier springless carriages. It may have been a closed vehicle, though that is not known. That new vehicle, however, was so successful an innovation that, within the next hundred years, it was copied all over Europe. But wherever it was built it still retained the name of the Hungarian town where its first maker had lived. Like the "Conestoga wagon" of the United States a hundred years ago, so called because built originally in Conestoga, Pennsylvania, it was, in Magyar, a "*Kocsi szeker*," or "wagon of Kocs." Each country, of course, adapted the pronunciation of the Hungarian town to its own spelling. Thus, because of the sound of the name *Kocs*, the name became *coach* in English, when the first of these vehicles was built in England in 1555.

cobalt

According to old German folklore, every cottage had its own guardian spirit. This was a *kobold*, a name probably derived from *kobe*, cottage, and the stem of *welten* (English *wield*), to rule; thus, "the ruler of the household." In later times this familiar spirit came to be associated with mischievous pranks, thought to be responsible for curdled milk, fractious cows, kettles tipped into the coals, and other mishaps that vex housewives. Their misdeeds came gradually to be associated especially with matters affecting miners. Hence, when the German miner suffered in health (probably from some such disease as miner's worm or miner's phthisis), he blamed his misfortune upon the *kobold*, whom he had come to regard as a malignant demon. In the same manner, certain ores which looked to be metallic failed to yield any metal when they were smelted. The miners tossed them aside contemptuously, muttering, "*Kobold* (Goblin)." So common had this designation become that it was retained when the true nature of the ore was determined by Georg Brandt in 1735. The German name became *cobalt* in English.

coconut

The slang reference to one's head as a "coconut" is, of course, familiar to everyone, so familiar that we may not even wince when we hear the term contracted to "nut." The slang use isn't amazing, for, after all, the shape of the head does somewhat resemble that of the nut. In fact, that is just what Portuguese explorers thought when, in their successful attempt to reach India in the late fifteenth century by sailing around the southern tip of Africa, they found this fruit growing upon islands of the Indian Ocean. Not only was the nut about the shape and size of a small head, but the base of it, with its three dark holes, strikingly resembled a grinning face. And that is what led the Portuguese to call the nut a *coco*, for in their language that means "a grinning face."

cockatrice (ichneumon)

Like the basilisk, with which it was sometimes identified, this fabulous creature was formerly supposed to be able to kill man or animal just by a glance from its deadly eyes. The actual existence of such a creature was believed even into the seventeenth century. It was then thought to be a kind of serpent; so considered by Shakespeare (in *Romeo and Juliet*) and by the translators of the King James Version of the Bible (in the Psalms and in Jeremiah). It could be killed, people said, by the sound of a crowing cock, so travelers were wont to carry a rooster with them when going through regions where they were thought to dwell. The only mammal unaffected by the baneful eye of the creature and which could attack it successfully was the weasel, because this animal could cure its own injuries by rue, the one plant which the cockatrice could not wither. Like the basilisk, the cockatrice was believed to hatch from an egg laid by a cock, a belief probably influenced by the first part of the name. But *cockatrice* is actually a corruption of the Latin *calcatrix*, and this, in turn, was a translation of the Greek *ichneumon*. This was and still is an Egyptian quadruped resembling a weasel. It is a mortal enemy of the crocodile, devouring its young and searching for its eggs. Hence its name, for *ichneumon* means "a tracker." It was anciently believed that when the ichneumon found a crocodile asleep, it would dart into its open mouth, into its stomach, and kill it by eating through its belly, but this is not true. So little was actually known of the creature that any fantastic story was accepted by credulous persons.

coin, coign, (quoin)

Although the minting of metals into currency has sometimes been done by casting—that is, by pouring molten metal into molds—the general practice has been to stamp the metal. Nowadays, as it has been for some centuries, the stamping is done by powerful presses.

Formerly, it was done by hammering, with little change in method back to the times of ancient Rome. The Roman practice, after blanks of uniform size had been procured, was to place the blank upon a die which carried the design of the reverse side. A wedge-shaped tool, with the design of the obverse face upon its small end, was then used to receive the blows of the hammer. Now this wedge-shaped tool was called a *cuneus*. In Old French, this Latin word became corrupted first into *cuigne*, then into *coing*, and finally into *coin*. The last form, though variously spelled, was carried into England. By that time, however, *coin* meant not only the wedge-shaped tool used in the minting of currency, but it was also a general name for currency produced by stamping. The old sense of a wedge has since died out in English usage. But it is interesting to observe that the old Roman meaning of *cuneus*, a wedge, is still retained in our architectural terms *quoin* and *coign*, both of which words developed along the same lines from the same Latin source.

collation

From its Latin source, *collatio*, the basic meaning of this is "a bringing together, a conference." It is from the participle, *collatum*, of the verb *confero*, confer, compare, collect. Most of its present various meanings are directly derived from the Latin meanings, but there is one use of *collation* that has come to us in a curious fashion. Back in the fifth century there lived a French priest, Joannes Cassianus. He is especially noted as being one of the first to introduce monastic orders into western Europe; he himself founded two large orders in Marseilles, one for monks and one for nuns. Little was known in France at the time about the proper conduct and way of life of those who took monastic vows, but Cassianus had lived for many years in several of the monasteries of Palestine and Egypt. He was requested, therefore, to write a memorandum which should serve as a guide to those who followed him. One of the most notable of the treatises that he then wrote had the title, *Collationes Patrum in Scetica Eremo Commorantium* (Conferences with the Fathers Dwelling as Hermits in Egypt). This was a series of twenty-four dialogues. Subsequently it became the custom in Benedictine Orders at the close of day to read aloud from the passages of these *Collationes* or from passages of the

Scriptures and to confer over them. After the reading or conference it became a further custom to have a light supper. This supper or light repast thus being associated with the reading from the *Collation*, as the treatise was called in England, or from the conferences that attended this or similar readings, became itself referred to as the *collation*. This usage was then extended to any light repast served at any time.

colonel

Our spelling of this word comes from Italian, from the "little column" or company of infantry which this officer formerly led at the head of a regiment. Such a little column was, in Italian, a *colonello*, or later in France, *colonelle*. The French word, however, became corrupted to *coronel*, and it was in this form that the word was introduced into England in the sixteenth century. The spelling was corrected to *colonel* within the next century, and strenuous efforts were made to reform the pronunciation also to accord with the reformed spelling. But the early influence was too great. Even by 1780 the pronouncing dictionaries had given up the battle and showed *colonel* to be pronounced like the former word *coronel*, that is "kurnel," just as we say it today.

colossal, Colosseum

Ancient sculptors were accustomed to make their statutes somewhat more than life size, especially those which were to be mounted upon high pedestals or as architectural ornaments upon lofty buildings. Thus, when viewed from the roadway, the figures appeared in proper proportions and the fine details of the artist's handiwork were not lost through the distance. Any such enlarged statue, however little it exceeded man's ordinary size, was, in Rome, a *colossus*; in Greece, *kolossos*, though no one knows the earlier source of the word. But some of these *colossi* were of such vast proportions that they would be notable objects of interest even in our present day of eye-filling skyscrapers. The most famous was the celebrated statue of the Sun, created in bronze by Chares of Rhodes, most widely known as "The Colossus of Rhodes." Its size was so great that the statue became counted as one of the seven wonders of the ancient world. This famous statue gave rise to our present interpretation of *colossus* as something of huge or vast proportions, and *colossal* like something vast, huge, tremendous, immense. From ancient descriptions, the statue was 105 feet in height; it stood at the entrance to the harbor at Rhodes, and was completed, after twelve years in the erecting, in 280 B.C. But it stood only about sixty years before it was destroyed by an earthquake. The broken fragments remained on the ground for more than nine centuries and were finally sold by the Turks. Nine hundred camels are said to have been required to transport the load. Another famous *colossus* was a statue of Nero, executed by Zenodorus and 110 feet in height. It stood near the huge amphitheater subsequently erected by the emperor Vespasian, and because of the proximity to the statue, the amphitheater got the name *Colosseum*.

comedy

Comedy among the early Greeks was for men only. In fact there were but few occasions when women were permitted to attend any of the public festivals or to appear outside of their homes. But the early comedy, or *komodia*, derived from *komos*, revel, and *oide*, song or ode, was a type of drunken revelry alongside of which the modern burlesque would be rather tame. The jokes and witticism were of the coarsest nature. Persons of important position were caricatured and lampooned freely. The utmost license prevailed, and the participants, who might include anyone, were careful only that their faces were concealed by masks or stained with wine to avoid discovery of their identities. In later periods much of the license and vulgarity disappeared from the Greek comedy. The term was retained, but the earlier festivities were replaced by well-written plays which were light and amusing and by eminent writers.

commando

Although it was the Portuguese who were first to colonize South Africa, no extensive development of the region took place until the Dutch East India Company founded Capetown in the latter part of the seventeenth century. Dutch settlers immediately began to have difficulties with the natives. The Hottentots, first to be encountered, were either enslaved, slain, or driven out, but as the colonists extended their settlements within the next hundred years they came against the more hostile and warlike Bushmen. Here, adopting a strategy of the earlier Portuguese, they organized their military parties into small units or commands capable of effecting quick raids against Bushmen villages. It is said that within six years they thus killed or captured more than three thousand Bushmen. The name of such a military unit, *commando*, meaning a party commanded, was also borrowed from the Portuguese, and came into English knowledge when the British began to establish colonies in southern Africa in the early nineteenth century. The British revived the term in World War II and applied it to each of various military units specially trained to effect quick raids into enemy-held country, usually at night, either to secure information, to destroy some menace, or to engage in some military undertaking involving great risk and requiring unusual courage, skill, speed, and initiative.

company, companion (accompany)

When we speak of, say, "John Smith & Company," we do not think of a body of men sitting down and partaking of bread together, but, in its original sense, that is precisely what the word *company* indicated. It, and its associated word, *companion*, though originating in France, were derived from the Latin *con*, together, and *panis*, bread, thus conveying the notion of friendship so true as to share bread, each with the other. And the derived word, *accompany*— from the Latin *ad*, to, plus *company*—had the original meaning, to go along with one and share bread together.

complexion

Back in the Middle Ages a person's disposition or temperament was thought to be dependent upon the proportions of the four humors which were combined in his body (see HUMOR). It was this combination that was said to determine his *complexion*, a word formed from the Latin *con*, together, and *plecto*, to braid. Thus if a man's countenance were ruddy and he was of an active nature, it was thought that blood was the predominant "humor" or liquid in his system, and his *complexion* was therefore said to be "sanguine." Or the combination of the four qualities—cold or hot, and moist or dry—might determine the *complexion* of a substance. Thus, in olden medical practice, gristle was said to be of cold and dry *complexion*, while flesh was of a *complexion* hot and moist. That is, formerly *complexion* was the habit or temperament revealed by the natural color and appearance and quality of the skin (especially of the face); the "braiding together" of those qualities was thought to indicate disposition.

comrade

We borrowed this word, three and a half centuries ago, from Spain. There, in the form *camarada*, it was used chiefly by soldiers to mean one who shares one's sleeping quarters or, as we would say, a roommate. It came originally from the Latin *camera*, chamber, room.

constable

When the Roman Empire was divided upon the death of Theodosius the Great, in A.D. 395, the eastern part had its court at Byzantium, a city that was later named Constantinople and is now called Istanbul. This empire, sometimes styled the Byzantine Empire, the Eastern, the East Roman, or the Greek Empire, lasted a thousand years. But its emperors were usually weak and vacillating; the court was torn with palace intrigues, feuds, and conspiracies. In course of time the emperors began to confer titles upon some of their young attendants of noble birth in order to retain their services, though the duties attached to those titles were often nominal. One of these titles was *comes stabuli*, two Latin words that meant simply "master of the horse, head of the stable." Eventually the head of the stable, however, like his underling, the groom of the horse (see MARSHALL), became a great officer of state, one of the most important in the retinue of the emperor, literally the leader of the king's troops. This title, along with those of other officers of the court, was embodied in the Theodosian Code of A.D. 438, and thus passed to the Roman Empire of the West at Rome. Hence, when France broke away from Roman domination in 486, the *comes stabuli* became one of the officers of its first king, Clovis I. This functionary gradually assumed increasing powers. The imperial master of the horse became the principal officer of the imperial household. From that office he rose to commander in chief of the army. In the meantime, the Latin spelling of his title had given way to the Old French single word *conestable*, and in this form it was introduced in England after the Norman Conquest, ultimately becoming *constable*. The Constable of France and the Lord High Constable of England are both now defunct offices, though both were once of great importance. In England, as in America, the title survives only to denote an officer of the peace.

copesetic

In a letter to the author, the noted tap dancer, Bill Robinson, stated his belief that he had coined this word or expression when a boy in Richmond, Virginia. Each morning the patrons of his little shoe-shining stand, he said, would say, "Well, Bill, how do you feel this morning?" To which he would respond, "Oh jes' copesetic, boss; jes' copesetic!" By which he intended to convey to them that he was feeling just fine and dandy, that all was right with him. The expression is one that he continued to use on the stage and which became almost his trade-mark.

But when that statement was published some years ago in the department, "The Lexicographer's Easy Chair," of *The Literary Digest*, a number of Southerners or persons of southern descent, perhaps a dozen in all, voiced their doubt of that origin. They had themselves heard it, they wrote, before Bill Robinson was born, or when a child, had heard it used by a parent or grandparent who could not have known Bill Robinson and who had never been in Richmond. The probability is, therefore, that the term, of unknown origin, was an expression current in some family, maybe a hundred or more years ago, and thus became familiar among acquaintances and friends of that family. Bill Robinson may have heard it as a young-ster; its orotund polysyllabism may have stuck in his mind, and, unconsciously, he may have appropriated it, perhaps ascribing to it a meaning of his own.

copper

Because of its extensive occurrence throughout the globe in native form and the ease with which it can be hammered or drawn into a desired shape, this metal was known and used by the human race in remote periods of time. Alloyed with tin into bronze, it was the first metallic compound, so commonly employed before the days of recorded history that an extensive period of early civilization is known as the Bronze Age. The Greeks called it *chalkos*; the Romans named it *aes* and used it from early times for the manufacture of coins. The Roman supply came chiefly from the island of Cyprus, in the eastern Mediterranean, though this island did not come under the control of Rome until 58 B.C. To distinguish it from other sources, supplies of the metal from Cyprus became known as *aes cyprium* or, eventually, just *cuprum*, because the Greek letter *y* was equivalent to the Roman *u*. We still retain this Latin form in scientific terminology, but in the speech of the common man in the Dark Age of the early English people it became corrupted to *coper* by the time of Chaucer, finally assuming the present *copper* in the sixteenth century.

cornucopia

When Zeus was about to be born, according to ancient Greek tradition, his mother was anxious to save him from the fate of all his brothers and sisters who had been swallowed by their father, Cronus, at their birth. So she gave birth to him in a cave, concealing him there, and gave the father a stone wrapped in a cloth which he swallowed, believing it to be the child. The infant, according to one of several accounts, was then given to the care of the nymph Amaltheia, who fed him with milk from a goat and honey from the bees. When the goat once broke off one of its horns, Amaltheia took the horn and filled it with fresh fruit and herbs for the child. The horn thereafter always replenished its supply of such food, no matter how much might be taken from it. The Greek artists of old often depicted this horn in their paintings, calling it the horn of Amaltheia. Roman artists, taking the same theme, gave it the name *cornu copiae* or *cornucopia*, from *cornu*, horn, and *copia*, plenty.

coroner

Back in the twelfth century, when this English office was established, the full title of the person who held it was the Latin phrase, *custos placitorum coronae*, guardian of the pleas of the crown. His duties were to record all criminal matters occurring within his province, primarily with the view of securing to the king his proper fines and dues. His office, next to that of the sheriff, was the highest in a county. But the only one of the duties which survives about as it was in olden times is that of holding an inquest, with a jury, over the body of a person who has died by violence or in an unaccountable manner. The original Latin word, *coronæ*, "of the crown," became early corrupted to *coroner* in the common speech of the people, and has so remained.

credence

From the time of its first use in English, *credence* has had as its prime meaning, confidence, belief, trust—from the Latin *credo*, believe. But there has also been a secondary meaning which arose from a cautionary measure back in the Middle Ages. In those days, when the preservation of meat was unknown and the food might readily become tainted and poisonous, or deliberately poisoned, it was the custom for the servants of a royal or noble house to carry the prepared dishes from the kitchen and place them on a small side-table in the dining hall. There, under the observation of the master and his guests, one of the servants or an official of the household tasted each dish before it was served at the table. (See also SALVER.) That tasting or assaying of the food and, by transference, the table at which it was performed, were known as *credence*. (A side table or buffet is called *crédence* in France, *credenza* in Italy, to this day.) In later days, when the needs for such precautions had passed, the name of the table was retained and applied, in Roman Catholic and Episcopal churches, to a small table near the altar which holds the bread and wine previous to consecration.

criss-cross

Our ancestors treated learning with reverence and respect—possibly because most of the teaching, three and four centuries ago, was performed by men trained for the ministry. So it is not amazing to find that when children learned the alphabet, the little "hornbooks" from which they studied were almost invariably decorated with a cross. Sometimes there was just one cross, preceding the letter "A." Sometimes there was one at the beginning of the alphabet and another at the end, and sometimes the alphabet itself was arranged in the form of a cross. The cross was itself referred to as *Christ-cross*, to distinguish the figure from the letters that followed, and the row of letters forming the alphabet came to be known as *Christ-cross-row*. Along with the pronunciation of Christmas, Christian, Christopher, *Christ-cross* was always sounded *criss-cross*, and was often so spelled. Ultimately, in this form, it took on the special meaning which we now give it, a series of crossing lines.

culprit

The story that is sometimes told to explain the origin of this word is that it was formed in the last quarter of the seventeenth century from two legal abbreviations. It is said that when a prisoner stood for his trial and pleaded "Not guilty," the Clerk of the Crown, using Anglo-French legal phraseology, contradicted by saying, "*Culpable: prest d'averrer nostre bille*," that is, "Guilty: (we are) ready to prove our charge." This became a court formula and was entered on the roll in the abbreviated form, "*Cul. prit*." The story is entertaining and may be correct, but has not been proved. All that is certain is that in the earliest record it appears that *culprit* was first used when the Earl of Pembroke was on trial for murder, in 1678. When he had pleaded "Not guilty," the Clerk responded, "*Culprit*, how will you be tryed?"

curfew

In the medieval towns of Europe, fire was an ever-present danger. The houses were of timber, usually with thatched roofs, and the household fire, in a hole in the middle of the floor, sent out its smoke and sparks through an opening in the center of the roof. Naturally, the danger was greatest at night. Therefore, the authorities of each town had a signal sounded, usually a bell, at about the time that folks were about to go to bed, to warn them to take care of their fires for the night. In many places of Europe this signal was known by the Latin words *pyritegium* or *ignitegium* (from *pyra* or *ignis*, fire, and *tego*, cover), but in olden France the signal was called *cuevre-feu*, cover-fire. The custom was taken from France to England several centuries before the Norman Conquest, and the people undoubtedly thought they were still speaking its French name when they called it *curfew*.

curmudgeon

It may be said at once that the source of this word is unknown. It is of interest, however, because of the several speculations that have been made of its source. In his *Dictionary of the English Language*, back in 1756, Dr. Samuel Johnson said that an "unknown correspondent" had suggested the French *coeur méchant* as a possible source. This, amusingly, was wholly misread by John Ash, twenty years later, who said, in his *New and Complete Dictionary of the English Language*, that *curmudgeon* came from the French *coeur*, unknown, and *méchant*, correspondent. Actually, of course, *coeur* means "heart" and *méchant* means "avaricious" or "evil," and it is not impossible that this may be the true origin. The renowned etymologist, Walter W. Skeat, in 1882, dismissed this possible source and gave it as his opinion that the original word had been *corn-mudging*. He based this upon a translation of Livy, in 1600, in which the Latin *frumentarius* was rendered *cornmudgin*, in a passage that speaks of fines paid by "certain cornmudgins for hourding up and keeping in their graine." The second element of the word he believed to be derived from an old French word, *muchier*, to hide, conceal. Thus, *corn-mudging* would be explained as "corn concealing," a miserly concealing of corn. But Skeat did not know that *curmudgeon* had been in literary use twenty-five years before this translation of Livy appeared, nor did he reckon with the fact that no one other than this one translator, Philemon Holland, ever wrote the word as *cornmudgin*.

currant

The plants which we grow in our gardens under this name, as well as the berries produced upon them, are really sailing under false colors, for the name *currant* should never have been given to them. The real currant is the dried seedless fruit of a certain variety of grapevine; a raisin, that is, but a particular kind of raisin. The grapevine from which it is produced came originally from Corinth. For that reason the dried fruit from these vines were known, in the thirteenth century, as *raisins de Corauntz*, raisins of Corinth. Gradually, the delicacy became known chiefly from its source, and the name of that source, already transformed to *Corauntz*, passed through many forms, becoming *currants* in the sixteenth century and settling into *currant* in the seventeenth. But the plant which we call "currant" is a bush, not a grapevine. When this bush was introduced into England in the sixteenth century, it was popularly but erroneously thought to be the source of the fruit that, in dried state, came from the eastern Mediterranean.

cynic

Among the students of Socrates was one named Antisthenes, a man who, as time went on, never abandoned the teachings of his master, but, rather, extended them and applied them to a philosophy of his own devising. But because his mother was not an Athenian by birth, Antisthenes was obliged to meet his own students in a gymnasium outside the city of Athens, known as the Cynosarges. He was not popular; he never had many pupils, although the celebrated Diogenes remained steadfast among them. Furthermore, the philosophy which he taught required too great an asceticism to be pleasing. It required a contempt for sensual or intellectual pleasure, holding that virtue was the ultimate goal in life. Ultimately, therefore, his followers became noted for insolent self-righteousness. It may be that originally the followers of Antisthenes were called *Cynics* through some reference to the gymnasium at which he taught, but the name early became associated with the habits that became outstanding characteristics of his disciples. These were a doglike insolence, a doglike disregard of social customs, a doglike use of tubs or kennels for sleeping, and a currish insistence upon one's own opinion. It may have been a coincidence that the Greek word for "doglike" is *cynikos*.

cynosure

Zeus, according to one of the many traditions surrounding his infancy, desired especially to honor the nymph to whose care he had been entrusted when a babe. (See CORNUCOPIA.) So he placed her in the sky and made one of the stars which form her constellation of great brilliancy and to be stationary in the heavens, so that all other stars and constellations appear to rotate about it. But to the more practical minds of Greek mariners, the last three stars in this constellation seemed to have the curve and upward sweep of the tail of a dog, so they gave the entire constellation that name, Dog's Tail or, in Greek, *Cynosura*. And the brilliant star, the one that appears to be the center about which all others rotate, they also called *Cynosura*, from which we get our figurative sense of *cynosure*, something which is the center of attention. The constellation is more familiar to us under the name *Ursa Minor* or Little Bear, and the star as *Polaris*, the Pole or North Star, still the guiding star of mariners in northern seas.

dædal

Among the traditions of the ancient Greeks the earliest developments in the arts of sculpture and architecture were accredited to the legendary personage, Dædalus. However, it is said, he was obliged to flee from Athens at the very peak of his genius when, jealous of a skill that threatened to surpass his own, he killed his nephew and pupil, Perdix. Dædalus fled to Crete where the wife of Minos gave him her patronage. When she gave birth to the monster Minotaur, half bull and half man, Dædalus built the labyrinth in which the creature might be kept. (Compare CLUE.) But this so enraged king Minos that Dædalus was again forced to flee. Unable to take a ship, he constructed wings for himself and his son, Icarus, attaching them to their shoulders with wax. But the young Icarus flew too close to the sun, the story runs; its heat melted the wax from his wings, and he plunged to his death in the sea below. Dædalus made his flight in safety and continued to exercise his skill in various lands about the Mediterranean. He was said to have originated carpentry and to have invented the tools essential to that trade, the saw, the ax, the gimlet; he invented the mast and yards for sailing vessels; in sculpture, he was the first to give an appearance of life to his figures, showing them with opened eyes and with hands and limbs extended; he built a reservoir and an impregnable city in Sicily, a temple at Memphis, and his sculptures were said to have abounded among all the coastal towns. So skilled an artist and workman was he that our poets continue to use *dædal* in describing workmanship which, in cunning, invention, or variety might be compared with that of Dædalus.

damask, damascene

Although Chinese weavers had long engaged in the production of beautiful woven designs in their silken fabrics, it remained for the weavers of Damascus, in the eleventh or twelfth century, to outstrip all other countries in the creation of silken textiles of unusually rich and curious design. These fabrics, sometimes with colors woven into the pattern, became the choice possessions of such nobles and others as could afford them, and were carried by traders to all parts of Europe. English merchants, after their usual practice of describing each cloth by the name of the city or town from which it came, gave this the name *damask*. The name has continued in use, although fabrics bearing it are now rarely of silk and do not often come from Damascus.

Damascus was formerly also noted for a certain beautiful and blush-colored rose. This, too, was called *damask* when introduced into England, and poets, Shakespeare among them, told of fair ladies with *damask* cheeks.

But the city was, as well, the habitat of many artificers in fine metal. Some of them possessed the rare skill of beating steel and iron together into a combination of curious elasticity and fine temper. Swords of such metal were especially prized; the best could be bent without injury until the point touched the hilt and could be used, with a powerful blow, to cut through an iron bar. Such steel, or a blade produced from it, was also known as *damask*. Other workers in metal created a type of beautiful inlay known only in Damascus. First, making fine incisions in the surface of the steel or other metal to be decorated, the workman would then beat a silver or gold wire into the depression until it became firmly united. By the use of both gold and silver, or gold of varying shades, skilled artisans were able to produce masterpieces of delicate elegance. Again, from the city of its source, such figured surfaces were said, in England, to be *damascened* or *damaskeened*.

damson

The damson plum was one of the fruits which the Crusaders of the twelfth and thirteenth centuries tasted on their weary travels in the lands bordering the eastern shores of the Mediterranean, found to be good, and took back with them for cultivation in their own countries. Because it was one of the products obtained from the gardens about Damascus, it was first known as *damascene* or *damesene*, when introduced into France and England. In the common speech of the countryside of England, however, the name underwent various changes and *damson* emerged as the one to be finally retained. Other fruits from Asia Minor, introduced to western Europe by returning Crusaders, included the orange, lemon, citron, apricot, and melon, some of them adaptable to the warm climates of southern Europe. Hence, although the several Crusades failed ultimately in the attempt to restore Jerusalem to Christian control, they did widen the knowledge of the western countries to the products of the East and were an important step in the establishment of extended commerce. (See also DAMASK.)

daphne

Old Greek and Roman writers tell of a chaste nymph, Daphne, who was so beautiful and graceful that the god Apollo, when he saw her, fell in love with her charms and would have taken her for himself. But she, fearing that he would harm her, fled from him. Apollo pursued, but as he was about to catch her, she prayed to the earth goddess, Gæa, to rescue her. Gæa heard the prayer and opened the earth to receive the frightened maiden. Then, to appease Apollo, she caused to grow from the spot a flowering bush that was thereafter sacred to him, the laurel, which in southern Europe is still known as *daphne* from the name of the nymph. The leaves of this plant were made into a garland by the young god and worn by him in memory of his lost love.

debauch

In the Middle Ages it was no more difficult to persuade a man to leave his work, perhaps for conversation or a convivial drink, than it is today. The French of that period had a word for that. It was *desbaucher*, literally, to lure from one's place of work or from one's duty to a master. The French meaning altered in the course of years, and by the time the word entered England, where it was eventually spelled *debauch*, it had acquired the meanings with which we use it now.

debut

Literally, when this was two words in French, *dé but*, it meant "from the mark." It was used just as we say, "your first stroke," in billiards, "your lead," in cards, or "your first throw," in dice. In other words, it signified the opening move or play in a game. From that expression, a French verb was coined, *débuter*, to lead off in a game. This meaning was then extended into to make one's first appearance (upon the stage, into society, or the like). The French verb and the noun created from it, *début*, retain the original and the extended senses, but we borrowed the noun only, now Anglicized to *debut*, and retained only the extended senses.

defalcate

In its original sense *defalcate* meant "to cut off by a sickle." Its Latin source, *defalco*, was formed from the preposition *de*, off, and *falx*, sickle, and that was the literal sense in which the word was employed in Medieval Latin. After its introduction into English speech, however—possibly from the notion that grasses cut with a sickle are then to be taken away—*defalcate* was used in the extended sense, "to take away." This has become its usual meaning, chiefly applied to the embezzlement of money.

delirium

The ancients employed figures of speech just as we do. Thus, if a person in the days of Cæsar wished to say that another was suffering from vertigo or was wandering in mind or speech, he might use the Latin verb *deliro*. The literal meaning was "to stray from the furrow," *lira* being "furrow." Naturally, no farmer in his senses would deliberately turn his oxen aside from the furrow previously plowed or the row that he was harrowing, and the term therefore came to be applied to anyone not in his senses, to a person suffering from a disordered mind.

demijohn

Possibly, back in the seventeenth century, there was in France a buxom barmaid of such portliness and jollity that her fame spread throughout the countryside. Her name, it would appear, was

Jeanne, known to all as *Dame Jeanne*. We may further surmise that at this period some wine merchant of the region began to use flasks of an unusual size for bottling his wine, bottles that would hold 20 liters or so. Some wag, it would seem, seeing these large bulging bottles encased in rush and with rush-work handles at the sides, was reminded of the neighborhood barmaid in her peasant costume with arms akimbo. Struck by the resemblance, he shouted, "Dame Jeanne!"

That story is entirely conjectural. All that is certainly known is that the bottles were known by the name *dame-jeanne* in France in the late seventeenth century and are still so called. The Spanish name is *dama-juana*; the Italian, *damigiana*, both meaning "Dame Jeanne." When introduced into England, they were first known by the French name, *dame-jeanne*, which, thanks to the English difficulty with French pronunciation, became corrupted to our present *demijohn*. (See also JUG.)

demon

The Greek verb *daiein*, which meant "to divide," had the special sense "to distribute destinies." Thus *daimon*, which is probably connected with it, meant "a divine power." It was nearly always used in a good sense; Socrates, for instance, spoke of his *daimon*, meaning very much what we should call "guardian angel." But when the worshipers of the old gods became Christians, they could not grasp the idea that their former deities had never existed; yet at the same time they were taught that they must cease to worship them. So they tended to compromise, regarding the *daimones* as real enough, but spirits of evil. Hence the deterioration of the meaning of *demon*.

denizen (foreign)

In the days of William the Conqueror, the French distinguished between a person living within a city and one living without. They described them as *deinsein* and *forain* respectively—the first word being an Old French corruption of the Latin *de intus*, from within, and the second from Latin *foras*, without. Both words were brought into England within the next few centuries and both meanings were at first retained. Later, under the influence of "citizen" the old *deinzein* became altered to *denizen*, and its meaning enlarged to include any inhabitant of a place, whether native-born or an alien entitled to the privileges of residence. The original *forain* became, at first, *forein*; then some one in the sixteenth century, probably an ignoramus thinking to exhibit great learning, stuck a meaningless *g* in the word, mistakenly influenced by "deign" and "reign," perhaps. Thus it has come down to us as *foreign*. We still use it in the original sense, but more generally apply it to a person or thing of another nation or another country than our own.

derrick

The device must have been new about the year 1600, although no historical account of its use or appearance has yet been found. Whatever its nature we do know its purpose, because it was named for the man who used it. His name is recorded as Godfrey *Derick* or *Derrick*. His profession was that of hangman at Tyburn, that place of public execution formerly just outside of London, where many famous and infamous persons were executed between the fifteenth and eighteenth centuries. Possibly, because the gallows generally used at that time had three posts set in triangular form, connected by crossbars at their tops, the hangman Derrick extended and slanted one of the legs and suspended a pulley from its top, thus constructing in rude form the mechanism since known by his name. The most famous of those executed by Derrick was Robert, Earl of Essex, the young and handsome nobleman who, after enjoying for fourteen years the favor and protection of Queen Elizabeth, presumed once too often upon her affection. He was condemned for treason and hung at Tyburn in 1601. By chance Essex had himself previously pardoned Derrick for an offense, an act long remembered in a ballad of the times called *Essex's Good Night*. In this, while on the gallows, the Earl is represented as saying:

> Derick, thou know'st at Cales I saved
> Thy life lost for a rape there done;
> . . . .
> But now thou seest myself is come,
> By chance into thy hands I light;
> Strike out thy blow, that I may know
> Thou Essex loved at his good-night.

derring-do

Chaucer, when writing *Troilus and Criseyde* in 1374, used the language of his day in describing his hero as "in no degre secounde in *dorrying don* that longeth to a knyght." He meant that Troilus was second to no one in "daring to do" that befitting to a knight. But a succeeding poet, John Lydgate in 1430, who borrowed extensively from Chaucer thought that *dorrying don* was some manly quality, and said that Troilus was a second Hector in *dorrying do*. At least he wrote it *dorrying do*, changing it slightly from Chaucer's *dorrying don*. But greater mischief was done when Lydgate's book was reprinted after his death, because the printer changed it still further to *derryinge do*. The poet Edmund Spenser completed the misinterpretation in 1579. Relying upon the language of Lydgate's reprint, not only did he use *derring doe*—the reformed spelling of his time—in the text of *The Shepheardes Calendar*, but he told, in a glossary, what he understood it to mean, "manhood and chevalrie." That is the sense in which our poets and romanticists still use it, though arrived at deviously from what Chaucer wrote.

despot

Nowadays when we apply *despot* to a person, we mean to imply that he, whoever he may be, uses his position or power in an oppressive or tyrannical manner. We don't like him—or her, as the case may be—and we don't want to be subject to his domineering authority. But this meaning is one that has developed within the past few centuries. The original Greek, *despotes*, meant merely master, lord. During the Byzantine Empire, *despot* was used as a title of the emperor and, later, was a title bestowed upon princes or rulers of dependent countries. A bishop or, especially, a patriarch of the Eastern Church was also addressed as *despot*. The word carried no connotation of tyrannical mastery. But because the old Greek master of a household usually had absolute authority over his slaves and his family, *despot* began to carry the notion of tyrannical power some two hundred years ago. Its frequent use in that sense during the French Revolution led to our present ordinary interpretation.

desultory

Expert horsemen have been greatly admired through all the ages. Even in the days of Homer there were some who, in their skill, could vie with those we see in our modern circus rings. Those of the greatest skill were those who, with three or four horses at full gallop, could skip nimbly from the back of one to the back of another. Usually, however, especially in the Roman circus, these equestrians used but two horses and rode them sitting, because such exercises were a part of military training. A soldier supplied with two horses was able, when one became wearied, to vault to the other, losing no time in the chase. In the circus, greater interest was evoked by charioteers who, driving two chariots abreast, would expertly leap from one to the other. Each such performer, horseman or charioteer, was known as a *desultor*, that is, a leaper, from the Latin *de*, from, and *salto*, to leap. Because these equestrians stayed but a moment upon each horse or chariot, seeming to flit like the butterfly from one aim to another, the word *desultory* acquired its present meaning.

deuce

This is the expletive, as in "What *the deuce*!" It has come to be synonymous with "the devil," and is often used euphemistically for the stronger expression. But there is every reason to believe that originally it meant the throw of two at dice, the lowest throw that one can make. In Low German that would be *de duus*. A player after a series of such unlucky throws might become sufficiently irritated to exclaim, "*De duus!*" or "*Wat de duus!*" The English expletive, "the *deuce*," now three hundred years old, is believed to have come from this Low German exclamation.

devil

The Hebrew "Satan," which appears in the Old Testament as the name of the enemy of mankind, means literally "adversary." When the Old Testament was rendered into Greek the translators looked for a word to reproduce this literal meaning. They hit upon *diabolos*, the noun from *diaballein*, which was compounded of *dia*, across, and *ballein*, to throw. *Diaballein*, from meaning "to throw across," had come to mean "to slander or accuse"; and *diabolos*, therefore, meant "accuser." Accordingly, the *Devil*, whose name is derived from *diabolos*, is properly to be regarded as the accuser of the soul.

diadem

When Alexander the Great, ruler of Greece, defeated Darius, king of Persia, in 331 B.C., he became thereby the ruler of all Persia. Until his death in Babylon eight years later, it was then his ambition to unite East and West into one world empire with Babylon as its capital. To that end he founded many cities throughout his new empire, habiting them with Greek settlers. And he himself began to adopt Persian and Oriental customs, persuading his officers to follow his example. To please his new subjects, Alexander also affected the costume of a Persian monarch, especially the fillet about the head that was a symbol of royalty. This fillet was a white band trimmed with blue, which encircled the head, its two ends descending to the shoulders. The Greeks called this a *diadema*, literally, a binding over, from *dia*, through, and *deo*, to bind. This same emblem of sovereignty was later assumed by rulers of the Western world and affixed by sculptors to their statues of the Greek and Roman gods. For further decoration the *diadem* became enriched with gold and gems and at length was transformed by the monarchs of Europe into a rich crown of gold, ornamented with gems, and worn especially as a symbol of royal dignity.

diaper

Although this has been the name of a textile fabric from its earliest introduction into western Europe, the fabric was not always intended to be converted into breechcloths for babies. Quite the contrary. In the earliest Greek reference to the cloth, in the tenth century, the fabric was probably made in Byzantium and woven of silk, its surface flowered with gold threads, though its name, from Greek *diaspros*, would indicate that originally it was "pure white" throughout. The material was then used for ecclesiastical robes. In England, however, from the fourteenth century, *diaper* was applied to a fabric, usually of linen, so woven that its main lines when viewed under reflected light formed innumerable small lozenges. The fabric was then employed chiefly as a cloth for the table. Later a similar fabric was made of linen and cotton, and eventually of cotton alone. Because of its softness and absorbency, it then became generally used for and its name transferred to, babies' breechcloths.

dicker

When we attempt to obtain a bargain by *dicker*, we have no thought that a unit of ten is involved in the transaction, nor do we remotely conceive of a bundle of hides in connection with the bargaining. But such, nevertheless, is the history of the word. In European languages its various transliterations still show such connections. It comes from the days after the Roman legions had conquered the German tribes and demanded regular tribute. The chief items which these barbaric races could supply as tribute were furs and skins. For convenient reckoning, the Romans demanded that such skins be in bundles of ten. Such a unit of anything was, in Latin, a *decuria* (from *decem*, ten). But among the Germans, who corrupted the word first to *decura* and eventually to the present *decher*, it meant only ten hides. This was its meaning also when, in the form *diker* or *dyker*, the German term came into English use about the thirteenth century. The British later applied it to any group, set, or bundle of ten or even twelve, such as dishes, knives, necklaces, etc. But when English colonists began to settle in America and to trade with the Indians, the old sense of the word was brought back into use, because skins and furs were commodities which the Indians had and which the colonists wished. So they began to bargain for *dickers* of skins, offering beads or cloth or knives in exchange. The notion of bundles of ten became lost through the years, and American traders among the Indians started our present use of *dicker*, treating it as a verb and equivalent with barter, or, especially, with haggle.

diploma, diplomatic, diplomacy, diplomat

During the days of the Roman Republic and of the later empire a person upon whom certain rights or privileges were conferred received an official document, signed and sealed by the consuls and senate or, later, by the emperor or such magistrate as he might designate. This document or state letter consisted of two leaves, either two tablets of wax or a folded sheet of writing material, and it was therefore known by the Greek name for such a twofold sheet, *diploma*, from *diploos*, double. Public couriers especially, on errands to foreign cities or countries, carried these tokens of authority. Because a *diploma* was essentially a state document, the term carried that meaning among the scholars of Europe.

Therefore when a German writer of the seventeenth century undertook to compile a collection, in the original texts, of the important public documents between the eleventh and fifteenth centuries, he coined the Latin adjective *diplomaticus* to indicate the nature of his collection. This provided us with the English adjective, *diplomatic*, which, though it first pertained to original official documents, came to refer to documents relating to international affairs, the usual nature of such official documents. From the adjective in its revised sense came the noun *diplomacy*, the art of conducting affairs between nations. Then, but not until the early nineteenth century, the nations found it expedient to rely upon persons who possessed certain skills in handling foreign relations, and the term *diplomat* was created. The original notion of a state paper is retained by all these terms. We are more accustomed to the use of *diploma*, however, as an indication of scholastic attainment; but here, too, it was originally a state paper, and is still issued under the license of the state.

dirge

Among the customs coming down through the ages has been that of chanting or singing a mournful or memorial song at the funeral service for the dead. In the Roman Church, from the Middle Ages, the response to the chant that was so used was based on the eighth verse of the fifth Psalm. In English, the words are, "Guide, O Lord, my God, my way in Thy sight." But the service was sung in Latin. The line was, accordingly, *"Dirige, Domine, Deus meus, in conspectu tuo viam meam."* Through the frequent repetition of the line, the service became known by its first word. The early English pronunciation of that Latin word gave us *dirge*.

disheveled

Nowadays we speak of a person being *disheveled* whose clothing is disarranged or very untidy or whose hair is badly disordered and uncombed, and such a person is more than likely to be a woman. In Chaucer's day, however, though it might apply to either man or woman, it referred more correctly only to the state of one's hair. Chaucer used it to mean either bareheaded or baldheaded, if a man, or with hair flying loose, if a woman. (He wrote it *discheuel, discheuelee, disshevely*, or as the spirit moved him.) The word was borrowed from the Old French *deschevelé* (modern French, *déchevelé or échevelé*), meaning stripped of hair, bald. It was formed originally from the Latin *dis*, not, and *capillatus*, having hair.

dismal

Two accounts have been advanced to explain the origin of this word. Both are plausible, and neither is absolutely certain; therefore the dictionaries usually content themselves by saying, "probably thus and so," or "origin uncertain," or the like. One account connects it with an early English phrase, "in the *dismal*," meaning "in the blues, depressed," and believes it to be derived from the Old French *disme*, meaning "a tenth," from Latin *decem*, ten. It would thus refer to the practice of feudal lords in exacting one-tenth of the harvest produced by their vassals, just as tithes were demanded by the church. Thus the phrase, "in the *dismal*," would indicate such depression as that experienced by people compelled to submit to the cruel extortionate measures of feudal barons at the time when these tithes were to be paid.

The second account ascribes its source to the Latin *dies mali*, evil days, of the medieval calendar. Such unpropitious days were also known as "Egyptian days," because their occurrence, it was believed, had been computed by Egyptian astrologers. These days of misfortune or gloom occurred on January 1 and 25, February 4 and 26, March 1 and 28, April 10 and 20, May 3 and 25, June 10 and 16, July 13 and 22, August 1 and 30, September 3 and 21, October 3 and 22, November 5 and 28, and December 7 and 22. It was considered unlucky to begin any new enterprise upon any one of those days. In Old French these days were called *dis mal*, and some scholars contend that it was from this that English *dismal* was formed.

divan

The countries of western Europe borrowed *divan* from Turkey, which in turn borrowed it from Arabic or Persian. In early times it signified a collection of written leaves, such as a compilation of poems or even a register of persons. It thus came to denote an account book or an office where accounts, especially accounts of state, were maintained. Eventually, in Turkey, *divan* meant a council of state, or the hall in which this council met. (In India, a minister of finance or a native prime minister is known as *dewan*, from another form of the same word.) But European visitors to the Turkish council chamber were impressed by the long, low seat or step, furnished with cushions, which ran around the walls of the chamber and upon which the councilors sat. This seat afforded ease for meditation and deliberation. To the western mind, *divan* thus became associated with easy comfort. Hence, though the Turkish meaning was also retained, the western countries adopted *divan* as a somewhat grandiloquent name for a deeply cushioned couch or sofa.

doily

We shall probably never know anything more than his surname, and we cannot even be sure that he spelled it *Doily*, *Doiley*, *Doyley*, or *Doyly*. He lived, however, in the latter part of the seventeenth century and we are told that he was the proprietor of a linen shop in the Strand, in London. His chief claim to popularity through the early part of the eighteenth century resulted from his introduction of some form of lightweight fabric for summer clothing, fabric which, as one writer for the London *Spectator* put it, was at once cheap and genteel. Probably this material was a loosely woven woolen cloth which could be converted into garments for men or women. But it seems to have been fabricated especially for his shop and for that reason to have been known as *Doily*. However, Mr. Doily did not limit his genius to the production or selling of material for clothing. He also put before his patrons a small table napkin for use when serving desserts. These were fringed and perhaps otherwise ornamented. At first, the purchasers proudly referred to them as "*Doily* napkins," but in the course of frequent use the name became abridged to *doilies*, by which we know similar articles today. The name of the clothing fabric has long been in disuse.

dollar

Silver was discovered in the valley of the Joachim, a few miles west of Prague, in 1516. This valley was then part of the vast estate owned by the Count of Schlick and, as was then the custom, the Count decided to mint his own coins. The first of the coins was produced in 1518 and was intended to have the value of the gold florin then in circulation. Because the valley, and the town within it, had been named in honor of St. Joachim, the new coin bore a picture of the saint upon its face. For that reason the coin could be readily identified and, from the name of the valley where it was produced, was known as *Joachimsthaler*, literally, "of the valley of Joachim," from *thal*, valley. The name was contracted to *thaler*, and this in turn became *daler* in some of the German dialects and in the speech of the Low Countries. Thus the name came to England as *dollar*. Forgetful or ignorant of the source of the term—that it meant "of the valley"—and thinking of it only as the name of a coin, the English used it to designate the Spanish *peso duro*, better known to us as "piece of eight" because of the large figure 8 on its face. This silver coin was widely circulated in colonial America, and thus the name *dollar*, already familiar, was applied to the unit of value in the United States when the first currency was minted in 1787. Our common expression, "two bits," meaning 25 cents, or "four bits," meaning 50 cents, is a survival from the time when pieces of eight were in circulation. One-eighth of that coin was the equivalent of the English shilling and was commonly known as a "bit." The value of a "bit" was thus 12½ cents; of "two bits," 25 cents, and so on.

dragon, dragoon

In the *Iliad* Homer describes a reptile of huge size, of blood-red or dark color shot with changing hues, and sometimes with three heads. This monster he called a *drakon*, which became *dragon* in English. Agamemnon, leader of the Greeks in the Trojan War, according to this ancient story, bore a shield with a picture of this creature painted upon it. But belief in dragons was not confined to the Greeks. They are pictured in the ancient art of China and Egypt, and even the Norse Vikings, in their day, carved dragons' heads on the prows of their ships. Generally, but not always, dragons were thought to be huge four-legged monsters with large fan-shaped wings extending on either side; sometimes from their wide jaws they shot a blood-red and venomous forked tongue against an attacking foe, and sometimes their nostrils breathed out fire.

Or again they attacked an enemy with their sharp claws, or struck at him with long and scaly forked tail. Some had but one head; others two or even three. Many legends describe how heroes of old fought and killed such a fabulous monster to rid the neighborhood of his baneful presence. In English history the most renowned is the legend of the holy knight, St. George, who became the traditional patron and protector of the English nation. He was supposed to have been a prince of Cappadocia, who, passing by, rescued the lady Aja from the jaws of a fierce dragon and slew the dread creature. The Crusaders of the twelfth and thirteenth centuries were so impressed by this heroic deed that, likening the dragon to their Mussulman foes and themselves to St. George, they felt themselves safe from danger if their banners pictured St. George killing the dragon.

In later years, after firearms were invented, the early muskets were called *dragons* because of the fire and smoke they emitted. In English spelling the term became *dragoon* and, like "lancer" for men armed with a lance, the name was also applied to those who carried the weapon.

dumbbell

Some two hundred and fifty years ago someone noticed that bell ringers attained a remarkable muscular development of the chest, shoulders, and arms, thanks to repeated exercise in pulling the ropes which put the great weight of the bells in motion. Whoever the person was, he figured out a scheme for erecting a device which would simulate the bell ringer's gallery, but without the bells. This device could be installed in the corner of a room or in the attic. The English essayist, Joseph Addison, had one in his room. The rope was probably attached to weights suspended over a pulley from the ceiling. A wooden bar, knobbed at the ends to keep the hands from slipping, was knotted to the other end of the rope and hung just within the reach of the exerciser. He could thus duplicate the physical activity of the bell ringer and, by regulating the weight, get whatever degree of exercise he might wish. Because there was no bell attached to this apparatus, it became known as a *dumb bell.* Later on someone else discovered that one could get much the same kind of exercise by dispensing with most of the cumbersome contrivance, using only the wooden bar or a heavier one of metal. This simpler device, because originally a part of the earlier equipment, continued to be known as *dumbbell*, though no longer associated otherwise with the art of bell ringing.

The modern *dumbbell* of American slang does not get its meaning from either of the above devices, other than by a play upon words. It was applied originally only to females, to the belle of the beautiful-but-dumb type.

dunce

John Duns Scotus was one of the greatest philosophers and scholars of the Middle Ages. He was still a young man when he died, suddenly, in 1308, though the year of his birth and the place where he was born, Ireland or England, are both unknown. He had attained great renown as a teacher at Oxford University before being appointed regent of the theological school at Paris in 1307. A member of the Order of Franciscans, his career was largely spent in contradicting the arguments advanced by the Dominican Order, especially those of Thomas Aquinas a quarter of a century earlier. So successful was he that his works on theology, logic, and philosophy became the accepted textbooks in the universities of the fourteenth century. His followers, called "Scotists," continued to dominate scholastic learning for two hundred years after his death. In the early fifteenth century, however, the Scotist system began to be attacked, first by argument and then by ridicule. The methods of the Scotists were condemned as sophistry, and the "Dunsmen" or *Dunses*, as the adherents of Duns Scotus were now termed by their foes, were said to be hairsplitters and stupid obstructionists. Eventually, after a long and bitter struggle, the cause of the reformers was victorious, but not until the term *dunce*, the ultimate spelling, had become a synonym for a blockhead incapable of learning.

dungeon (donjon)

If one looks at a picture of an ancient castle of medieval days, it can be seen that one of the towers, usually the central one, dominates all the others and the countryside around. It was also the strongest part of the castle, the part where the defenders, if forced back, might withstand a long siege or regain their strength. For this reason, this tower was often called a "keep" in England, meaning a place that could be held or "kept" against attack. But in France, and sometimes in England, the tower had its name from its dominant position and was known as a *donjon*. *Donjon*, in Old French, was a corruption of a Medieval Latin word, *dominio*, which meant dominion or mastery; in England, the spelling was usually *dungeon*. Moreover, because of its impregnability, the *dungeon* or "keep" served as a lodgment for prisoners, who were kept in the dank, gloomy vaults beneath the massive structure. To them and to all who feared such cheerless confinement, *dungeon* meant a dark, underground cell, rock-walled and comfortless. It is this meaning that has survived, and the archaic *donjon* is now used to designate the tower above.

easel

In all countries people have been wont to bestow the name of some animal upon a tool or implement which in some way resembled it. Thus tailors of old, seeing that their heavy smoothing iron, with its curving handle, somewhat resembled the heavy body and curved neck and head of a familiar barnyard fowl, called it a "goose." The housewife saw a resemblance to a wildfowl standing on one foot, its other leg stretched behind, in the upright iron rod alongside her hearth, its leg swinging over the coals, and called it a "crane." The old-time fire-"dog" or andiron looked somewhat like the short-legged hunting dogs of the English peasant. And of course, the bench commonly employed by the carpenter takes little imagination to see in it a "horse." Dutch painters familiarized English artists with a similar word from their own language. It was the stand upon which their canvas rested while they were painting. In those days this framework was not unlike a smaller copy of the carpenter's horse. They likened it to an ass. Accordingly they called this stand an *ezel*. Perhaps the English ear would have been hurt had English painters translated the name into "ass." But instead the Dutch name was adopted, modified into the English spelling, *easel*.

Easter

Early Christian missionaries, spreading out among the Teutonic tribes northward of Rome and Italy, found many pagan religious observances. Whenever possible, the missionaries did not interfere too strongly with the old customs, but quietly transformed them into ceremonies harmonizing with Christian doctrine. Thus they found that all the Teutonic tribes did homage about the first of April each year to the goddess of spring. Her name among some of the tribes was *Ostara*; among the Angles or Saxons she was known as *Eastre*. The day was one of great rejoicing; old and young celebrated with dancing, feasting, and games. Bonfires were lighted. Children gathered eggs, which they colored, and searched for newly born hares, both of which were ancient offerings to the goddess of spring. Christian missionaries were quick to see that the occurrence of this festival corresponded with the time of the observance of the Paschal feast, and that its occasion could be readily altered into one of rejoicing over the rebirth of Christ. The old customs remained unchanged. Thus, in most of the Teutonic countries, it happens that the name of this long forgotten pagan goddess— *Oster* in Germany, *Easter* among English-speaking people—is still given to the day that commemorates the Resurrection of Christ.

echo

One of the stories of old Greek legend relates that the great god Zeus was fond of the society of a certain group of nymphs. His wife, Hera, however, tried to keep him devoted to her alone. Through jealousy she followed him wherever he went. To outwit her, Zeus arranged with a nymph named Echo to waylay Hera when he sought the others and to hold her in conversation. This ruse succeeded on a number of occasions, but eventually Hera saw through the scheme. In her wrath, then, because Echo was such a chatterer, she condemned her forever to wander over the earth, but unable to speak until someone else had first spoken, nor to remain silent when another had spoken, and then to repeat only that which had been said. Echo wandered long and mournfully over the hills, repeating only what others might chance to say in her hearing, but not otherwise able to converse with them. One day she saw the beautiful young Narcissus admiring his reflection in a pool. She fell deeply in love with the lad, the story goes, but her love was not returned. In sadness the poor nymph pined away until nothing was left of her but her voice. It is this voice, according to this tale, which we still hear coming back to us in certain spots. We still call it *echo* in memory of the lovelorn nymph.

egis (ægis), (titanic)

It was a part of Greek belief that Zeus, when an infant, had been suckled by a goat, or, in some accounts, had been raised upon the milk of a goat (compare CORNUCOPIA). At least Zeus was believed to feel that he had been especially protected by a goat. For that reason, therefore, when Zeus and his brothers arose in rebellion against the Titans in rulership over the universe, again he looked to the goat to make him impregnable. The struggle lasted for ten years; all the gods on each side of the conflict loosed all of their weapons against their adversaries, to the extent that nature itself seemed involved in the fray. The ferocity of the battle and the magnitude of the efforts put forth by the Titans have since been signified by our word *titanic*. But Zeus was eventually victorious. For his own escape he gave credit to the shield of goatskin with which he protected himself from the thrusts of the enemy. This shield was said to "flash forth terror and amazement" among the foe. The name given to it was *aigis*, a word of uncertain origin, but thought by the Greeks to mean "goatskin." The Latin transliteration was *ægis*, a form often used by English writers, although *egis* is now more common. Of all the other gods Athena alone was permitted to carry an *egis*, which she wore as a breastplate. We owe our present interpretation of the word to the English writers of the eighteenth century who assumed, poetically, that the *egis* of Zeus or Athena—or their Roman counterparts, Jove and Minerva—shed its protection to all who might come under its influence.

eldorado

Within twenty-five years after Spanish captains had begun to explore the northern coasts of South America, they began to hear tales of a marvelous king who ruled over a great and wonderful city somewhere in the interior. The streets of this city, it was said, were paved with gold, the roofs of its buildings shone from afar with their surfaces of gold; the king controlled vast golden treasures and wore robes glittering with gems and golden threads. No one knows when the legend was started nor how it was spread, but it came to be firmly believed. The Spaniards, avid for gold, sent out expedition after expedition. One lieutenant, in 1531, claimed to have seen the city and to have been entertained by its king, but was unable to lead others to it. Other parties, led by unwilling natives, either died from exhaustion, hunger, or disease, or with decimated ranks returned with tales of the utmost hardship. Among the Spaniards, the fabulous king became known as *El Dorado*, "the Golden One." The natives spoke vaguely of a city somewhere in the interior which they named Manoa or Omoa, though none knew its whereabouts. Search for the elusive city, to which the name *El Dorado* had been transferred, led subsequent parties to explore much of the interior of northern South America. Even as late as 1595 Sir Walter Raleigh headed an expedition into interior Guiana in a vain attempt to discover the mysterious city. From this sixteenth-century dream, *eldorado* has come to mean any place of untold richness or, figuratively, of untold opportunity.

electric

We may sometimes think that the word *electric* and its derivatives are of recent coinage, perhaps no older than Ben Franklin's experiments with his kite and lightning, but they are much older. They were in use three hundred years ago. Probably as far back as the seventh century B.C., it had been known by the Greeks that amber, after being rubbed, acquired the property of attracting extremely light substances, such as the dried pith of reeds. The Greek name for amber was *electron* (Latin *electrum*). Hence, in 1600, when the English physicist, William Gilbert, published, in Latin, his researches on magnetism which were based upon experiments with amber, it was natural that he should use the Latinized word *electricus*. Through his own later lectures in English this he translated as *electric*, and the agency through which magnetism was effected he named *electricity*.

elixir

We are indebted to the Arabs for the beginnings of the science of chemistry, starting perhaps in the seventh century. Their knowledge was extremely limited, however, and was based on the theory that all the metals are composed of mercury and sulphur in different proportions. It was this theory that found its way into Europe, through Spain, and which, under the name of alchemy, flourished through the Middle Ages and until the sixteenth century. Gold was the pursuit of all the alchemists. It was the one perfect metal, they held, all others being inferior. But since gold itself was basically composed of the same elements as the lesser metals, there must be something, they argued, many times more perfect than gold which entered into its composition. Therefore, this unknown substance was the chief object of their search. If found, they believed, it could be mixed with any of the other metals in proper proportion, drive out their imperfections and turn them into gold. This mysterious substance was named by the Arabs, *el iksir*, or *elixir* by the alchemists of Europe. Its Arabic meaning was "the philosopher's stone," because the olden alchemists regarded themselves as philosophers. Some of the later alchemists believed that this undiscovered substance might be a liquid or a powder and, when found, that it would also have the property of prolonging life. This accounts for the present use of *elixir* in denoting a medicinal preparation.

emancipation

In Roman law part of a formal contract of sale consisted in the buyer's actually taking hold of the thing that he was purchasing. Such a purchase was called *mancipatio*, from *manus*, hand, and *capio*, take. The proceeding was carried out even in the purchase of a slave, and the owner's power over that slave was almost as absolute as over any other purchase. Similarly, a Roman father's power over his son was like that of a master over a slave, but the son could be released from it by legal process when he became of age. The father took his son solemnly by the hand, as if he were buying him as a slave, and then let go. This was ceremonially performed three times to complete the release. It was termed *emancipatio*, the letting out of the hand, with the prefix *e* meaning out.

enchant (incantation)

From earliest times and among all primitive people the solemn chanting of songs has been supposed to have magical properties, to influence the gods, to avert evil, to cast spells, to bring sunshine or rain, to cause or remove disease, to foster the growth of crops or to ruin them, or to bring success in love or war. In fact, every mortal function, it was believed, could be favorably or adversely affected by the repetition of some poetic formula. Traces of these ancient superstitions still linger among civilized people, as when children chant over and over, "Rain, rain, go away. Come again some other day." For ordinary singing, among the Romans, the verb *canto*, was used, but when the song was intended to work magic against another, they used *incanto*, literally "to sing against." This verb, through French, became our term *enchant*. The song, such as attributed to sirens in luring men to harm, or in averting or bringing about evil, thus became an *incantatio*, from which comes our word *incantation*. *Enchant* we now use chiefly in a pleasant sense, as of rapture, though we no longer associate the term with song. But *incantation* still carries a suggestion of muttered rhythm and is usually associated with witchcraft and evil.

enthusiasm

Annually, in ancient Athens, groups of play-writers, poets, musicians, and other skilled artists competed with one another among their group for the plaudits of the populace. In their day the men of greatest renown thus had their work reviewed by the great throngs attending these festivals. A successful contestant or one who showed remarkable attainment was said by his admirers to be *entheos*, that is, to have a god (*theos*) within, or to be *enthousiazo*, inspired or possessed by a god. Thus our English word, *enthusiasm*, if used in its purest sense, which is rarely the case, would denote a God-given fervency, divine inspiration.

epicure

The Greek philosopher, Epicurus, who was born in 342 B.C., held that pleasure constitutes the highest happiness. He argued, however, that pleasure was not a transitory or momentary sensation; it was rather something lasting and imperishable. It was attained chiefly by pure and noble thoughts. Freedom from pain and from all influences which disturb the peace of one's mind resulted in happiness, and his teachings were directed to the attainment of such peace of mind. After the death of Epicurus in 270 B.C., his pupils and disciples maintained his school, under fourteen masters, for more than two hundred years, despite violent attacks upon his theories by later philosophers. Some asserted that his theory provided an excuse for the greatest debauchery and sensuality. And it was from these distorted notions that some men, who had devoted their lives to such vices, called themselves Epicureans. Cicero was one who held such a mistaken thought. It is therefore largely through him that *epicure* came to denote, rather than a true follower of Epicurus, one given over to sensual pleasures, especially gluttony. (We do not now imply gluttony in our use of the term, but rather one who shows a refined taste in his eating and drinking.)

ergot

Sometimes, as many farmers have observed, a seed of rye becomes diseased and is transformed into a fungus growth of dark purple color, in shape strongly resembling a cock's spur. The condition was noted by French farmers many centuries ago, and because of the shape they gave this fungus the name *argot*, cock's spur. In modern French this has become *ergot* and was thus borrowed by us.

escape

As the dictionary says, this is from the Latin *ex*, out, and *cappa*, cape. In olden days the meaning was literal. One slipped out of his cape or threw it aside in order to free himself for running, or, it might be, he left it in the clutch of a would-be captor and made away from the spot. One is reminded of the young man mentioned by St. Mark who, when the servants of the high priests attempted to seize him by the garment he was wearing, "left the linen cloth, and fled from them naked."

esquire

In the Age of Chivalry—that is, in the period between the tenth and fourteenth centuries—young men of gentle birth who aspired to be knights were accustomed to attach themselves to the services of the knight of their choice and attend him in his travels. The chief duty of such a voluntary servant was to act as shield-bearer. Because of this duty the young man was called an *esquire*, a word of French origin, but tracing back through the Italian *scudiere*, shield-bearer, to the Latin *scutum*, shield. In later days the title was transferred to men of gentle birth, such as the younger sons of a peer, who ranked immediately below a knight, and ultimately became a courtesy title to any man who, through birth, position, or education is considered to be a gentleman.

etiquette

Elsewhere it has been shown how the expression, "That's the ticket," arose from a mispronunciation of *etiquette*.* But the French word itself means "ticket," among other things, and in Old French was used to designate the ticket that prescribed a soldier's lodging place, his billet. Just how the sense became transferred to prescribed conduct is not known.

eureka

The Greek mathematician, Archimedes, who was born in Syracuse in 287 B.C., was so far in advance in the practical application of geometry to mechanical devices that he may be called the Thomas Edison of his day. It is hard to comprehend that more than two thousand years after his death we are still making use of his discoveries and inventions and have done little more than effect improvements upon them. Faced one time with the problem of determining the amount of silver a dishonest goldsmith had used in making a crown for the king which had been ordered of pure gold, Archimedes hit upon the solution one day when he stepped into his bath. The bath was full and a certain amount of it overflowed. This suggested to him what is now known as a law of hydrostatics, that a body surrounded by a fluid is buoyed up by a force equal to the weight of the fluid which it displaces. Thus by weighing out an amount of gold equal to the weight of the crown and by putting them separately into a basin full of water, the difference in the weight of the overflow would denote the amount of alloy. It is said that Archimedes was so excited by his discovery and so eager to test its proof that, forgetting his clothes, he sprang from the bath and rushed home, shouting to astonished passers-by, "*Eureka, eureka*! (I have found it, I have found it!)"

* See the author's *A Hog on Ice, and Other Curious Expressions.*

explode (applaud, plaudit)

The Roman populace expressed their opinion of the abilities of their actors in manners that were unmistakable, and their ways were not unlike our own. If they liked an actor's performance, they clapped their hands at the end of his lines, when the action permitted; if they liked the entire play, they continued to clap after the performance closed. But if an actor gave a poor performance, he was literally clapped off the stage; that is, the clapping and hissing, begun at each appearance on the stage, continued until he was forced to retire. These judgments, all accompanied by clapping, were all based on the word *plaudo*, to clap. They were *applaudo*, from *ad*, to, thus meaning "to clap to," which became our word *applaud*. The second came through appeal by the actors— *Plaudite!* Please clap!—which has given rise to our English word, *plaudit*, acclamation. The action of disapproval was expressed by *explaudo*, from *ex*, off, meaning "to clap off," especially with a loud noise. Our English word, *explode*, derived from that, was still used, though rarely, with the Latin sense into the nineteenth century. The sudden burst of loud noise and the ejectment of the actor brought about a figurative usage, applied to anything that burst forth suddenly and with noise, and this in turn led to our present usages of *explode* and *explosion*.

expunge

In old Roman days, when a soldier had retired from service and his name was to be carried no longer on the lists, the fact was indicated by a series of dots or points pricked over or beneath his name. In this manner it was said to be "pointed out." The Latin term for "to point or prick out" is *expungo*. In English use *expunge* carries the sense of deletion by erasure, blotting, omission, or striking out in any form.

extravagant

Formed from the Latin words *extra*, outside, and *vagor*, to wander, *extravagant* has the literal meaning, "tending to wander outside the usual path; hence, astray, roving." Such were the senses of the term in Shakespeare's time. But it soon became extended in meaning, and "straying beyond reasonable bounds" became the usual intent of the word. Thus one who is *extravagant* with money or in statement goes beyond the bounds of reason.

fad

In certain regions of England, the local people, when they fondle or caress a child, or make a pet of it, say that they "faddle" it. That word has been known and used for three hundred years. From it, about a hundred years ago, the curtailed word, *fad*, was formed and used to indicate a pet project, something that one took up as a hobby. It is not known who originated the contraction.

fake

Until a hundred years ago this was one of the words frowned upon by the schoolmasters. It was slang. Not only that, but it was the slang used by thieves and gypsies, not by reputable speakers and writers. The true history is therefore unknown, but some suppose it to have been picked up long before by English soldiers during the Thirty Years' War (1618-48) when they were in long contact with German allies. If so, the German source was *fegen*, to clean, sweep, or, in a slang sense, to take the contents of something, such as a purse. But it seems more likely to me that *fake*, obsolete for many centuries in literature, came directly from *faken*, a term used in England until the fifteenth century, meaning fraud, guile, dishonesty.

fan

In the popular sense of an enthusiast, a *fan* is a follower or devotee of a sport or special interest, or an ardent admirer of some person. One of my elderly friends, an early baseball *fan*, insists that the term originated through the fact that the spectators at baseball games, back in the 1880's, seated in the hot sunshine, usually carried with them common palm-leaf fans with which to cool themselves. Players and reporters, he says, constantly reminded of the spectators by their large waving fans, began to refer to the spectators as *fans* for that reason. His account is plausible, but no proof of the theory has yet been found. Another entertaining theory is that *fan*, in this sense, was a contracted form of "the fancy," an expression which, a hundred years ago, was a popular term for those people who followed some sport or interest, such as prize fighting, dog breeding, or the like. This theory also lacks proof. The accepted opinion, therefore, is that *fan*, in this sense, is a contracted form of *fanatic*.

fanatic

It is said that Sulla, while leading the Roman army in Asia Minor against Mithradates in the early part of the first century B.C., was visited in a dream by a goddess. She appeared to urge him to return to Rome to forestall enemies who were plotting against him at home. He followed the advice and was in time to save his reputation. In gratitude, Sulla caused a temple or fane to be erected to this goddess, who, like an old Italian goddess, was named Bellona. He brought priests and priestesses from Asia Minor to establish the rites sacred to her and conduct services in her worship. At the annual festivals these rites were peculiarly grim. All the priests were clad in black robes from head to foot, but some among them, inspired by religious frenzy, would tear their robes aside, seize a two-edged ax, and gash themselves about the arms and loins, scattering the blood upon the spectators. These priests were believed to be inspired into excessive zeal by the goddess or by the fane or temple at which she was worshipped. Such zeal, accordingly, was said by the Romans to be *fanaticus*, from which our *fanatic* was derived. Its literal meaning is, therefore, "inspired by the fane."

farce

In the churches of medieval France and England, back in the thirteenth century, it became customary to insert various phrases in the litanies sung by the monks between the words *Kyrie* and *eleison* in the supplication, *Kyrie eleison!* "Lord have mercy!" Such an insertion, borrowing a term already used in cookery, was called a *farce*, from Latin *farcio*, to stuff or pad. (The cookery term survives in present use, slightly altered, in "forcemeat," finely chopped meat used for stuffing.) Later, when religious dramas, such as the mystery plays, became so popular, the actors who had comic parts began to introduce impromptu ludicrous gags into their lines to fit some local event or condition. Because these inserted remarks also padded out the lines of an actor, to his amused audience his buffoonery became known, in turn, as a *farce*. It was but a natural sequence then that any short dramatic work which had the production of laughter as its sole object should be given the same name, and that we should carry the term still further to apply to any sham or piece of mockery.

farm

The history of this word, especially of its change in meaning, is curious. It is derived, through the French *ferme*, from Latin *firmus*, fixed, settled, and when first used in England, as in France, it denoted the fixed annual rental, tax, or revenue payable by a person, town, or county to the overlord. A *farmer* was then the person who collected such payments. In France, even up to Revolutionary times, the *fermes générale* or "general farmers" grew inordinately wealthy by pocketing the difference between the annual sum paid by them in advance into the royal treasury and the sum subsequently collected by them through taxes and customs levied upon towns and individuals. In England, however, *farm* commonly designated the fixed annual rental paid by a tenant upon a tract of land leased for agricultural purposes. Most of such tracts were not, and still are not, owned by the persons who operate them. Later, but not until the sixteenth century, the meaning of *farm* was transferred from the rental upon land to the modern sense of a tract of land devoted to agricultural purposes. In England a *farm* is still held under lease, but in the United States it may be operated by the person who owns it.

faro

In the early eighteenth century various card games which became popular at the gambling tables were introduced into England from France. Little is now known about some of these, and others, such as basset (or bassette) and lansquenet, lost their popularity many years ago. But among these was the game now known as *faro*, although the name of the game, when first brought into England, was correctly spelled *pharaoh*, a translation of the French name, *pharaon*. The reason for the original name is not positively known, but the assumption is that the name was taken from one or all of the king cards in the deck which bore a likeness to the Egyptian monarch upon its face. Possibly that likeness appeared only upon the king of spades. *Pharaoh* means "king," and it is customarily the spade suit, beginning with the king, which is reproduced upon the painted cloth upon which the game of *faro* is played.

fascinate

From earliest times, and even today among superstitious people, it has been believed that certain persons, if so inclined, have the power to injure or even kill other persons or animals or to destroy crops or commit other injury by no more than a malignant glance. Such a person is held to possess the "evil eye." In ancient Greece, the power of the evil eye was called *baskania*, in Rome *fascinatio*. Because no one knew who that he might meet had the power and the wish to do him injury, it was an almost universal custom, in olden times, to wear an amulet of some kind which was believed to protect the wearer. Even the cattle were sometimes so adorned. Children were thought to be especially susceptible to the power of the evil eye, and no Roman mother, in classical days, would permit a child of hers to leave the house without first suspending from its neck, under the robe, a certain amulet called *fascinum*. Actually, therefore, our word *fascinate*, when first brought into English use, meant to cast the evil eye upon one, to put one under the spell of witchcraft. We use the word rarely now in such a literal sense, but employ it rather to mean to hold one's attention irresistibly or to occupy one's thoughts exclusively by pleasing qualities.

February

Among the oldest of the annual festivals of Rome was that known as the Lupercalia. It was celebrated on February 15 in honor of Lupercus, an ancient Italian god of fertility, sometimes identified with Pan or Faunus. He was the god of shepherds; thus the festival was connected with Romulus and Remus, the kings of shepherds, and thence introduced into Rome. In the ceremony, goats and dogs, noted for strong sexual instincts, were sacrificed by the priests. Two youths of noble birth were then touched upon the forehead with a sword smeared with the blood of the goats. Other priests then wiped the foreheads clean with wool dipped in milk. Whereupon the two youths were then obliged to shout with laughter. After that the priests, all of whom were of patrician birth, cut the skin of the goats into strips and, holding the strips in their hands and clad only in a loincloth of goatskin, they ran through the streets of the city touching or striking all persons whom they met. Women sought the runners eagerly, because the thongs were thought to be charms against barrenness. These thongs were called *februa*, purifiers, derived from *februo*, to purify; and the day upon which the festival occurred was called *dies februatus*, day of purification. From this most important festival in its period, the name *februarius*, month of purification, was given to the month. Thence our term, *February*. (See also JANUARY.)

ferule

In southern Europe there is a perennial plant which, though not a true fennel, is called "giant fennel" because it somewhat resembles the fennel and belongs to the same order. Unlike the fennel, which runs about three or four feet in height, this plant sometimes reaches a height of fifteen feet. Its Latin name is *ferula*. The old Romans prized it, as do their descendants, because the dried pith of the stem made an excellent tinder. But the *ferula* had other uses. The plants were plentiful, the stalks were pliable, and they were early found to be handy switches for the punishment of small boys. Such rods came to be known as *ferulæ*, from their source, and the schoolmasters of Shakespeare's time turned the name into *ferule* for the rod or flattened piece of wood they used to chastise refractory scholars. (*Ferule* and *ferrule* should not be confused. The latter is the name of the metal ring about the end of a cane or the like; it is corrupted from an earlier *verrel*, which goes back to the Latin *viriola*, little bracelet.)

fiasco

This Italian word means, in its literal sense, a flask or bottle. But at some time there became current among theatrical people of Italy the expression, *far fiasco*, which, though it actually means nothing more than "to make a bottle," was used with exactly the same meaning that we convey when we say, "to make a mess of; to fail," or in popular speech, "to pull a boner." So *fiasco*, in English use, came to mean complete and ignominious failure, but not even the most profound scholar in Italy can explain why "bottle" became a synonym for "flop."

fib

"Fable," from the earliest appearance of the word in English, six hundred years ago, not only meant a pleasant narrative, but also meant a downright lie, and we still use the word in either sense. Some three or four hundred years ago, however, an unknown parent thought to soften the word, probably, by accusing her small child of telling a "fibble-fable" when she caught him (or her) in a story which she knew to be nonsense. At any rate, this expression caught the popular fancy at about that time as a term for a slight falsehood. But, according to best conjecture, the expression proved to be too long a name for a slight sin, and soon became shortened to *fib*.

fife

Back in 1515, when Francis I of France was leading his army against Milan, he found twenty-five thousand Swiss soldiers, the bravest in Europe at that time, drawn up against him ten miles north of the city. They had been hired by the Milanese government to assist in defending the city. The brave Swiss, however, armed with their old-fashioned pikes, were no match against the new arquebuses with which the French troops were then supplied. Hence, though they fought by the light of the moon until midnight, only three thousand of their number were left to escape, as best they could, after the second day of battle. Milan fell. But this battle, aside from proving the superiority of the firearm over sword and pike, introduced a new instrument into military music. The drum had long been used, but with it the Swiss also used a kind of flute having a loud and brilliant tone. German musicians of the period, to distinguish it from the shrill pipe (German *pfeiff*) which it somewhat resembled, called it *Schweizerpfeiff*, Swiss pipe. The instrument soon became generally popular in army use because its tones carried well, and it is believed to have been carried to England by German musicians of the sixteenth century. The English, unable to pronounce *pfeiff*, called it and wrote it *phife*, *phyfe*, *fiphe*, or *fyfe*, and finally, in the seventeenth century, settled upon *fife*. (See also MAGENTA.)

filibuster (freebooter)

Piracy flourished in the seventeenth century, probably more successfully and openly than ever before or since. Spain had secured all of the rich new countries bordering the Caribbean Sea, and, although nominally at peace with the other maritime nations of Europe—France, Holland, and England—rigidly excluded those nations from establishing colonies in her domain. Her own American colonies, moreover, were supposed to trade with Spain alone, a trade that was usually extortionate, and she ruthlessly seized any vessel caught within the "Spanish Main" to enforce her rule. Such a condition could not be tolerated by Dutch, English, and French shipmasters, who knew the wealth that awaited them among the colonies. Their governments conveniently looked elsewhere while they armed themselves and set sail to capture Spanish ships, sink any that might interfere, and bring back wealth from New Spain. Ultimately such a captain or a member of his crew, of whatever nationality, became generally known as a "buccaneer," but one from Holland was first called a *vrijbuiter*, literally, a "free robber" or corsair. This, because of its sound and its resemblance to "free" and "booty," became "freebooter" in English. In French, however, it became first "fribustier" and then *flibustier* (the *s* probably inserted to show that the preceding vowel was long). These French forms were rarely used by English writers, who favored "freebooter" or "buccaneer" in telling of the pirates of the sixteenth and seventeenth centuries. But the French term passed into Spain, and there it suffered another alteration into *filibustero*. It was but natural, then, that the American adventurer, William Walker, of the 1850's should have been called a *filibustero* by Central Americans, a term that was shortened to *filibuster* in English. Walker, it may be recalled, was the young fellow who, in 1853, led an expedition of American adventurers in an attempt to capture the State of Sonora, Mexico. The attempt failed, but two years later a similar expedition against Nicaragua succeeded to such an extent that he was able, briefly in 1857, to proclaim himself president. Driven out of the country later in the same year, he then attempted to capture Honduras in 1860, but was caught and shot by the Honduran government. Our modern use of *filibuster* in legislative halls is harmless by comparison. At least it doesn't involve piracy or acts of violence. It probably arose through a mild comparison of the actions of legislators seeking to block a bill with the actions of Walker who sought to block international law.

flapper

It is perhaps just as well that this slang term for an adolescent young woman, the equivalent of the later "bobbysoxer," has just about disappeared. It was never complimentary, even if, as some think, the name was borrowed from the hunters' term for a young wild duck in ungainly flight. But there was an earlier slang use of *flapper* which preceded the twentieth-century use by only a few decades, and which was more probably the direct antecedent, somewhat altered in meaning. The late nineteenth-century slang meant an immoral young woman. Immorality was not implied in the later slang.

fork

The ancient Romans ate with their fingers, conveying food with such grace as they could master from plate to mouth. So, for that matter, did all European people until about the eleventh century A.D. The Roman *furca* (from which *fork* is derived) was an agricultural implement with two tines, like the hayfork of today, and it was used for various similar purposes. An instrument of punishment was also called *furca* because, shaped like an inverted V, it resembled the farm tool greatly enlarged. This device, of heavy wood, was hung over the neck of the person to be punished, usually a runaway slave, and his hands were fastened to the two ends. The inventor of the table fork is unknown. The implement is said to have been introduced into Vienna in the eleventh century by a Byzantine princess, who may have had it designed for her. Like many of the forks of today, it probably had but two tines. The Viennese promptly dubbed it *furca* from its resemblance to the agricultural implement which had descended to them. The rest of Europe was slow to adopt this novelty, and even as late as the sixteenth century its use in France was ridiculed. Forks came into use by English nobility early in the seventeenth century, though even at the close of that century few nobles possessed as many as a dozen. The English name *fork* came from the Old English corruption, *forca*, of the Latin word.

fortnight (sennight)

The Angles and Saxons who conquered Britain in the fifth and sixth centuries A.D. had not yet fully adopted all of the Roman devices for marking the passage of time. Thus, though it is probable that they had already accepted the Roman method of naming the days of the week, modified to honor corresponding Teutonic gods, it is not certain that "week," as we use it today, was understood by them to mean a period of seven "days." They clung, instead, to the ancestral practice of referring to such a period as "seven nights," because, with them, night, when the world was dark and men were asleep, marked a distinct division of time. Their term became *seofon nihta* in Old English, and this, through the centuries, became corrupted to *sennight*, now almost entirely out of use. The more convenient term for a two-week period, roughly half a month, is still in current use in England, though not often heard nowadays in America. In Old English it was *feowertene nihta*, fourteen nights, which became contracted into *fortnight*.

foyer

In these days of comfortable living we are likely to forget the discomfort that our ancestors took as a matter of course. The theater of today, regardless of outside winter temperature, is pleasantly warm, both for audience and performers. Such was not always the case. Even so recently as a century ago, no matter how warmly dressed, the audience welcomed the intermissions between acts to walk about and get the blood back into circulation; those especially cold retired to the lobby or entrance hall of the theater where a large fire burned upon the hearth. The actors congregated about a similar hearth in the greenroom. In France, the name for hearth is *foyer*, and the sense of this word gradually came to include the large hall or room in which the hearth was located. The need for the hearth and the hearth itself vanished long ago, but the name was borrowed into English usage for both the greenroom and the lobby.

franc

After the battle of Poitiers in 1356, John II, king of France, sometimes called "John the Good," was taken prisoner by the British. He remained a prisoner in London until 1360. Then, upon a promise to cede certain French provinces to the British crown and to pay a ransom of three million gold crowns, he was permitted to return to France to evolve ways of raising this huge sum. His attempt failed and he returned to England voluntarily to resume a not too onerous captivity. During his brief period of freedom, however, which was spent largely in debasing the currency in order to raise money, he caused a new gold coin to be struck. It was actually equivalent in value to the livre then in use, merely having a new legend and new design upon its face. The design was presumably an effigy of King John on horseback; the Latin legend read, *Johannes Dei gracia Francorum rex*, "John, by the grace of God, King of the Franks." Because of the legend and the effigy, this coin became popularly termed *franc à cheval*, "a franc *with a horse*." The term was given additional impulse when Charles V, successor of John II, issued another coin of the same value bearing an effigy of himself standing upright. This became *franc à pied*, "franc on foot." The new name for the livre persisted, and from then on French writers used *franc* or *livre* indiscriminately until, in 1795, the gold coin was superseded by the silver franc and the livre was dropped from currency.

frank

In the late sixth and early seventh centuries A.D., a warlike German tribe living along the lower stretches of the Rhine, moved steadily southward. The Roman legions had at one time conquered this tribe and had used its forces as honored allies, but now the Roman power had become weak and the tribe finally occupied all the coastal country north of the Pyrenees. The members of this tribe were known to the Romans as *Franci* (plural of *Francus*), after the javelin with which they were efficiently armed. The English equivalent is *Frank*, and the tribe is referred to in English accounts as the *Franks*. After their conquest of the country the Franks imposed their own laws, subjugating the natives and arrogating all the privileges to themselves. Thus they became the only free people in the land. Hence their name, having lost the old Roman meaning, came to be used as meaning "free." And because of this and their power, they scorned the use of subterfuge in their dealings among themselves or with others. Thus the Franks became noted, not only for their freedom, but also for integrity. Hence, *frank* came to denote the characteristics attributed to these people, straightforwardness and candor. Part of the country which they occupied still honors this old free tribe by the name it bears, *France*.

Frankenstein

In 1818, Mary Wollstonecraft Shelley, second wife of the romantic young poet, Percy Bysshe Shelley, published her first piece of writing. It is said that she had undertaken such authorship two years before when she, Shelley, and Byron had agreed that each was to undertake to write a tale dealing with the supernatural. Mrs. Shelley was the only one to complete the task. Her tale bore the title, *Frankenstein, or The Modern Prometheus*. The story tells about a Swiss student, Victor Frankenstein, who found a way to create life artificially. After making the discovery he visited dissecting rooms and graveyards and constructed a body in human form and endowed it with life. The soulless monster thus created had muscular strength and animal passions, but was shunned by all other living creatures. Made frantic by its unsatisfied desires and by Frankenstein's unwillingness to create a mate for it, the monster revenged itself upon its creator. After committing many atrocities, including the murder of Frankenstein's friend, brother, and bride, it finally slew Frankenstein himself. The book became very popular, and the term *Frankenstein* came into the language as indicating any person whose work brings about his own ruin. Unfortunately, Mrs. Shelley did not give a name to the monster, with the consequence that *Frankenstein* has often been misapplied to the monster itself, and, thus, to the agency that brings about the ruin of its creator.

Friday

When the Egyptian system of a week of seven days was adopted by the Roman Empire during the reign of Constantine, the sixth day of what is now our week was named *dies Veneris*, day of Venus, in honor of the planet that was presumed to influence that day, according to Egyptian astronomers. But the Teutonic tribes of the north, when adopting the seven-day week, knew nothing of the planetary reason for naming the days, and, supposing the Romans to have merely honored their chief gods and goddesses, gave to this day the name of their own chief goddess, *Frigg* or *Frigga*. She was the wife of Odin (or Woden); she presided over marriages and over the skies, and knew the fate of all men. Later myths, however, introduced a new goddess among some of the Teutonic tribes, a goddess of similar name. This was *Freya* or *Freyja*. She, with her brother, Frey, were the children of Njord, the god of the winds and sea. Freya was the goddess of love, and therefore corresponded more closely with the Roman goddess, Venus, than did Frigg. In Old English literature her name appears as *Freo*, of which the possessive is *Frige*. Consequently, because of this similarity, some scholars believe that *Friday*, which appears as *Frigedæg* (Freo's day) in Old English, also honors the goddess of love, just as, by way of the planet, the Romans did with *dies Veneris*. (See also SATURDAY.)

fudge

There is, unfortunately, no certainty about the origin of this word. But Isaac D'Israeli (the father of the statesman, Benjamin Disraeli), in *Curiosities of Literature*, published in 1791, quoted a story that went the rounds of the British navy in 1700 which was then thought to explain the source. The quoted explanation ran: "There was, sir, in our time one Captain Fudge, commander of a merchantman, who upon his return from a voyage, how ill-fraught soever his ship was, always brought home his owners a good cargo of lies, so much that now aboard ship the sailors, when they hear a great lie told, cry out, 'You *fudge* it.'" The story may be true, for there was a real Captain Fudge living in the seventeenth century, and he was said to have been known by some as "Lying Fudge," but the explanation is not generally accepted as the source of our word.

fun (fond) (fondle)

We know that "son" is pronounced as if spelled "sun," so it is not surprising to learn that *fun* was spelled *fon* back in the days of Chaucer. The meaning of *fon*, however, was not quite the same as that which we give to the later spelling. It meant "a fool," and when the word was revived in the early part of the eighteenth century in the present sense and spelling, *fun*, after two centuries of disuse, the learned Dr. Samuel Johnson called it "a low cant word." In the early use, *fon* was also a verb, meaning "to act the fool; become foolish." Its past participle, though sometimes spelled *fonned*, was then usually spelled *fond*. So when Shakespeare and earlier writers speak of "fond old men" or "fond maydens," they actually described foolish or silly old men or maids. This past participle didn't fall into disuse, as did *fon*, but its meaning gradually altered from "foolish" to "foolishly tender," and finally to "tender and sentimental," although fond young men, and especially fond old men, still often look and act foolish. Toward the eighteenth century someone felt the need of a verb to indicate the action of being fond, and thus created *fondle*. Sometimes it, too, carries back to the original *fon*, for a doting grandmother sometimes acts foolish when fondling a grandchild.

furlong (mile)

Before the days when Edward I ruled England (1272-1307), an acre of land was understood to be such amount of tillable land as a yoke of oxen could plow in a day. The size was indefinite, just as was the Latin *ager*, field, from which *acre* is derived. It was several times the size of our present acre, usually ten times the size, because in some regions at least the extent was measured as the amount which a team of eight oxen could plow in a day. This latter ideal field was a square which measured an eighth of a Roman mile, or a *stadium*, in each direction. The furrows were therefore each a stadium in length and, with the primitive plow then used, there were probably 320 furrows across the field. The length of a furrow thus became a convenient measure of distance—a *furlang*, it was called in Old English, from *furh*, furrow, and *lang*, long. But for the sake of standardization, the size of the acre was reduced under the statutes of King Edward. Thereafter it denoted an area which measured forty rods in length by four rods in breadth, although neither the rod nor the yard upon which it was based were of standard size. Then when the Roman mile of a thousand paces (*mille passus*), or about 1,618 yards, was replaced by the standard English mile of 1,760 yards, and the length of the yard became a standard measure, *furlong* became merely a term for a unit of distance an eighth of a mile or 220 yards in length, no longer equal to the Roman *stadium.* (See also ACRE.)

galvanism

Luigi Galvani was only a young man of twenty-five when in 1762, through the merit of his studies in medicine, he was appointed professor of anatomy at the University of Bologna, Italy. One day, a few years later, it is said, while his wife was watching him dissect a frog, she saw something that astonished her. She saw the skinned leg of the frog twitch as though alive when, accidentally, the scalpel which her husband had just picked up from the table came into contact with an exposed nerve. She called it to his attention. Upon investigation they found that the scalpel had become charged by an adjacent electric machine. Further experiment showed that the phenomenon was repeated as long as the nerve remained fresh at every such contact with a charged instrument. Galvani continued this new line of experimentation for some twenty years before publishing his findings. His conclusions—that the nerves are sources of electricity and that the scalpel or other metal served only as conductors—were subsequently proved to be wrong by Volta, but his experiments opened up a new line of electric research in the development of electricity by chemical means, and the name of the Italian physician has been perpetuated through the name given to the process, *galvanism.*

gamut

Guido of Arezzo was the greatest musician of medieval times. He lived in the eleventh century, although few details of his life are known. He is credited with the first systematic use of the lines of the staff and the spaces between them, but is now chiefly remembered from the names that he gave to the notes of the scale, six of which are in present use. It is said that when teaching his choristers the hymn addressed to St. John the Baptist he was struck with the regularly ascending sounds of the opening syllable of each hem-

ıstich in the first three verses. These verses, separated into hemi-
stichs, were:

Ut queant laxis   *re*sonare fibris
*Mi*ra gestorum   *fa*muli tuorum
*Sol*ve polluti   *la*bii reatum

The hymn closed with "Sancte *I*ohannes," the initials of which—
si—provided the seventh note of the scale when, in later days, the
heptachord of seven notes replaced the hexachord of six notes used
by Guido. The first syllable, *ut*, has been replaced by *do* in English-
speaking countries, but is still used in France. In his written music
Guido used the Greek letter *gamma* (Γ) to indicate the note one
tone lower than A, which from classical times began the scales,
and this note was accordingly designated *gamma ut*. It became contracted to *gamut*, and ultimately became the name by which the
entire "Great Scale" of Guido's invention was known. Because this
scale was intended to cover the entire singing range of both bass and
treble, *gamut* early acquired a figurative usage denoting full range
or entire sequence—such as we say of an actor who may be able to
assume expressions that run the full *gamut* of emotions.

gantlet (gauntlet)

During the Thirty Years' War, which lasted from 1618 to 1648,
the English forces observed a form of disciplinary punishment used
among their German allies. It looked highly effective, so it was not
long before it was adopted by English disciplinarians. The Germans
said that it had originated in the Swedish army, in which it was
known as *gatloppe*, literally, "a running of the lane." In this punishment, the severity of which could be regulated, a soldier guilty of
an offense was compelled to strip to the waist and run between two
lines of his fellows, each armed with a lash or rod. As he passed,
each was supposed to strike him across the back. Depending upon
the severity of the punishment to be inflicted, the lines of men might
be short or long, and the lashes might be knotted for maximum
severity. The Swedish word became corrupted into *gantlope* by
the English, but was later altered to *gantlet* or *gauntlet* because of
the resemblance of the word to the name of the glove.

gardenia

Alexander Garden was born in Charleston, South Carolina, and went to Scotland to study medicine. He returned to Charleston in 1755 as a young physician of twenty-five. He was also a profound student of botany, as a young man, and it was in his honor that the Royal Society, in 1760, gave the name, *gardenia*, to a newly discovered tropical shrub. Throughout the Revolutionary War, Dr. Garden remained a Tory, and was still opposed to the formation of an independent country when the war closed. Accordingly, in 1783, he emigrated to London where he again took up the practice of medicine. His estates, confiscated during the war, were returned to his son Alexander, a volunteer in the American army, serving with distinction under General Lee and General Greene.

gargantuan

When the great French writer of the sixteenth century, François Rabelais, wished to satirize the extravagances of the French court of his period, he chose to do so by allegory. This he wrote in the form of an account of the life of an enormous giant, whom he named *Gargantua*, taking the name from that of a legendary giant of the Middle Ages. At birth, he explained, the huge infant required the milk of 17,913 cows. For his education he rode to Paris on a mare as large as six elephants, and about the mare's neck he hung the bells of Notre Dame as jingles. The mare's tail was as great as the bell tower of San Marco, and when stung by wasps near Orleans, the mare swung it so furiously as to knock down all the trees in the neighborhood. *Gargantua* was so huge that he combed his hair with a comb 900 feet long; his shoes required eleven hundred cowhides for the soles alone. His appetite was prodigious. To this day our expression, "a *gargantuan* feast," refers to the occasion when *Gargantua*, being hungry, made a salad from lettuces as big as walnut trees and, inadvertently, ate up six pilgrims who had taken refuge among them.

garret

If one recalls the French expression so commonly heard during the recent World Wars, "*C'est la guerre!*" a clue may be seen for the origin of the word *garret*. The ancient French spelling was *guerite*, and the term meant a watchtower or place of observation, as under the roof of a building where a sentry could be on the lookout for an approaching enemy. Taken to England by the Norman conquerors, its original meaning became altered to our present sense and its spelling, thanks to similarity of pronunciation, transformed to *garret*.

gas

Until about the end of the sixteenth century chemists, or alchemists more properly, still held to the theory of Aristotle that the four primary properties of matter were fire, air, water, and earth. At that period, however, some such experimenters as Galileo, Harvey, and others were beginning to discard the old theories, and the alchemists themselves were finding flaws in their ancient beliefs. Among the critics was the Belgian physician, Jean Baptiste van Helmont, born in 1577. Although he believed that he had himself transmuted mercury into gold with a small piece of the "philosopher's stone," he was obliged to fall back upon supernatural agencies to find an explanation for certain phenomena that he discovered in his other experiments. He observed that when he applied heat to certain things, water especially, a vapor would arise. He believed this vapor to be fundamentally water in ultrararefied form, and, as he says, "for want of a name, I have called that vapor *gas*, not far disassociated from the *chaos* of the ancients." Thus, although van Helmont had no more than a vague understanding of the nature of gases, we are indebted to him for the word.

gazette

Back toward the early part of the sixteenth century there circulated in Venice a small coin of low value, made chiefly of tin. Probably it was worth no more than half a cent in our currency. The Venetians called it a *gazzetta*. This name may have been a diminutive of *gazza*, a magpie, or, as some scholars believe, a diminutive of *gaza*, which denoted the treasure of Persian kings. If the latter, the Venetian *gazzetta* was an extremely small treasure. Be that as it may, the Venetian government began to issue official leaflets, about the middle of the sixteenth century, which dealt with battles, games, elections, and other matters of general interest. (Some of the material was supplied by merchants returning from foreign ports. Much of the information was based upon unreliable rumor and hearsay.) The price set upon this paper—or for the privilege of reading it in such public places as it was displayed—was one *gazzetta*. The leaflet itself thus became known as a *gazzetta*. This term was brought into England in 1598 by John Florio in his Italian-English dictionary. He described the contents of the paper as, "running reports, daily newes, idle intelligences, or flim flam tales that are daily written from Italie, namely from Rome and Venice." Our present spelling came about through French influence.

gerrymander

Elbridge Gerry, born in 1744, was a member of the group of the American patriots who stirred the townspeople of Boston into active opposition toward the Acts of George III, resulting in the War for Independence. Subsequently he was a member of the Continental Congress and a signer of the Declaration of Independence. He continued to serve in this Congress until 1786, and was elected to the First and Second Congresses after the adoption of the Federal Constitution in 1788. Twice he was elected governor of Massachusetts, but was defeated when running for the third time in 1812. Instead, however, he was elected vice-president of the United States in that same year and served in that capacity until his death in 1814. But despite this honorable record, Gerry's name has come down to us in association with one dishonorable episode in his career. While running for his third term as governor of Massachusetts, he permitted the state legislature, in accordance with customs of the times, to divide the electoral districts of the state into new districts in such manner that the strength of the opposing party was concentrated into a few districts. A map of one of the districts thus arbitrarily created was seen by the painter, Gilbert Stuart. Stuart saw in it a resemblance to the body of an elongated animal. With a few strokes he added a head, claws, and wings, and remarked, "That will do for a salamander." "Better say a *gerrymander*," growled the editor in whose office the map was hanging.

gin

Credit for the introduction of the juniper berry into wine in the sixteenth century is given to the Count de Morret, one of the illegitimate sons of Henry IV of France. The beverage, subsequently known as juniper wine, was found to be pleasing and it led others to try the effect of the berry when added to spirit distilled from fermented liquors. Previously, ginger, pepper, and other aromatic ingredients had been used. The addition of the juniper berry, however, was found to be far more agreeable, and the older experiments were dropped. The new beverage became known in France by the name of the berry—*genevre* (in modern French, *genièvre*). In Holland, where manufacture was largely centered during the following century, the name became *genever*. The English, who marketed vast quantities of the liquor, altered this to *geneva*, after the Swiss city of that name. It was not long, however, before they shortened the general term *Holland geneva* into *Holland gin* in accordance with the customary British penchant for contraction, and this then soon became more commonly further shortened to *gin*.

glamour

Until the seventeenth century there was no necessity for anyone to speak of "Latin grammar," because that was the only kind of grammar that was taught. Anyone who knew his "grammar" necessarily knew Latin. Even in these days, among untutored folk, any learned person is regarded with something akin to awe. But in those days, when few men in any community could read or write, one who was so learned that he could read and speak Latin was believed, by common folks, to possess occult powers, to be capable of witchcraft or of working magic spells. Accordingly, in the speech of England, such a person was said to have *gramary*, that is, ability to effect charms through a knowledge of grammar. In Scotland he had *glamer*, a corruption of the same word and with the same meaning. Various Scottish writers, spelling it *glamer*, *glamor*, or *glamour*, used the term in that sense, but it was Sir Walter Scott who explained it and brought it into English usage slightly more than a century ago. Since then we have extended the earlier sense by glorifying the enchantment, though we no longer imply that one possessing *glamour* is necessarily learned.

gorgon

Three hideous sisters, according to Greek mythology, lived in the region of Night at the extremity of the Western Ocean. They were known as *gorgons*; their separate names were Stheno, Euryale, and Medusa. The latter, the only one of the three who was mortal, had once been a beautiful girl, but having had the misfortune to enrage the goddess Athena, her aspect was changed so that she became even more fearsome and deadly than her sisters. The sisters are described as being girded with winged serpents which had brazen claws and enormous teeth which they gnashed viciously. The hair of Medusa was changed by Athena into writhing serpents, which gave her head so fearful an appearance that anyone who looked at it was changed into stone. According to other tradition, the *gorgons* were formidable animals with long hair, and of such frightful appearance as to paralyze anyone seeing them. In modern usage, a *gorgon* repels more by a forbidding manner than by repulsive appearance.

gorilla

In the fifth or sixth century B.C., a Carthaginian navigator, Hanno, set out upon a westward voyage along the north coast of Africa, through the Pillars of Hercules, which we now call the Strait of Gibraltar, and thence southward along the west coast of Africa. He wrote an account of his voyage in a small book called *Periplus*. It is not now possible to identify the points at which he touched nor to determine the actual extent of his expedition, though he is supposed to have reached what is now Sierra Leone. He says that an object of the trip was to establish Carthaginian colonies along the way, and that he took with him 30,000 men and women for the purpose. That number, however, is probably an exaggeration introduced by translators when the book was circulated in Greece. Among the strange things that he encountered on the trip was a wild creature which he believed to be a large hairy woman. This he called *gorilla*, using the native name. It is probable that the creature described by Hanno was either the chimpanzee or the baboon, however, for it is not believed that he traveled far enough to the southward to encounter the fiercer creature that we now call *gorilla*.

gospel

A missionary to any heathen country must first learn the language of that country. He then tries to deliver his message in that language, translating the words that are familiar to him into new words that will carry the same meaning. Thus the Latin *evangelium* was turned into *gōd spell*, good tidings, when Roman missionaries came to England, for that was the literal translation. These were two separate words, *gōd* and *spell;* but through carelessness or ignorance early writers began to join the words into *god-spel* or *godspel*, the literal meaning of which was thereby altered to "God story." In speech and eventually in writing, this became *gospel*, though the true meaning of the missionaries is still to be found in such titles as "The *Gospel* (Good Tidings) according to Saint Matthew."

gossamer

The story of St. Martin is briefly told under CHAPEL, originally the sanctuary in which his *capella* or cloak was preserved. He became the patron saint of France, but was also honored elsewhere in Christendom. In Germany his festal day, November 11, was especially celebrated with eating, drinking, and merrymaking, probably, in part, because it replaced the old pagan festival of *vinalia*, noting the time when wines had reached their prime, and in part because it occurred in November when, through long custom, fat roast goose was the favorite dish, goose being then in season. In fact, the period was so given up to the consumption of roast goose that the month itself, in Germany, was called *Gänsemonat*, goose month. This Teutonic association of the goose with St. Martin was carried into England, to the extent that "St. Martin's summer" was also called "goose summer" in olden times. At such a period of unseasonably warm weather, which in America is called "Indian summer," finely textured cobwebs may be found on the grass or floating in the calm air. Such a delicate web, which we call *gossamer*, is now generally believed to have taken its name from the period—"goose summer"—in which its occurrence was most marked. From *"goose-summer* webs," the term was eventually corrupted to *gossamer*.

gossip

Sponsors for infants in the rite of baptism were, at one time, held to contract a spiritual kinship with the infant in whose name they took the vows. We still observe that kinship by the terms we use for sponsors—"godparents," parents in God; "godfather," "godmother." Such godparents thus were held to be spiritually related to the other members of the family. Hence, in a family containing several children, there would be a number of men and women who, though not related to each other by blood, could claim kinship through their ties with this family. Such folks were said to be *godsib* in olden times, that is, "related in God," for *sib* means "related." That gave them the privilege of talking with each other about the family to which they were mutually akin, and about its various members—probably also about such of their own number as might be absent. Undoubtedly they exercised the privilege—to such an extent, in fact, that *godsib* became a term for anyone who entertained others with rumors, idle talk, and tattletales. And, just as *gōd spell* became corrupted to "gospel" through assimilation of the letter "d," so *godsib* became corrupted to *gossip*.

graham

Sylvester Graham was born in Connecticut in 1794 and, after studying at Amherst College, entered the ministry in 1826. Within a few years he became an ardent advocate of temperance and of vegetarianism. He held that the two were related, for it was his belief that one who followed a diet composed wholly of vegetables would have no desire for alcohol. Along with his dietary principles he favored the use of unbolted wheat flour in the making of bread, and had this flour especially prepared for him. Others tried the product upon his recommendation and created a demand for it. His name thus became inseparably associated with the flour and any of its products. One may buy *graham* crackers or *graham* bread in any grocery in the country.

Greenland

We know little about the character of Eric the Red except what can be judged from episodes in his life related in the sagas of Iceland.

He must have been hot-tempered. His father and he fled from Norway to Iceland after killing a man. But in Iceland Eric was so continually in trouble with his neighbors and involved in other killings that he was finally obliged to flee from that country as well for a term of years. He had heard of a country lying further west and determined to sail for it. After he found it he explored the coast until he discovered a place that was habitable, spending three years in the search. He must have been a humorist also, because when he returned to Iceland and sought to persuade others to help colonize the new country, in 983, he called it *Greenland*. He gave it this name, he said, because "people would be more willing to go there if it had an attractive name." He did, in fact, start a colony and helped in the foundation of others. These grew until, according to estimates, there were four or five thousand people living in them at the height of the prosperity of the country in the twelfth or thirteenth century.

gregarious (aggregate, segregate, congregate, egregious)

Among any primitive people the care of one's livestock is, next to oneself, the most important duty. Such people therefore become very familiar with the ways of their livestock and, naturally, compare the actions of their fellowmen with the actions and habits of dumb creatures. So it was among the Romans, and so did they pass down to us words with meanings for which we must search among farm animals in explanation.

The Latin word for herd, whether sheep, goats, or cattle, was *grex* (the root of which is *greg-*). Hence, when a band of men joined together into a military company, the people saw that this band, when grouped together, looked like a herd of sheep; so they called the military company *grex* also. The way the men flocked together, they said, was *gregarius*, the way of a herd. This has become *gregarious* in English, and we still use it to describe a person who is not happy unless with a number of other persons.

The same root has given us the verb *aggregate* (from Latin *aggrego*, to add to a herd), which means to collect into a total; and the verb *congregate* (from Latin *congrego*, to assemble into a flock or herd), which we use to mean to assemble into a body; and the verb *segregate* (from Latin *segrego*, to set apart from the flock or herd), which has come to us with little change in meaning.

From the same root we have also the word *egregious*. The Latin word, *egregius*, with the literal meaning, "surpassing the rest of the flock," was always used in a favorable sense. This was also the sense in which it was first employed in English, but it then became ironical and is now usually employed in a bad sense; an *egregious* blunder is one that tops all other blunders.

grenade (garnet, grenadier, pomegranate)

Granum is the Latin word for grain or seed, and is the source of a number of the words we now use. Not only *grain* and *grange* and *granary*, but also *garnet*, *grenade*, and *pomegranate*. The latter words came from the Latin adjective, *granatus*, "having many seeds." Anyone who has eaten a pomegranate will readily see why the Romans called it *granatum*, for it is certainly filled with seeds. They also called it *Punica granatum* and *malum Punicum* (Punic apple), believing it to have originated in Carthage. (Our present name, *pomegranate*, from *pomum*, fruit, apple—hence, fruit of many seeds—was of later formation.)

The pulp of this fruit has a deep, transparent, reddish color, very similar in appearance to that of the gem, garnet. Either because of the color or because of the general resemblance between the seeds of the fruit and the crystals of the gem, the precious stone was called *granaticus* by the Romans. This became *grenat* in Old French and, when taken to England, *gernat*, *gernet*, and, ultimately, *garnet*.

After the invention of gunpowder, experimentation began with various explosive missiles. One of these used by the English army in the late sixteenth century was a small bomb, shot from a gun or thrown by hand into a cluster of the enemy. This missile was facetiously called a *granate* or *granade*, perhaps because it was about the size of a pomegranate and was filled with "seeds" or grains of powder. The name became fixed as *grenade*. Later, a company in each regiment or battalion was specially trained in the handling and hurling of grenades and, quite properly, each member of such a company became a *grenadier*.

grog

In 1738, the British House of Commons was stirred by a story related by one Robert Jenkins. Jenkins, a master mariner, said that he had been peacefully trading in the West Indies when his vessel had been boarded by a Spanish guard, his hold had been rifled, and as a crowning indignity one of his ears had been lopped off. So many incidents of Spanish aggression had occurred that the government decided that it should be suppressed. Thus occurred what is sometimes called, "The War of Jenkins' Ear." As the first step, Vice Admiral Edward Vernon—whose name was later given by Lawrence Washington, who served under him, to his estate in Virginia, Mount Vernon—was sent to the West Indies. In 1739 Vernon captured the small and poorly defended garrison at Porto Bello, in what is now Panama and, though his subsequent encounters with the Spaniards were failures, he was given a great ovation in London upon his return in 1743. Vernon was not popular with his crew, however. They called him "Old Grog," in allusion, it is said, to the grogram cloak that he habitually wore. He was a stern disciplinarian, as were most naval officers of the period, and, historians say, he was arrogant and self-conceited. His popularity was not improved among those under his command by an order issued by him in August, 1740. Previously, according to long custom, all sailors received a daily ration of undiluted rum or brandy. Summarily, Vernon ordered that after that date the rum should always be diluted with equal parts of water before it was served. The incensed sailors contemptuously called this piffling watered beverage, *grog,* taking the name from the nickname they had bestowed upon the admiral.

guillotine

Joseph Ignace Guillotin did not invent the machine that bears his name, nor did he die by it, although both statements are sometimes made. He was a physician, born in 1738, and was practicing in Paris at the outbreak of the French Revolution. He then became a member of the National Assembly. In 1789, three years before the beginning of the Reign of Terror, the Assembly was considering the matter of capital punishment. Dr. Guillotin, who had probably seen one or another of the beheading machines used in other countries, proposed that all executions in France should be on some similar machine, which he described. His ideas gradually took hold, and the method that he had suggested was adopted in 1791, after Dr. Guillotin had retired from the Assembly. The machine that was built was actually designed by Dr. Antoine Louis and built by a German named Schmidt. The first execution by it was that of a highwayman, in April, 1792. At that time it was known as a *Louisette*, after the name of its designer, but the public, remembering the man who had first proposed the machine, insisted upon calling it a *guillotine*. Dr. Guillotin died in 1814, fifteen years after Napoleon had suppressed the Revolution.

guinea

In 1663, the Royal Mint of England made a special gold coinage of twenty-shilling pieces "in the name and for the use of the Company of Royal Adventurers of England trading with Africa." These coins, and others of the same value afterward coined for general use, were called *guineas*, because the trade of the "Royal Adventurers of England" was actually along the coast of Guinea. At this period in English history the standard of value was not gold, but silver, and the silver coinage was in bad state owing to the activities of "clippers," who mutilated coins by paring the edges. The value of the gold guinea therefore increased to more than twenty-shillings' worth of silver coin, or more than its face value. Accordingly, in 1717, its value was fixed at 21 shillings. After the establishment of the gold standard in 1816 no more guineas were coined.

guy

In early November, 1605, a plot, long under preparation, was about ready to be put into execution. It was to blow up King James I of England and the entire House of Parliament when the king was to address the opening session of that body on November 5. The gunpowder, covered with faggots to fire it, was in readiness in the cellar of the building, and the man selected for resolution and bravery was stationed in the cellar ready to light the fire. He was provided with a slow match which, it was hoped, would allow him to set the fire and make his own escape before the explosion. The plot—later called the "gunpowder plot"—would undoubtedly have succeeded had not one of the conspirators recalled that a dear friend would be among those killed. So he wrote that friend an unsigned note, urging that he absent himself from that first session and giving an inkling of what was about to happen. The friend immediately took steps to start an investigation, with the result that late in the evening of November 4, the plot was discovered and the man charged with setting off the gunpowder was arrested. That man was Guy Fawkes. He was later tried, with some of his fellow conspirators, and all were hanged. "Guy Fawkes' Day," as November 5 has since been known in England, is celebrated by carrying grotesque effigies of Fawkes clad in ragged garments through the streets. From these effigies, any person faintly resembling them in dress or appearance became referred to as a *guy*.

gymnast, gymnasium

Among the Greeks a sound body was considered to be equally as important as a sound mind. Thus physical training was as much a part of the general education of boys and young men as was mental training. Buildings were set aside for the purpose and officials were especially selected for their fitness in supervising all athletic activities. But that their charges might receive the best instruction for the proper development of their bodies, as well as have the greatest freedom of movement when exercising, all the young athletes were naked while undergoing this training. "Naked," in Greek, is *gymnos*; "to train naked" is *gymnazo*. Thus, in its literal sense, a *gymnast* is one who is naked while exercising, and a *gymnasium*, from the Greek *gymnasion*, is the place where such exercises are held. The terms lost those literal senses, however, before being adopted into our language.

halcyon

Greek legend relates that Halcyone, whose name sometimes occurs as Alcyone, threw herself into the sea when she found the drowned body of her husband. She was one of the demigods, a daughter of Æolus, but had married a mortal. The couple were blissfully happy and their wedded life had been compared with that of Zeus and Hera. Hence, after their tragic death the gods changed both husband and wife into birds, thereafter known as *halcyons* by the Greeks. These are the birds that we call kingfishers. The ancients believed that these birds built their nests upon the sea and that the sea was charmed by them into calmness while they brooded upon and hatched their eggs. The times chosen for building the nests and hatching the eggs were supposed to be the seven days preceding and the seven days following the winter solstice. This period became known, therefore, as *"halcyon* days," an expression now referring to any period of peace and tranquil serenity.

halibut

In Old English the common name for any of the flatfish—skate, turbot, plaice, flounder, or whatever—was "butt." The most highly regarded of all, however, the one that was reserved for eating upon holy days, was the largest of the flatfishes, so large that fish weighing three and four hundred pounds are not uncommon, running up to seven or eight feet in length. This they named the *haly butt*, for *haly* was the old-time spelling of *holy*. The consumption of the *halibut* is no longer limited to feast days of the Church, despite our designation of the fish as "the holy flounder."

halloween

The thirty-first of October was the last day of the year, according to old-time Celtic reckoning. Ghosts walked until the midnight of that evening, and all witches held their annual festivals, riding to them on their broomsticks in the company of their black cats. Many of our present customs and sports in observance of the day trace back to the time when it figured as the Celtic New Year's Eve. But with the introduction of Christianity, New Year's no longer was observed on November 1 and belief in witches was discouraged. However, as with other pagan observances in old England, the Church transformed the occasion of celebration into one of sacred character. Instead of celebrating "all witches," as in the past, the occasion was transformed into one for celebrating "all saints." Thus, because *hallow* was the term used in England for "saint," or "holy man," until the fifteenth century, the celebration became *All Hallows' E'en*, literally, "All Saints' Evening." The contraction to *hallowe'en* followed as a matter of course.

handicap

Gamblers of the fourteenth century had a sport which they called "Newe Faire." Three players were required, one of whom served as umpire. All three put some forfeit money into a cap held by the umpire. Then one of the other two offered some article that he had in exchange for something held by the other. It was then the umpire's duty to appraise the two articles and state how much should be offered to boot for the better article. The two other parties then reached into their own caps or pockets, in which there were loose coins, and drew out their hands. If both drew out money, the exchange was effected, and the umpire took the forfeit money for himself. If neither drew out money, the umpire again took the forfeit money, though the exchange was not made. But if only one drew out money, he was entitled to the forfeit money, even though again the exchange was not made. The game later became known as "hand in the cap" or "hand i' cap," whence *handicap*. The game was later modified and transferred to horse racing, probably in the seventeenth century.

hangnail

Here is an instance of a word being formed first, through mispronunciation, and a meaning then devised which would account for the word. Anciently the English word on which this was based was *angnægl*, which then meant "a painful corn or wart on the foot." It was literally, "a painful nail," because at that time *nægl* or "nail" meant not only the ordinary metal nail with rounded head, but anything that resembled it, such as a corn or any other hard, rounded growth upon the skin, as well as a fingernail or toenail. But the spelling gradually became *agnail*, and its meaning was enlarged to include a whitlow, or painful swelling about a fingernail or toenail. In British dialects, however, the older pronunciation still lingered, "angnail." Then, like many another English word, an "h" was added and a new word was born, *hangnail*. This required explanation; so *hangnail* became a term for the small strip of skin that occasionally breaks away or "hangs" from the epidermis covering the root of a fingernail. *Agnail* was then reserved for the older meaning for a while, but then it embraced the new meaning also, although *hangnail* is the more usual term.

harvest

The Old English word from which this was derived, *haerfest*, had the same source and original meaning as the present German word *herbst.* Its meaning, that is, was the season in which crops were ripe. It was the name of the season, the third quarter of the year, the season now known by the later name, "autumn." That original English sense has now almost passed out of use, and now *harvest* usually covers, not only such crops as ripen in autumn, but also those that may be gathered at other seasons, such as fruit and vegetables that may ripen in the spring.

hazard

This term originated as the name of a gambling game which, at least in its later form, somewhat resembled the American game of craps. The name itself is from the Arabic *al zahr*, the die. This became *hasard* in Old French, and the English borrowed both game and name shortly after the Norman Conquest, it would seem. The game became very popular and was played for extremely high stakes in some of the most famous gaming halls of London. The chance of great loss associated with *hazard* thus caused its name to become synonymous with peril, risk or danger.

hearse (rehearse)

After he had plowed, the old British agriculturalist raked his land with a "harrow." The Norman invaders of England in the eleventh century called this implement a *herse*, a term which had come down in French from the Latin *hirpex*, rake. This was a heavy, triangular affair of wood, with spikes projecting from the lower side. When this instrument was overturned, it closely resembled the framework for holding lighted tapers used in certain religious ceremonies, with the tapers taking the place of the spikes. Consequently, the ecclesiastical device came also to be called, in France, a *herse*, a term that was later brought into England. The framework, though still called a *herse*, began to assume greater elaboration. More candles were added than the original thirteen used in Holy Week, and the structure was placed over the bier during the funeral services of distinguished persons. Such structures went out of use in England in the sixteenth century or shortly thereafter, but the name, which folks were beginning to spell *hearse*, was now applied to the vehicle that transported the coffin at a funeral.

Our word *rehearse* more nearly retains the sense of the Old

French *herse*, a harrow or rake. The act of repeating something that had been previously said was likened to the act of raking a field previously raked; hence, "to *herse* again," or *rehearse*.

hectic

The Greek physician Galen, who lived in the second century B.C., discovered that the cheeks of certain of his patients were continuously flushed as if by fever. He described that condition as *hektikos*, which meant "habitual." Later the condition was recognized as a disease, and the physicians of the fifteenth century, using Galen's term, called it *hectic fever*, though we now call it consumption from the fact that the disease gradually consumes the tissues of the body. (The broader term, tuberculosis, is more accurate.) Doctors use the term *hectic fever* nowadays, however, for a type of fever which, though usually associated with tubercular disease, also accompanies some forms of septic poisoning. An accompanying symptom of this fever is a nervous excitability in the patient, the appearance of which is heightened by flushed cheeks and abnormally bright eyes. In consequence of this air of excitability, the ancient medical term, in recent years, has acquired a meaning that would astonish poor old Galen. He would find it difficult to believe that a term meaning "habitual" could have had its meaning so distorted as to be used in place of "wild, reckless, excitable."

hector

In Homer's *Iliad*, the chief hero and champion among the Trojans was Hector, the son of their king, Priam. He was described as being an ideal son, husband, and father, loyal to his friends, and a man of the highest courage and bravery. He was feared by the Greeks above all others among their Trojan enemies. But when Hector, taking advantage of Achilles' withdrawal from the Greek camp, drove the Greeks back to their ships, which he almost succeeded in burning, and killed Patroclus, the friend of Achilles, the wrath of Achilles knew no bounds. He returned to the conflict, armed himself, routed the Trojans with fearful slaughter, and sought out Hector in single combat. Hector's courage failed him and, hotly pursued, he fled three times round the walls of Troy. But Achilles caught and slew him. and to complete his revenge dragged the body of Hector from his chariot once more about Troy. The story became a familiar one to the Romans, who looked upon themselves as descendants of the Trojans, and in due course *Hector* took his place in the minds of English schoolboys as a paragon of valiant courage. In the seventeenth century, however, the name came to be applied less worthily to a set of bullies who frequented the streets of London. These *Hectors* are described as swashbucklers or swaggering ruffians who, traveling together, insulted wayfarers, broke windows, and, in general, behaved with the utmost insolence. It is from their actions rather than from the Trojan hero that we owe our present use of *hector*.

helpmeet

Although this is another word for "helpmate," it was formed through a misunderstanding. If one turns to Genesis 2:18, one reads, "And the Lord God said, It is not good that the man should be alone; I will make him an help meet for him." The meaning of *meet* in this passage is "suitable, fitting, proper." Hence the biblical intent was "a suitable helper for him." But the two words were consistently read as one, many years ago, and resulted in an unneeded word.

hermetic

The ibis-headed god Thoth, in Egyptian theology, was the god of wisdom, science, magic, religion, and art. The Greeks identified him with Hermes, and he was therefore often known as Hermes Trismegistus (Hermes Thrice-greatest). He was the reputed author of the 42 books that constituted the sum of Egyptian learning, books which were therefore known as the "*Hermetic* Books." Because they dealt largely with the occult sciences—magic and alchemy—*hermetic* acquired the significance of "secret, hidden," and, in one usage, "airtight."

hobby, hobbyhorse (morris dance)

Among the amusements in England of the fifteenth and sixteenth centuries, especially in the May-day celebrations, was one known as the morris dance. Its original name had been "Moorish dance," and some of the features, probably borrowed from the Moors of

Spain, were long retained. Thus, although the group of characters costumed for the dance always included a Robin Hood, a Maid Marian, and a Friar Tuck, others, fantastically arrayed, were intended to represent Moorish dancers, some garbed as clowns, some with bells dangling from long hoods, and some with bells on their ankles. Usually also one of the Moors was represented as riding on an Arabian steed. The "steed" was a figure made of wicker, covered with hide or cloth to resemble a small horse, but actually fastened about the waist of the person supposed to be riding it. Its "rider" pranced about to show off the spirited nature of the steed. This make-believe steed became known as a *hobbyhorse*, probably because *hobby* had long been the term for a small horse, just as "dobbin" indicated a farm horse. From the use of the hobbyhorse in the morris dance, someone got the notion to convert it into a plaything for a child. Thus, since the sixteenth century some such imitation, variously constructed, has been a childhood favorite. Sometimes a child gets such enjoyment from his toy horse as to abandon all other playthings, and whenever awake, will furiously ride his *hobbyhorse* or *hobby*, which early became the shortened name. This favorite pastime was likened, even in the seventeenth century, to the devotion some men exhibit to a subject or an occupation that was at first taken up for amusement. Thus *hobbyhorse*, later shortened to *hobby*, came to denote any pursuit which is of great interest to an individual, though followed only for pleasure.

hobo

Little more may be done with this word than to repeat the several theories that have been advanced to explain its origin. Any one of them might be true, but there is no proof as yet.

Slightly less than four centuries ago the French musical instrument, the *hautbois*, came into English use. Its name was literal, from *haut*, high, and *bois*, wood, for the instrument was made of wood and its tone was high. (Later, from Italian spelling, it came to be called, as at present, the "oboe.") The English, as they frequently did with French words, corrupted the spelling into *hautboy* or, often, into *hoboy*, giving it the latter pronunciation in either case. There are, therefore, many people who think that our term *hobo*, which is of American origin, came somehow into use through itinerant players of the *hoboy*. Jack London, who had a lot of first-hand experience among tramps and vagabonds and who wrote much about them at the turn of the century, gave this theory the stamp of his approval.

Another explanation credited the source to the lumber camp. French-Canadians, they say, when felling a tree, instead of giving the shout, "Timber-r-r!" would cry, "*Haut bois!*"— literally, "high timber." From this cry, which might be rendered "*ho bo*" in English, it has been suggested, the itinerant Canadian lumberjack came to be called a *hobo* by his English-speaking fellow workers.

Another theory, advanced by a recent authority, is that the word may be derived from an ironic use of the word "beau," together with the word of greeting, "Ho." Thus, "*Ho, beau!*"—just as, in present popular speech, we hear, "Hi, fella!"

It is my own thought that the source might go back three hundred years. There is record of a slang term in use about that time applied to a man engaged in the most menial of all labor—one whose work it was to go about London at night and clean latrines. Such a man was called a *hoboy*. Possibly the name was of gypsy origin, as was much of the underworld slang of that period and some that is still alive. It is therefore possible that *hoboy* persisted among gypsies, changing to *hobo* through the years, and applied either to a tramp or to a migratory worker.

hollyhock

Because the name is actually a corruption of *holy hock*, in which *hock* is an old name for mallow, an ingenious scholar of the past century (Hensleigh Wedgwood) made the statement that it "was doubtless so called from being brought from the Holy Land, where it is indigenous." This statement has been repeated by others, but it lacks foundation. It is much more probable that the affix *holy* came about through an early association of this plant with some holy man. The plant has also been known as "St. Cuthbert's cole," thus warranting the inference that its later name was derived in some way either from that holy man, or from the island, Holy Island, off the northeast English coast which he made his retreat in the seventh century.

horde

Genghis Khan, great leader of the Mongols, died in 1227. He left his vast empire to his sons and grandsons, dividing it among them. To one of the grandsons, Batu Khan, fell the leadership in 1235 of the Mongol invasion of Europe. Without meeting much resistance his armies crossed the Volga River, where one part turned northward toward Moscow and Poland and the other southward into Bulgaria and Hungary. City after city fell before the invaders, was burned and leveled and the inhabitants massacred. An historian, writing of the taking of the Bulgarian capital in 1237, says: "The inhabitants, without regard to age or sex, were slaughtered with the savage cruelty of Mongol revenge; some were impaled, some shot at with arrows for sport, others were flayed or had nails or splinters driven under their nails. Priests were roasted alive, and nuns and maidens ravished in the churches before their relatives." Similar fates were met by those of other cities until, in 1241, satisfied with his conquests, Batu retired to the Volga to set up his capital. Wherever he had camped he had set up his own gorgeous tent, richly covered with embroidered silk and gilded leather. His followers called it the *sira ordu*, or "silken camp." The Poles put an initial *h* on the second element, making it *horda*. From this the name "Golden Horde" was applied to the tent or camp of Batu. This name in turn came to include the entire army of the Mongols. Thus, because of the great terror inspired throughout eastern Europe by this vast Mongolian army, *horde* became a general term for any Tatar tribe, and ultimately was applied to any large group of persons, savage in appearance or actions, or to a pack of fierce animals, likened to the savage and brutal Mongols.

hoyden (hoiden)

The most interesting story of the probable source of *hoyden* is the one that connects it with *heathen*. Formerly the word did not apply chiefly to a boisterous or ill-mannered girl, as it does now, but denoted an awkward lout, an ignorant boor of either sex. Persons of such uncouthness, in olden days, were commonly those who dwelt far from the villages and towns and had little contact with persons of refinement. Such were the folks who dwelt far from neighbors upon the heath; they were the last to hear of new things, and, thus, being the last to learn of Christianity, gave rise to our word *heathen*. (See PAGAN.) Now the former Dutch word for *heathen* was *heyden*. Thanks to the nearness of Holland to the English coast, it is likely that the Dutch word, slightly altered in pronunciation, passed over to England. There, although still applied to the rustic clown, male or female, who haled from the lonely heath, it became *hoyden* or *hoiden*.

humor (choleric, melancholic, phlegmatic, sanguine)

Ancient physicians—Hippocrates, Galen, and others, and even the physicians of the Middle Ages—believed that the body was governed by four primary fluids, or *humors*, as they said, using the Latin term for "fluid." These four fluids were the blood, the yellow bile, the black bile, and the phlegm. The nature of the four fluids was supposed to be hot and sweet, hot and dry, cold and dry, and cold and clammy, respectively, the Latin terms for these (some taken from the original Greek) being *sanguineus, cholericus, melancholicus* (from Greek *melas*, black and *chole*, bile), and *phlegmaticus*. The meanings of our words *sanguine, choleric, melancholic,* and *phlegmatic* accordingly trace back to those original senses. Thus, in olden days, a person said to be of *sanguine humor* was of ruddy countenance and had a courageous, hopeful, and amorous temperament; one of *choleric humor* was bilious and jaundiced, and of irascible temperament; one of *melancholic humor* was characterized by sullenness, sudden outbursts of anger, and fits of depression; and one of *phlegmatic humor* had a marked inclination toward indolence and apathy.

By a natural extension, *humor* thus became a synonym for temperament or disposition. In the sixteenth century the meaning of *humor* was further extended to unreasoned preference, capricious fancy, and at this period it became one of the most overused words in the language. Shakespeare poked great fun at this tendency to run the word into the ground when, in *Merry Wives of Windsor* and in *Henry V*, he has the character, Corporal Nym, interlard almost every sentence with "*humor.*" From this use developed the further extension that we understand chiefly by *humor* today, the quality of being amusing or of perceiving that which is droll or whimsical.

hyacinth

Once there was a Spartan youth, son of a king, who possessed such extraordinary beauty as to win the affection of the god Apollo. The name of this remarkably beautiful lad, according to Greek legend, was *Hyacinthus.* But he was also beloved by the West Wind, Zephyrus. And one day, when Apollo and Hyacinthus were playing quoits, Zephyrus in jealousy caused the heavy disk thrown by Apollo to stray from its course and strike Hyacinthus upon the head, with such force as to kill the lad. Great was the remorse of Apollo, but he could not restore the life of his friend. In grief, therefore, he caused a flower to spring from the blood-soaked earth, thereafter called *hyacinth* in memory of the handsome lad. It is believed, however, that the Greeks included several flowers under this name, especially the iris, the gladiolus, and larkspur. It is otherwise difficult to account for the variety of colors ascribed to the flower by various Greek writers.

hydraulic

About the year 200 B.C., an inventive genius, named Ctesibius, lived in Alexandria. He is supposed to have conducted experiments upon air pressures, but his chief invention was a water organ or clypsydra. It is not certain how this organ was operated, but it is likely that water served to regulate the air pressure within the tubes of the organ. The instrument was named *hydraulis,* or *hydraulikon organon,* from Greek *hydor,* water, and *aulus,* pipe. Later instruments operated by water power or through the utilization of water became thus classed as *hydraulic* by virtue of this first invention.

hymeneal

There is an ancient Greek legend of a youth of such delicate beauty that he might have been taken for a maid. His name was *Hymen* or *Hymenæus.* The girl with whom he fell in love spurned him, but in the disguise of a girl he followed her into the country to a festival. On the way he and all the real maidens in the gathering were carried off by a group of brigands to a foreign shore. But upon landing, the weary robbers fell asleep, whereupon Hymen, throwing off his disguise, seized a weapon and slew all of them. Then, leaving the maidens, he returned to Athens. There he got the promise of the citizens that his own beloved should be given to him in marriage if he were to bring the maidens back to Athens. The request was granted gladly, and he soon restored the girls safely to their homes. From that time onward Hymen was praised in the bridal or marriage songs of the nation, thenceforward described as *hymeneal* songs in honor of his exploit.

iconoclast

The word means "a breaker of images," from Greek *eikon*, image, and *klastes*, breaker. It originated in a great struggle within the Christian Church, beginning in the eighth century and lasting for one hundred and sixteen years. For a number of generations there had been discussion over the appearance of works of art—pictures and statuary—within church edifices. Some held that they should be excluded, because they were reminiscent of idol worshiping; others held that they merely increased the spirit of reverence in the mind of the beholder. Among the latter was Pope Gregory the Great, who had said, "What those who can read learn by means of writing, that do the uneducated learn by looking at a picture." But the emperor of the Eastern Roman Empire, Leo III, took the opposite view. He was a zealot, of such decided views that he had forcibly baptized all Jews and Mohammedans within his empire. In 726, therefore, he decreed the abolishment of all paintings and images from the churches of the realm. The ensuing struggle, carried on even more aggressively in the reign of Constantine V, who succeeded his father in 740, assumed the proportions of a crusade. In 765, images and relics were destroyed on a great scale throughout the Eastern Empire. The tide changed with succeeding monarchs, but the issue was not finally settled until 842 when the patriarch of the Eastern Church, assisted by clergy and court, solemnly restored the images in the church of St. Sophia in Constantinople. The term *iconoclast* is now usually employed figuratively, and is applied to one who destroys cherished illusions or declares the falsity of long-credited beliefs or superstitions.

idiot

When we say that *idiot* is derived from the Greek *idiotes*, it must be understood that the Greek term had no such meaning as we give to *idiot*—not remotely. Its stem—*idio*—is the same as that which gives us "idiom," one's own personal or individual language, and "idiosyncrasy," one's own personal or individual characteristics. So the Greek word originally meant nothing worse than a private person, an individual, a person occupied in his own affairs as distinct from one holding public office. It acquired an extended meaning from this—one who lacked professional knowledge, whether of politics or other subjects; a layman—but in Athens there was no reflection upon one's mentality when referred to as an idiot.

When the Romans borrowed the term, giving it the form *idiota*, they gave it a slight stigma, however. In their view, a man who failed to take enough interest in the affairs of state as not to hold any public office, must be one who lacked the brains for the job. They held that contact with public life was indispensable for the full development of the intellect, and thought that none but a weak-minded person would refuse an opportunity for such service. So, to the Romans, an *idiot* was a person who, through lack of mental ability, was unfit for public office; hence, an ignoramus. Early English writers were somewhat confused as to the meaning when *idiot* was introduced into our language. Some used it in its Greek sense and some gave it the Latin meaning, but others went further than the Romans had gone and gave it just the meaning that we give it today—a person so deficient in mental powers as to be incapable of reasoning or of self-protection.

ignoramus

Literally, this is a Latin plural, meaning "we do not know." The term was introduced into the courts of law in England in the sixteenth century. When used by a grand jury it was written across the back of an indictment presented to the jury if the members thought the evidence was too weak to warrant prosecution. The term might have been confined to legal usage if, in 1615, it had not been for a play written by George Ruggle. He gave the play the title, *Ignoramus*, after the name of his chief character, a lawyer. It was a satire written "to expose the ignorance and arrogance of the common lawyers" of his day. The wits of the period took up the name of the character and thus spread the application of the term to ignorant persons, regardless of profession.

imp

In the days of King Alfred—that is, in Old English—an *imp* was a sapling or offshoot of a tree. This meaning gave rise to a figurative use, the scion of some noble house or, especially, a male child. Then, in due course, probably because most male children are mischievous, *imp* became synonymous with a young demon. Thus since the sixteenth century an *imp* may be a mischievous child, a young demon, or one of the petty fiends of hell. The original meaning has passed completely out of use.

impede (expedite)

Those who were slaves in ancient Rome were usually left unfettered, their hands and feet unbound for the better performance of work. Severe and sometimes barbarous punishments for those who attempted to run away, involving scourging, mutilation, or even death, were generally sufficient to make it unnecessary for the owners to chain them. It was customary, nevertheless, to employ fetters or chains when the nature of the work was such as to make escape fairly possible. Thus the slave whose duty it was to attend the door of a Roman house was chained to his post, and those who worked in the fields or woods were compelled to have their feet in fetters. The Latin word that meant "to put fetters on the feet" was *impedio*, from *in*, on or upon, and *pes*, *pedis*, foot. Thus, because one who has his feet shackled together is hampered in his movements, *impede* came to signify "to check the motion of; to hinder." But a Roman slave who had been placed in chains, either at the time when he was taken into captivity, or in punishment, or at his work, found that he could move actively, apparently even with greater ease than ever before, when his fetters were removed. Therefore our word *expedite*, from the Latin verb *expedio*, literally "to release the feet, as from fetters or a trap," came to mean more broadly, "to hasten the progress of; to accomplish more rapidly."

inaugurate (augur)

When the twins, Romulus and Remus, decided to found a city along the banks of the Tiber, according to ancient Roman legend, they disagreed upon the hill on which the city should be laid out. Romulus preferred the hill later called the Palatine, Remus the Aventine. They agreed, however, to leave the decision to the gods, and each passed the night upon the hill of his choice to learn their will. Remus, it was said, saw six vultures as the day began. This was thought to be highly propitious. But just as Romulus received the information, twelve vultures flew over his head. The omens, therefore, appeared to favor him. Remus was unwilling to yield the decision, however, and in the struggle that followed, he was killed. Accordingly Romulus was the sole founder of Rome.

In those days and for many centuries thereafter, no important matter was undertaken by the Roman people until it was learned whether the gods favored the enterprise. This was often determined by watching the birds, for it was believed that they were the messengers of the gods. Certain men, wise and highly devout, were given the responsibility handed down to them by Romulus, and were thought to be able to read those messages. These were interpreted from various signs—the kinds of birds, their numbers, their appearance in certain quarters of the sky, the direction of flight, their songs in flight, and so on. A man able to make such interpretations was called an *augur*, a word partly derived from the Latin *avis*, bird, and *garrio*, to talk, or chatter. The interpretation that he made was called *augurium*, from which our word *augury* was derived. The verb *inauguro* meant, at first, "to consult the birds before undertaking an enterprise"; later it carried the meaning, "to consecrate (an official) by the ceremony of consulting the birds." Our word *inaugurate* comes from this verb; hence, when we use it we imply an accompaniment of special ceremony. (See also AUSPICE.)

incubus (succubus)

In the Middle Ages any woman who gave birth to a witch or sorceress was supposed to have been visited, in her sleep, by a male demon or evil spirit. The name given to this spirit was *incubus*, from the Latin *in*, upon, and *cumbo*, to lie. It was also supposed to be the

cause of nightmare. The feminine counterpart of this demon, bringing nightmares to men, was called a *succubus*, the first element
from *sub*, under. The existence of such demons was recognized in
those days by both church and state, but has long been known to be
entirely imaginary, except perhaps by highly superstitious persons. It
is because of the feeling of great pressure or heavy weight upon one
who is ridden by the supposed *incubus* that the term is now used
figuratively for an oppressive load.

indent, indenture

To prevent the likelihood of alteration in deeds and other contracts
between two parties, a certain practice was introduced into the
England of the late Middle Ages. The contract was written out in
duplicate upon a sheet of parchment or paper, with a blank strip
between, and then the two documents were cut or torn apart in
such manner as to leave a notched or wavy edge. At any time
thereafter the genuineness of either document could be proved by
matching the cut edge with that of the other. One was said to
indent the contract, from Latin *in*, in, and *dens*, tooth. The contract
itself was, and still is, called an *indenture*, from that original means
of identification. It was this form of contract that existed between
an apprentice or a servant and his master; the apprentice or servant
"took up his indenture" when he had completed his service. Thus,
many of the early settlers of the American colonies, lacking the
money for their transportation, voluntarily became *"indentured
servants"* in order to get to America. Usually after seven years
such a servant was table to "take up his indenture" from the master
who had bought it from the ship owner. (Compare KIDNAP.)

indolence

When Cicero coined the term *indolentia*, from *in*, not, and *doleo*,
suffer, he meant it to be the equivalent of the Greek word *apatheia*,
lack of sensibility to pain or passion, indifference. And this was the
sense in which *indolence* was first employed by the philosophers
of the seventeenth century. But because indifference is usually
accompanied by a disinclination to invite trouble or to disturb
oneself, *indolence* passed out of use in its initial sense and came to
be synonymous with laziness.

infantry

The literal meaning of *infant*, from the Latin word *infans*, is "one unable to speak." Though that literal sense actually applies only to the first year or two of babyhood, both under Roman law and those of our own country a person is referred to as an infant until he has reached such age as he may legally enter into certain forms of contract. That is, extending the literal sense, a person remains an infant until fully able to speak for himself in all matters. In Italy, some centuries ago, much as we today apply the word "maid" to any female servant, there began the practice of calling a personal attendant of a knight, or a foot soldier, or other similar retainer an *infante*. Possibly, though it is not known, the practice came about through the youthfulness of the early retainers. A collection of retainers or foot soldiers became *infanteria*, a term that, passing through French, produced our *infantry*.

ink (encaustic)

Artists of ancient Greece, employed in the painting of murals, sometimes used a process that is no longer fully known. As described by Pliny, the colors were mixed with wax and resin. The mixture was heated in a brazier and was then applied as needed to the wall or other surface with a spatula, which was also heated. Somehow the chemicals that were used and the application of heat caused the colors to sink into the surface of the stucco of the wall. The Greeks said that they were "burnt in," using the word *enkauston*, from *en*, in, and *kaio*, burn. Such *encaustic* paintings, as we now call them, from the Greek term, had remarkable life; one upon an open portico, *Stoa Poikile*, in Athens, was said to have retained its colors for more than nine hundred years. Others, protected by the ashes of Pompeii, are still visible after nineteen centuries. Because of that longevity the process was thought to be worthy of use by Roman and the later Greek emperors for their signatures upon royal documents. A purple dye was used for this purpose, and the dye in turn was called *encaustum* in Latin, *enkauston* in Greek. Through the Roman colonies in France, the Latin word became corrupted to *enche* or *enque* in Old French, giving rise to *enke* or *inke* in medieval English, and our present *ink*.

insolent

In its truest sense, *insolent* would mean "unusual, not according to custom." Its source was the Latin *in*, not, and *soleo*, to be accustomed. But even the Latin writers realized that one who violates custom is usually willing to offend and is, indeed, likely to be offensive. So they used *insolens* also to mean haughty and arrogant. It is thus from the latter use that our meaning of *insolent* is derived.

insult

The literal sense of the Latin *insulto*, from which *insult* is derived, was to leap at or spring upon a person or thing. A wild beast might spring upon its prey, ready to tear it apart; a soldier leap at his foe, prepared to take his life. But the ancients realized that they could tear a person apart, in a figurative sense, by a torrent of abusive words, or kill him with scorn and abuse, and thus *insulto* acquired such a figurative meaning, giving rise to the sense in which we use *insult*.

interloper

About the middle of the sixteenth century a group of British merchants formed a company for the carrying on of trade with Russia. The company, under the name of the Russia Company, was highly successful through the next thirty or forty years. Perhaps too successful, because toward the end of the century some Spanish traders operating from Holland, and other bands of Englishmen, began to break in upon the monopoly of the English company through bribes to Russian officials. The interference was settled within a few years, perhaps with adequate counterbribery, but the incident brought a new word into our language. The trespassing traders were called *interlopers*; the source of the new coinage being the English *lope*, to run, and the Latin *inter*, between.

intoxicate (toxic)

In ancient times some armies equipped their archers with poisoned arrows. Greek and Roman writers referred to it as a practice of barbarians, and, in order to describe it, the Greeks had to distort the meanings of some of their own words. Thus the Greek word for an archer's bow was *toxon*, and accordingly that which pertained to a bow was said to be *toxikos*. From that connection the poison with which an arrow was smeared, thus making the arrow ready for the bow, was called *toxikon*. The term was taken into Latin in the form *toxicum*, and in the Middle Ages this came to be a general term for poison of any kind, no longer connected in any way with the archer's bow. Hence, *toxic* now means "poisonous," and our verb *intoxicate* originally meant "to poison."

intransigent

After Queen Isabella of Spain was deposed in 1868 the country was without a ruler for some years. Members of the royal families of Europe declined to accept the vacant throne, but at last, in 1870, Prince Amadeo of Savoy accepted the offer. Three years later, however, he was glad to resign. Thereupon one branch of the party favoring a republic, made up, it was said, of the dregs of society, though calling themselves "volunteers of liberty," attempted to establish a form of communism within Spain. They were termed *los intransigentes* (from the Latin *in*, not, and *transigo*, to come to an agreement), because they refused every attempt to reconcile their political views with those of others. The press of England and America took up the name as *intransigent*. The party was put down in 1874 under force of a temporary dictator who ruled the country until Isabella's son, Alfonso XII, revived the monarchy in 1875.

investigate (vestige)

Hunters through all the ages have known that their game could be found by following its footprints or the traces that it left of its passage. Roman hunters used the word *vestigium* for footprint or trace—whence our word *vestige*, trace—and thus *investigo* meant to trace or track out, as a dog scents game. Our word *investigate* is not quite so literal in meaning, but the term does imply the thoroughness of search similar to that of a dog on a cold trail.

italic

Aldus Manutius was the Latin name of the noted Italian printer, Teobaldo Mannucci, who was born in 1450. He received an excellent education before establishing himself as a printer in Venice in 1490. There he surrounded himself with other scholars and set out to make Venice the center of literature, especially in the printing of Greek, Latin, and Italian classics. Aside from the merit of the works printed by the Aldine press, as his establishment had been named, was the excellence of the type that was used. Aldus experimented with various faces, cut either by himself or under his direction. The one type to which we are still indebted to his genius is that which he named *italic*, thus honoring his native land. Until this invention all type was erect, called "Roman" from the erect letters of the ancients. The first book to utilize the new type was an edition of Vergil, printed in 1501.

jade

A few hundred years ago it was believed that one need merely wear this stone to be free of colic or of disorders of the kidney. It was sometimes called "colic stone" or "nephrite" (from Greek *nephros*, kidney) for that reason. The Spaniards, who found much of the stone in Peru and Mexico in the sixteenth century, called it *piedra de ijada*, literally "stone of the colic," and the French, taking only the last part of the Spanish name, rendered it first as *l'ejade*, and later as *le jade*. From the French it was a natural step to the English name *jade*. (The homonym, *jade*, a term for an old horse or spiteful woman, is from Old Norse *jalda*, a mare.)

janizary

Turkey became an independent monarchy in the year 1300. Its army, however, was too feeble and poorly organized for the wars of aggression that the political leaders wished to wage against neighboring states. Hence, in 1330, it was suggested that a band of Christian youths be taken from their parents each year, and that this band be specially trained in the arts of warfare and maintained in the strictest discipline. The first levy was a thousand of these lads. They were enrolled as *yeni chéri*, or "new army," this term being ultimately corrupted into English *janizary* or *janissary*. The army was increased until it numbered 20,000 of these professionally trained soldiers, and this remained the normal strength until the sixteenth century. The janizaries received little pay, but had so many privileges that service in the organization ultimately became sought. Acceptance of Mohammedanism was not required, but the faith was regularly taught to them. After the sixteenth century the number became larger and larger until in 1825 there were 135,000 janizaries in the army. In that year this band thought it had the power to defy the government, against which it had been staging acts of violence for many years. But the sultan was in readiness with troops of Moslems that had been drilled. The struggle was short and bloody. In its course every janizary was massacred.

January

This month derived its name from the ancient Italian god, Janus— *Januarius* being the Latin name, which signified "the month pertaining to Janus." How old the worship of the god may have been cannot be determined, but it undoubtedly dated back prior to the foundation of Rome. Janus was the tutelary deity of doors and gateways—*janua* is Latin for "door." He was therefore always represented as having two faces, so that, it was explained, he might guard both entrance and exit. Upon one of the hills of Rome— named Janiculum, in his honor—the gateway of a temple to him was always open in time of war, according to legend, in order that the defending soldiers might not be delayed in seeking refuge, if in danger of defeat, or of marching into the city triumphantly, if victorious. Prior to the reign of Augustus, it was said, the gates had been closed but once in seven hundred years, at the close of the first Punic War, 241 B.C., when Rome was briefly at peace.

It is sometimes thought that January, being the first month of the year, was so named because Janus was also the god of beginnings. That is not so, however. In the oldest of the Roman calendars the year had only ten months, thus accounting for the names of the last four months in our present calendar—September (seventh), October (eighth), November (ninth), December (tenth). Some seven hundred years B.C., the calendar was readjusted and two months were added to the year. The names given to them were *Januarius* and *Februarius*; they were, respectively, the eleventh and twelfth months, and they were so named because the first contained a feast day in honor of Janus, and the second included the Roman festival of purification (*februum*). March continued to be the first month of the year until long after the Christian Era had begun and March 25th, because that date coincided with the vernal equinox (the beginning of spring) in the Julian calendar, was the day upon which the civil year began.

It was not until the adoption of the Gregorian calendar that January was accepted in all countries as the first month of the year and that January 1st was generally observed as New Year's Day. This calendar was prescribed by Pope Gregory XIII in 1582, to correct errors in the Julian calendar, but it was not adopted in England and its colonies until 1752. Hence, in England, the confusion that had existed through many centuries in matters of chronology was finally cleared away, for the popular practice and the practice of historians from the twelfth century or earlier had been to date the year from January 1 (or sometimes from Christmas), though in civil and church practice March 25 had been the beginning of the year.

jeep

It is regrettable that the story of the word *jeep* is not complete. In 1937 the cartoonist, E. C. Segar, began to use an animal in his comic strips about "Popeye," which he called "Eugene, the Jeep." This creature was described as being able to move at will between the third and fourth dimension, being invisible while in the latter, and being able to answer all questions about the future. Because of the popularity of this comic strip, the term *jeep* was somewhat in the public mind at the beginning of World War II. But the Willys-Overland people, although maintaining that the term *Jeep*, designating a type of vehicle prominent in that war, was first applied to the vehicle actually produced by that company, have been entirely unable to trace the reason for the application. In a small book, *Hail to the Jeep*, by A. Wade Wells, from which I am privileged to quote, the first use of the name is credited to Irving (Red) Hausmann, test driver for the Willys-Overland plant in Toledo, Ohio. Hausmann does not claim credit for originating the name. He drove the test model to Baltimore, for Army test and approval, and is quoted as saying:

Shortly after our arrival the Ford Motor Co. also sent their ¼-ton vehicle in for test. Some distinction had to be made as to a name for our vehicle. I took a lot of pride in the vehicle we had developed, and I didn't like people confusing it with the others and calling it a "Bantam," "Bug," "Midget," "Blitz-Buggy," a "Ford G.P.," "Quad," or "Peep," so I picked up the name "Jeep" from the soldiers who were tossing it around among themselves. I started calling our model a Jeep and called it Jeep at every opportunity.

Upon his return to Toledo, it is said, others in the Willys-Overland plant took up his use of the name. But in late 1941 when, as a lexicographer, I was investigating the word *Jeep* for dictionary inclusion, neither Army nor maker was able to satisfy my interest in its source. The best guess was that the name had been formed from the sound of the initials "G.P.," which indicated the "general purpose" for which the vehicle was designed, although proof is lacking that the design was ever so designated.

jeopardy

In the game of chess, as played in England until about the beginning of the sixteenth century, a problem which posed an even chance of winning or losing was known as a *iuparti*. This was from the Old French *iu parti*, meaning "divided chance" or "even game." The term was also introduced into other games in which certain positions offered an even chance of winning or losing, and thus came into general use for any situation in which safety hung in the balance, for any position of peril or possible harm. The initial letter, despite numerous variable spellings of the word through the centuries, seems always to have been consonantal, and so when the letter *j* came into general use in the seventeenth century the form changed from *ieopardy*, as Lord Francis Bacon wrote it, to our present *jeopardy*.

jeroboam (jorum)

Someone with a sense of humor, back near the beginning of the nineteenth century, must have remembered his Bible when he first beheld a huge brandy bottle. He was reminded of the verse which says, "And the man Jeroboam was a mighty man of valor" (I Kings 12:28), and the one, also about Jeroboam, "who did sin, and who made Israel to sin" (I Kings 14:16). This unknown wit thereupon christened this large bottle, *Jeroboam*, a name by which it is still known. It may have been the same man who gave the same name to an unusually capacious bowl or goblet at about the same time. Through confusion with a later biblical king, the latter vessel is also called a *jorum* or *joram*.

jitney

Usually a slang term baffles those who search for its source. By the time it has become popular, the person who invented it and the occasion leading to the invention are forgotten and cannot be located. *Jitney* acquired popularity throughout the United States in 1914 and 1915 as a slang term for a five-cent piece, a nickel. The meaning was then transferred to the passenger vehicle, other than a streetcar, for which the fare was, originally, five cents. A correspondent of the late Dr. F. H. Vizetelly, quoted by him in his *A Desk-Book of Idioms and Idiomatic Phrases*, suggested that *jitney* might be a corruption of *jetnée* in a catch song of the French-speaking Louisiana Negro:

> Mettons *jetnée* dans li trou
> Et parcourons sur la rue—
> Mettons *jetnée*—si non vous
> Vous promenez à pied nu!

Which is freely translated thus:

> Put a *jitney* in the slot
> And over the street you ride;
> Put a *jitney*—for if not
> You'll foot it on your hide.

The explanation is plausible, and *jetnée* itself may be a corruption of the French *jeton*, a token, counter.

joke

Like our words *bus* and *mob*, contracted by humorists of bygone years from the more pompous Latin terms *omnibus* and *mobile vulgus* respectively, *joke* came into our language in the seventeenth century as a contraction by some unknown wit of the Latin *jocus*, a jest. The legend that John Milton originated the contraction cannot be proved, for the word does not appear in any of his writings. He had the wit to have done so, however, as shown by his various facetious poems.

journey, journal

Through the fact that French *jour* means "day," it is not surprising to find that Old French *journée* meant the space of a day, or that which was accomplished in a day, such as work, employment, travel, or the like. It was the sense of day's travel, however, in which the word was carried to England. Thus at first a *journey* was usually understood to be a distance of twenty miles, or what a man could walk in a day, and greater distances were spoken of as *two journeys*, *ten journeys*, or sometimes as *two days' journey*, *ten days' journey*. Also from French *jour*, day, it is readily seen that *journal* was originally a record of the day. As first employed in England, however, a *journal* was a record of the ecclesiastical services for each hour of the day. In strict accuracy, in this sense of a written or printed record, the term should still apply to the occurrences of a single day, though many technical publications, perhaps issued not oftener than once a month, contain the word *journal* in their titles.

jug

From the early sixteenth century, in England, a popular nickname for anyone with the name Joan or Joanna was *Jug*. Especially was she called by that name if she were a servant or of unattractive appearance. No one knows why, any more than one can explain why the name "John" became altered to "Jack" as a nickname, or "Margaret" to "Peg," or "Mary" to "Molly" or "Polly." Be that as it may, it was during the same century that potters began to turn an earthenware vessel somewhat similar to, but larger than, a pitcher. Perhaps the squat shape of these early vessels reminded some wag of a popular barmaid named *Jug* who was of similar shape; or perhaps it was just because other drinking vessels were already known as *jack* and *jill*, from the nicknames of John and Gillian. The fact cannot be determined. The full name, Joan, which would be Jeanne in French, suggests the possibility that "Dame Jeanne" (demijohn) might have been a French translation of *jug*.

juggernaut

A huge grotesque image of the god Vishnu has been worshiped for the past eight centuries or more at Puri in Orissa, India. The local name of the god is *Jagannath*, a name which sounds to Occidental ears as *Juggernaut*. There are several curious customs connected with the worship of this god. Among them is that each summer he is taken from his temple to his "country house," a distance slightly less than a mile. The god is therefore placed on a large cumbersome wagon about thirty-five feet square and having sixteen wheels, each about seven feet in diameter. The god towers about forty-five feet in the air. Ropes are attached to the wagon, and to those carrying the images of his brother and sister which accompany him. Thousands of willing pilgrims drag the huge conveyances on their way. The path is so sandy and the weight so great that, despite the short distance, the journey requires several days. Early travelers, seeing this annual spectacle, brought back strange tales. Perhaps, seeing some weak or aged pilgrim faint under heat and exhaustion while pulling the ropes, he thought the man had thrown himself under the slow-turning wheels as a deliberate sacrifice. His report of one such victim, which may have been accidental, was magnified by later travelers. Some of these Occidental travelers, then, not knowing that even the accidental shedding of blood in the presence of the god is a pollution, reported that many devotees threw themselves each day beneath the wheels as the car moved slowly toward its destination. Thus, through these exaggerated tales and mistaken interpretation, brought about by ignorance of the real purpose of the journey, the "car of *Juggernaut*" became a literary symbol of relentless self-sacrifice to which one devotes himself blindly, and *juggernaut* was adopted into English speech as a figurative term for any powerful force that relentlessly moves to destroy all in its path.

June

One of the most prominent of the families in ancient Rome was that to which the members of the clan Junius belonged. Their ancestor, Lucius Junius Brutus, drove out the last of the Tarquin kings, 510 B.C., and was elected the first consul of Rome. We owe the name of our sixth month, *June*, to the name of this clan or gens, or, more likely, to the first consul who may have decreed that his name be thus honored.

junket

Originally this was a creel, a basket of woven rush in which to catch or carry fish. The Norman-French word was *jonket* or *jonquette*, from *jonc*, a rush. But even before the Normans invaded England some housewife had discovered that the same basket, before being contaminated with fish, could be used in preparing a kind of cheese. This cheese then became *junket*. Incidentally, when served with a dressing of scalded cream, the dish is known as "curds and cream" in some parts of England. The rush basket also suggested, to our forefathers, the meal that could be carried in it, with the result that *junket* came to denote a sumptuous repast or merry feast. We in the United States have carried that notion still further, and that which originally denoted a rush basket now embraces a picnic or, especially, a pleasurable excursion.

kaleidoscope (stereoscope)

Sir David Brewster, when a young man, had intended to follow his father's career in the ministry, but found within a few years after entering that field that his greatest interest was in science. Hence, at the age of twenty-seven he had become an editor of the *Edinburgh Encyclopedia*, writing upon scientific subjects. The study of optics was most fascinating to him—the reflecting powers of mirrors and the magnifying powers of lenses. But it was purely as a scientific toy that, in 1816, he devised an arrangement of mirrors within a tube, which would show by reflection a shifting pattern, multiplied symmetrically, as the tube was rotated. Because of the beauty of the patterns, when bits of colored glass were reflected, the toy was named *kaleidoscope*, from the Greek *kalos*, beautiful, *eidos*, form, and *skopos*, watcher. A few years later Brewster, with some associates, devised another type of optical instrument, consisting of two lenses, so ground that when mounted upon a rack before two identical pictures, the two pictures would blend into one, creating an effect of three dimensions. The name given to this instrument, which became very popular with advances in the art of photography, was *stereoscope*, from the Greek *stereos*, solid, and *skopos*.

kangaroo

A great controversy arose about the name of this Australian animal, a controversy that now may never be settled. Captain James Cook, the British explorer, and his shipmate, the noted naturalist, Sir Joseph Banks, both trained observers, understood that the Australian natives called this strange animal a *kangaroo* (which each of them subsequently spelled *kangooroo*). They saw the animal near Endeavour River, Queensland, while their ship, "Endeavour," was undergoing repairs on its northward voyage of exploration along the eastern coast of Australia in 1770. Later explorers within the next fifty years were unable to find any tribe along the coast that used this name, and concluded that the natives with whom Cook and Banks had tried to converse were actually saying, "I don't know," in their language. They reported that various other names were used by the different tribes, though none resembled *kangaroo*. Now, however, all the natives have adopted the English name, regardless of the name by which they had previously known the animal.

ketchup (catsup)

Manufacturers will continue to spell it *catchup* and *catsup*, but the spelling here shown is that which best resembles its source, the Chinese term, *ke-tsiap*. The Dutch, who were heavy importers of this Asiatic condiment in the eighteenth century, spelled it *ketjap*, indicating a pronunciation very similar to *ketchup*. The original importation, however, was a sauce composed from the juices of edible fungi, chiefly mushrooms, salted for preservation and spiced.

khaki

The British army borrowed both the material and its name from India, where the army first used it. The Indian name means "dusty," and the original material was a stout cotton drill of the color of dust. For clothing it served a twofold requirement. It was adapted to a warm climate, and its color was an admirable camouflage. It was first word in 1848 by the Guide Corps, a mixed regiment of frontier troops. Military use of today does not confine the material to cotton and permits the color to range from tannish-brown to olive-drab.

khan

Europe first heard this term in the year 1222. A strange band of invaders from the east had pushed across the Volga and the Don, and was threatening Galicia and Bulgaria. (See HORDE.) The Russian princes who opposed this invading force were destroyed with all their armies, and the inhabitants of towns and villages were massacred. This, Europe learned, was the army of the Mongolian emperor who became known to the West as Genghis *Khan*—that is, Genghis the Ruler, or King, or Emperor. The title became much more familiar to Europeans generally, however, in the latter part of the same century when the great Venetian traveler, Marco Polo, returned from his long expedition into China and wrote his memorable account of his travels and of his long stay at the court of the Great Khan, Kublai. This ruler was a grandson of Genghis, and therefore retained the title which his grandfather had been the first to assume.

kidnap

We like to think that all those who flocked to North America from England after the founding of Jamestown and Plymouth came eagerly and of their own accord. That was far from the case. Many of the early colonists, especially those in Maryland and Virginia, flocking into the country which, they were told, offered such great opportunities, were unaccustomed to manual toil and needed servants and agricultural workers. Craftsmen, skilled in trades greatly required by their fellows, needed more apprentices and labor than the villages could supply. To meet this varied demand for unskilled help, British shipowners began to offer free transportation to the new colonies in return for an agreement to work without wages for seven years. Many thousands accepted these offers. These were known as "indentured servants." (See INDENT.) After the seven years of service their master was required to supply them with certain agricultural implements, some clothing, and some seed, and the colony usually gave them fifty acres of land. There was nothing debasing in such indentured service and many of these settlers were

well educated and later became honored citizens. But the demand
for labor exceeded this willing supply. Some shipowners then began
to obtain passengers by unscrupulous measures. At first they induced young homeless waifs from the slums of London to board
their vessels, with great promises for a future in America. But later
their gangs ranged the streets of English towns and cities and, using
a term of the times, "spirited" the youngsters away. In the reign of
Charles II (1660-85) when this crime was at its height, the term
kidnaping was coined to describe it. This was composed of the
slang *kid*, a child, and *nap*, to steal. The full number of these unwilling colonists probably exceeded one hundred thousand. One
kidnaper confessed in 1671 that in the previous twelve years he had
himself annually transported an average of five hundred youngsters.
Another admitted that he had kidnaped eight hundred and forty
in a single year. In theory all of such kidnaped children had become voluntary indentured servants, but in 1682 the London Council
forbade any person under fourteen (the age of consent at that time)
to be bound into service unless with the knowledge and consent of
his parents.

knave

The history of this word is similar to the slow change we are wit-
nessing in the meaning of the word "boy," now often applied to
servants and grown men. Originally, back in Old English times, a
knave was a boy in a literal sense—a male child. It had the same
meaning as the German *knabe*, to which it was closely related. Then
people began to apply it to a boy who was employed as a servant,
one who might be apprentice to a cook or to a groom, or who
served as a potboy in a tavern or in any such form of work as a
boy could perform. In those olden days, however, the life of any
menial was hard; that of a boy was doubly so. His sleeping place
might be the stable or a drafty garret, without mattress or blanket;
his clothing any castoff garment that he could tie upon him; his
food any scraps that might be tossed to him from his master's table.
It is not surprising, therefore, that these boys, still called *knaves*
as they became older, developed a high degree of rascality. They
had to become crafty in order to survive. Thus the meaning of the

term gradually came to apply only to such a person, boy or man, who practiced dishonesty.

knickerbockers

Some time in the latter part of the seventeenth century, probably about 1682, a gentle Dutch farmer from Holland settled with his family near the site that was to become Albany, New York. There he prospered greatly and left sizable properties to his seven children. His name was Harmen Jansen Knickerbocker. The eldest of his children, Johannes Harmensen Knickerbocker, acquired additional property north of Troy, along the river Schaghticoke, and this estate and the great manor upon it descended in due course to his grandson, Harmen, born in 1779. This man, great-grandson of the original Harmen, entertained lavishly, for he had inherited great wealth. He became known as "the prince of Schaghticoke." But it is likely that he would have had little more than a local notoriety had it not been for the satirical writer, Washington Irving. Intending at first merely to burlesque a pretentious guidebook to New York written by Dr. Samuel Mitchell, Irving got carried away with his theme. He could not resist playing up the characteristics of the phlegmatic Dutch burghers, and wound up with a richly humorous book, *A History of New York from the Beginning of the World to the End of the Dutch Dynasty*. The two-volume *History*, published in 1809, was ascribed by Irving to "Diedrich Knickerbocker," a thinly disguised alias for the "prince of Schaghticoke," who, of course, had actually had nothing to do with the matter. The most popular edition of *Knickerbocker's History*, as the book came to be called, was illustrated with pictures showing Dutchmen clad in seventeenth-century costume, wearing knee breeches buckled just below the knee. These costumes were copied, especially for boys' wear, during the 1850's. The trousers, because of the distinctive cut and the buckle or button at the waist and knee, became immediately known as *knickerbockers*, a term now often shortened to *knickers*.

lace

Properly, as it was of old, a *lace* is a noose, a cord or the like with which to snare game or a victim. It was so used in the time of

Chaucer. The word comes to us from the Latin *laqueus*, noose, which in popular spelling was *lacius*. The latter term became *las* in Old French, and came in that form into the English language. The development into our present meaning came progressively. Because garments were formerly held together by loops, the cord that was used for the purpose was termed a *lace*, a meaning that survives with us in the word *shoelace*. Then when it became fashionable to decorate garments with fanciful nooses or loops of gold or silver wire or cord, these were in turn described as gold *lace* or silver *lace*. The further substitution of threads for the earlier cords into an intricate network was the final stage, an elaborate multiplication of nooses.

laconic

Spartan youths were all trained with the utmost rigor. But in addition to the activity, vigilance, endurance, and cunning which were practiced in all the land, those dwelling within the province of Laconia were also taught modesty of deportment and conciseness of speech. The Laconians thus became so noteworthy for their short and pithy way of speaking and writing that such a style became characterized as *laconic*, from the land where it was the native practice.

lady

It is a far cry from the woman of Old England from whom this title descended to the one who often calls herself a lady today. That remote woman was proud to be known as the breadmaker, *hlæfdige*, a word subjected to many changes, becoming *levedi* in the thirteenth century, *levdi* and *ladi* in the fourteenth, and *ladie* and *lady* in the sixteenth. By present standards of usage *lady* is a term of courtesy applied to any woman, but no longer necessarily implies an ability to make bread.

larva

Many years ago it was the popular belief that the caterpillar concealed within itself the complete butterfly in perfect form. It was then thought, that is, that the caterpillar served as a mask for the butterfly. For that reason it was called *larva*, Latin for "mask."

leech

From early English antiquity a physician has been called a leech, and from equally early times physicians have used the aquatic blood-sucking worm, known as *leech*, for bloodletting under certain conditions. It is impossible to tell which was first to receive the name. Etymologists believe, however, that present identity of spelling is accidental and that, originally, the words were different, although of similar form. They think also that through the use by the early physician of the worm for bloodletting, the name of the latter became altered to that of the physician through association.

legend

Toward the end of the thirteenth century the Archbishop of Genoa, Jacobus de Voragine (James of Viraggio), brought forth a book upon which he had long been engaged. It was, largely, a collection of the stories told about a number of the Christian saints within the several churches with which they were chiefly connected. The actual title was *Legenda Sanctorum*, literally, "things to be read of the saints," but the title by which it was and is generally known is *Legenda Aurea* or "Golden Legends." The book became exceedingly popular and was translated into many languages. The data were chiefly historical, although through the years the original facts had become somewhat magnified and distorted. Subsequent stories of the lives of saints, following the model set by this book, became more and more fanciful and imaginative. The consequence was that all these stories were viewed with skepticism. Hence the word *legend*, originally "something to be read," came to denote a story that, though apparently historical, was actually traditional and lacking in authenticity.

lethal, lethargy

There was a river in the lower world or the region of Hades, according to Greek mythology. Its name was *Lethe*, which signifies forgetfulness or oblivion; its water was believed to possess such properties that one who drank of it totally forgot all of the past. Shades of the dead, entering into the pleasures of Elysium, drank of the water and forgot all their mortal sorrow and suffering. Hence, from the likeness between this state of obliviousness and that of a deep slumber, ancient Greek physicians gave the name *lethargia* to a certain disease characterized by extreme drowsiness. From this has come our *lethargy*. The Romans took the meaning of the myth more implicitly and, reasoning that total and lasting forgetfulness came only with death, coined the adjective *lethalis*, whence our *lethal*, to signify deadly or fatal.

libel, liber, (library)

In legal use, a *libel* must be published. Otherwise the damaging statement may be slander, but not *libel*, although the latter word is often popularly used when "slander" should be employed. The legal interpretation emphasized the source of the word, for *libel*, from the Latin *libellus*, originally meant a "little book." Thus a *libel*, in its early English use as well as the Latin source, denoted written matter, especially matter that was shorter than that constituting a book. The basis of the Latin *libellus* was *liber*, which was actually the name for the inner bark of a tree. This inner bark was found to furnish an excellent surface upon which to write; hence, by transference *liber* came to denote "book." This Latin term is still used in reference to legal books and is the source of *library*, a collection of books.

libertine

In ancient Rome, *libertinus* denoted a slave who had been liberated, a freedman, and this was the meaning of *libertine* in early English use. But, just as a schoolboy released from irksome confinement of school is likely to break all bonds in his exuberance, so it was found that those released from slavery were likely to show no restraint in the observance of moral laws. Thus it came to be expected that a *libertine* would lead a life of unbridled license, and it was in this manner that the term came to refer to anyone, whether ex-slave or not, who lived such a life.

livery

Livery formerly corresponded exactly with our word "rations," except that it denoted the rations allotted to servants and retainers. The term, from Old French *livrée*, delivered, was taken to England by the Norman conquerors, and was meant to include food, clothing, or other provisions "delivered" to the servants. (In time it came to include allowances for the feed of horses; hence, *livery stable*.) Eventually, as the feeding of one's servants became a matter of course, *livery* was largely restricted to the clothing allotted to one's retainers or servants. Such clothing, in olden days, was marked by badge, color, or cut in some manner as to render it distinctive, so that anyone in the service of a prominent person could readily be identified when appearing in public. Well-informed persons with social pretenses prided themselves upon the number of such *liveries* they could place. Today the term is used for the uniform style of costume worn by the pageboys in a hotel, waitresses in a restaurant, elevator operators in a building, or the like.

lord

Just as "lady" was gradually formed through alterations in the pronunciation of the Old English original *hlæfdige*, so was *lord* formed from *hlaford* or *hlafweard*. The forms in which it appeared were also numerous, including the twelfth century *laford, leverd, lauerd,* and the fourteenth century *louerd, lhord,* and *lorde*. And just as the original meaning of "lady" was "breadmaker," so was the original meaning of *lord* "keeper (*weard*) of the loaf (*hlaf*)." The significance of the title was that he who was the keeper of the bread was master of the household. His servant, in those ancient days, was known as *hlaf-æta*, literally, "loaf-eater."

lottery, lotto

From remote antiquity disputes have been settled, ownership agreed upon, priority established, leadership determined, or the like, by casting or drawing lots. The emperors of Rome introduced a novelty into the old practice when, during the Saturnalia, or feasts to Saturn in mid-December, they awarded elaborate gifts to the person fortunate enough to hold or draw a winning lot. Similar customs were observed by European rulers during later centuries. Eventually the thought occurred to someone that people should pay for the chance to hold or draw a winning lot. So far as is known the earliest of these latter events was held at the city of Bruges in 1446. It may not have been until the following century, however, that a drawing held in Florence in 1530 was the first to be called by the Italian term, *lotteria*. The first *lottery* in England was a state affair for the purpose of raising money, in 1569, for the repair of harbors. The Virginia Company held another in 1612 for the benefit of the distracted colonists of Jamestown. Thereafter lotteries were frequent in England and throughout Europe. In Italy a numerical lottery was invented in 1620 by the Genoese, and was called *lotto di Genova*. It had been devised originally for the election of counselors, with wagers upon the outcome. But later the names of candidates were replaced by the numbers from one to ninety, with wagers, according to the ability of the gambler, upon the five numbers that were drawn. There were four different kinds of chances in this *lotto*, the lowest returned fourteen times the stake and the highest forty-eight hundred times the amount of the stake. This form of Italian lottery was transformed into a game, called *lotto*, often played for stakes, which became popular in France and England in the eighteenth century.

lounge

The story of this word is not certain; all that we can say is "perhaps." The name of the centurion who pierced the side of Jesus with a spear as He hung upon the cross was said to be *Longinus*, according to the apocryphal gospel of Nicodemus (7:8). This Longinus, by later legend, became converted and, in German and English calendars, was honored as a saint, his day being March 15. In medieval times his name was usually written *Longis*, and was popularly supposed to be derived from the Latin *longus*, long. Hence we may infer that in casting the characters for mystery plays dealing with the Crucifixion, the part of the centurion was given to a tall man. That this character was also depicted as slender and exceedingly indolent is highly probable, because Cotgrave, in 1611, thus defines *longis*: "A slimme, slow backe, dreaming luske, drowsie gangrill (a slim, indolent, dreaming sluggard, a drowsy toad); a tall and dull slangam (lout), that hath no making to his height, nor wit to his making, one that being sent on an errand is long in returning." If a person of that description were cast in the role of *Longinus* (or *Longis*), it is likely that, in the coarse humor of the period, he would be shown leaning indolently upon his spear, or sprawled upon the coat of Jesus. Thus, *lounge* is supposed to have been suggested by the attitude of *Longis*. The story cannot be proved.

lumber

Originally, the Lombards were a Teutonic people whose earlier name, *Langobardi*, long beards, was traditionally derived from the appearance, before the god Wotan, of their women with their hair combed over their faces. Startled, as he awoke from sleep, Wotan asked, "Who are these longbeards (*longobardi*)?" They were a warlike tribe, and in the year A.D. 568, with their families and possessions, moved southward into Italy where they occupied the plains at the head of the Adriatic, a region that became known as Lombardy. In the fourteenth century, enterprising traders and merchants from Milan and other parts of Lombardy (see also MILLINERY), found it profitable to move westward into England. There, through ingenuity, they became bankers, money-changers, moneylenders, or pawnbrokers. (The three golden balls, still marking a pawnbroker's establishment, are from the coat of arms of the Medici family, long the chief family of Lombardy.) They were so successful in these various enterprises, which then did not greatly differ, that the establishments themselves were popularly called "Lombards." From the various spellings employed in the early days, however, the name was usually pronounced *lumbard* or *lumber*. The latter became not only the usual pronunciation but also the usual designation of a Lombard pawnbroking establishment, sometimes also called *lumber-house*. Thence, because articles placed in pawn often consist of furniture or other cumbersome items that take up space, *lumber* assumed the meaning, "disused household furnishings." Thus *lumber-house* and *lumber-room* became places for storing such odds and ends. The reason for the American use of *lumber* instead of "timber" is difficult to determine. Possibly it derives from a practice of early settlers of storing rough timbers in the lumber-room for drying or until ready for use, although the *Dictionary of American English* says it "undoubtedly arose from the fact that ship-masts, sawed timber, barrel staves, etc., as important but bulky commodities, once blocked or *lumbered* up roads, streets and harbors of various towns."

lyceum

Among the epithets borne by Apollo was Lycean, an epithet of
such antiquity that it has never been determined whether it was
derived from the root *luce*, light, or *lyco*, wolf. In the one case it
would refer to the god as the giver of light; the other as the wolf-
slayer. Either explanation could be readily supported. Be that as
it may, the Athenians dedicated an enclosure to Apollo, which was
known as the *Lyceum*, in its Latin form. It was decorated with
buildings and sculpture by the leading artists and was a favorite
place of exercise by Athenian youths. But its significance to us lies
in the fact that it became also the favorite walk of the most noted
Athenian philosophers, especially Aristotle, who taught his followers most readily while strolling through its paths, and it was this
practice that caused the term to be adopted for certain of our lecture halls or meetings.

. lynch

Dispute has waged during the past century over the identity of the
man who achieved the doubtful honor of adding this name to our
language. Was it Colonel Charles Lynch, or was it Captain William
Lynch? The case for each has been stoutly maintained. Both were
Virginians and each was an officer of militia in the Revolutionary
War. They lived in adjoining counties, Colonel Charles in Bedford
(his brother, John, was the founder of Lynchburg), and Captain
William in Pittsylvania, and each was a justice in the court of the
county in which he resided. The description of the manner credited
to each in meting out justice, and the causes therefore, are almost
identical. At that period, the concluding years of the Revolutionary
War, Williamsburg was the seat of the only court in Virginia in
which certain felonies could be tried. But Williamsburg was some
two hundred miles from Bedford County, and the difficult roads
led through country held by the British or controlled by Tories.
Many of the offenders brought before Colonel Charles Lynch and
his three fellow magistrates were Tories; in any event they could
not securely be transmitted to Williamsburg for trial. After due
and deliberate consideration of the conditions, these four magistrates—Charles Lynch, James Callaway, William Preston, and Rob-

ert Adams—set up a court and, observing all of the practices of a regular court, tried such cases as came before them. In no instance save one, a case of proven manslaughter, did a convicted prisoner receive greater punishment than fine or whipping. Their actions were subsequently reviewed by the Virginia legislature which found them "justifiable from the imminence of the danger." It is likely that Charles Lynch was the leader of this group as he was a man of considerable prominence in his community. He had been a member of the House of Burgesses and had served in the Virginia constitutional convention in 1776.

The case for Captain William Lynch of Pittsylvania County rests largely upon the testimony of one man, and the attending circumstances of that testimony combine to make it of doubtful value. In *Harper's Magazine* for May, 1859, there appeared an article by one who signed himself "Cohee." This person related that, following some recent incident, he had had occasion to use the term *lynch law* in some conversation. Among the hearers was an old man, Richard Venables, who had "long been in feeble health, and often sat for hours to all appearance unconscious of what was said or done in his presence." This very old man was aroused by the expression, "lynch law," and said that as a young man he had known the "Mr. Lynch" for whom this form of justice had been named. Thereupon the author persuaded the old man to give him further information, but the remainder of the article is chiefly concerned with the activities of a gang of Tory horse thieves under one, "Captain Perkins," who was a sample of the villainy that "Mr. Lynch" tried to suppress. Nowhere in the article is the first name of "Mr. Lynch" given; in one place Mr. Venables is quoted as saying, "Our flourishing town of Lynchburg received its name in compliment to his worth." All in all, therefore, there are grounds for a suspicion that the account related by the aged Mr. Venables, if worthy of credence at all, might properly have been intended to refer to Colonel Charles Lynch. Perhaps some future historian may find additional proof to support the William Lynch claim.

macabre

This is often written *danse Macabre* and is sometimes Anglicized into "Dance of Death," in allusion to the common representations of the dance in paintings. The origin of *macabre* is disputed. Some think it to be merely a French corruption of the Arabic *makbara*, funeral chamber. Others think that it was the name of the first artist to depict the allegory. The paintings, or occasional sculptures, which first appeared in the fourteenth century, represent Death presiding over or in the midst of a group of dancers of all ages and conditions. For that reason some think the allegory to have been based upon the terrific plague, the Black Death, which swept over Europe in the middle of the fourteenth century, wiping out an estimated two-thirds of the population. The basis for that belief was provided by the fact that, almost literally, during that plague, man, woman, or child, aglow with health in the morning, might be stricken with the disease and be dead before night. But others, now the majority, hold the opinion that *macabre* is an Old French corruption of *Macabé*, the French equivalent of *Maccabee*. In this view the "Dance of Death" is thought to have been taken from an old morality play. Death and his victims, representing all walks of life—old and young, rich and poor, clown and scholar, male and female—have a long series of debates, in which each victim hopes to obtain a reprieve of Death's sentence. Death wins each argument, and the play ends in a weird dance, with Death escorting his victims off the stage. The dance is supposed to have received its name from, and to have been inspired by, the account in the second book of Maccabees, an apocryphal book of the Old Testament. The sixth and seventh chapters describe the torture and death inflicted upon the followers of Judas Maccabeus in his revolt against the laws of Antiochus IV which required all Jews to worship the Greek gods. The "seven brothers of the Maccabees," their mother, and the venerable scribe, Eleazar, were horribly tortured, under the king's orders; in the morality play they were especially prominent participants in the dialog with Death.

macadam

Although born in Scotland, John Loudon McAdam went to New York in 1770, at the age of fourteen, to work with an uncle. He returned to Scoltand when a young man of twenty-seven and bought an estate in Ayrshire. There he became interested in the improvement of roads. The French had been experimenting with the use of small broken stone as a surfacing material for some twenty years, spreading it to a thickness of ten inches upon a sublayer of large stones set on edge. The completed road was excellent, but its construction was costly. After considerable experimentation and study Mr. McAdam concluded that a base of heavy stone was unnecessary, that if drainage were good nothing was required but a layer of small broken stone, six to ten inches in depth. Appointed surveyor-general for the roads of Bristol in 1815 he was able to develop his ideas. The results were so satisfactory as to lead to general adoption, not only in England but for new roads built in France. From these "McAdam roads" came the general term *macadam* for any road surface constructed along the principles of this Scottish engineer.

mackintosh

In the early years of the nineteenth century numerous chemists and inventors were trying to find satisfactory ways to utilize the baffling substance known as "rubber." The substance got that name because the one thing for which a use had been found for the stuff was to "rub" out lead-pencil marks. The most notable success was achieved in 1823. In that year a 57-year-old Scottish chemist, already the inventor of various other chemical processes, found that rubber could be dissolved by the action of naphtha. The resulting solution could then be spread upon cloth, he discovered, and would produce a fabric that was absolutely waterproof. This new invention was immediately seen to be highly practical in the making of waterproof outer garments. Coats so made, taking their name, slightly altered, from that of the inventor, Charles *Macintosh*, gave us our present name for the garment, *mackintosh*. (Compare RUBBER.)

Machiavellian

The late fifteenth and early sixteenth centuries produced a great Florentine student of political affairs. He lived at the time of the Borgias and de Medicis and it is undoubted that his chief work, *Il Principe*, was greatly colored by his knowledge of the practical politics played by those two unscrupulous families. He was Niccolo Machiavelli. Actually Machiavelli was an ardent advocate of a united Italy and a sincere believer in political freedom, but, oddly enough, his book was heartily condemned some years after his death, in 1527, through the erroneous belief that it was intended to instruct tyrants in the art of oppression. Much of what he advocated toward obtaining good government is now in general acceptance, but his defamers alleged that he proposed duplicity in statecraft and that he justified the adoption of any means, however vicious, to obtain a desired end. Thus was formed *Machiavellian* to characterize political craftiness, cunning, or treachery. So heartily was this political writer condemned that perhaps the historian, Thomas Macaulay, was right when he wrote, "Out of his surname they have coined an epithet for a knave—and out of his Christian name (Niccolo) a synonym (Nick) for the devil."

maelstrom

This now means any strong power that seems to influence one irresistibly, especially a power composed of conflicting forces which seem to engulf one. That meaning is figurative. It is derived from the name, *Maelstrom*, which means whirlpool, given to a certain strong tidal current found near the island of Moskenes off the coast of Norway above the Arctic Circle. This current, under certain tides and winds, attains great force because of the vast mass of water that rushes past the island every twelve hours out of and into West Fjord. Differences in the depth of the channel also produce powerful eddies which, with the violent seas, cause the destruction of small vessels that may attempt passage. The entire current was formerly thought to be one vast whirlpool of such irresistible force, according to old fables, as to engulf whales and to suck into its depths any ship that might venture too close to its rim.

magenta (fuchsin)

On the morning of June 4, 1859, in the series of wars for a unified Italy, the French and allied Italian armies, though of inferior strength, fell upon the Austrian army defending Milan in the vineyards and mulberry groves about the small town of Magenta. (See also FIFE.) This battle, which subsequently was known by the name of the town, was momentous and a great victory for the French and their allies. It had a side effect, however, in a direction quite remote from warfare. In the field of chemistry a new aniline dye had recently been discovered. It produced a beautiful purplish-red color, not unlike the color of crushed unripe mulberries, and this new dye, though sometimes called "aniline red," had not yet received a distinctive name. When news of the battle in northern Italy reached the French chemists, the name *magenta* struck them as an excellent label for the dye in celebration of the victory. (The dye is now preferably known as "fuchsin," a name given to it because the color is like that of the blossom of the fuchsia.)

magnet (lodestone)

Homer and Plato knew about the magnet. The ancients, that is to say, had discovered a peculiar stone native to the neighborhood of the town of Magnesia, in Thessaly, which had the power of attracting small pieces of iron. They called it *magnes*, from the name of the town, or more frequently, *lithos Magnetis*, stone of Magnesia, whence our term *magnet*. There is no certainty, however, that the Greeks put the peculiar properties of this stone to any use; in fact, the first European record of the use of the directive properties of the magnet is not found before the end of the twelfth century A.D. This record, made by Alexander Neckam, foster brother of Richard I of England, makes it certain, however, that the mariner's compass, which depends upon the magnet, had long been familiar to English navigators. Perhaps in some mysterious way the knowledge had been brought from China, for the Chinese are thought to have made such use of the stone many centuries earlier. Through the use of the compass this "stone of Magnesia" or *magnes*, as it was also called, came to be known as a *lodestone* because, like the lodestar, it pointed the way (from the Middle English word *lode*, way). Many curious beliefs were attached to the magnet or lodestone. William Gilbert, who, in 1600, was the first to produce a scientific study of magnetism, related some of the "figments and falsehoods" which had once been taught. People were told, he says, that "if a lodestone be anointed with garlic, or if a diamond be near, it does not attract iron"; "if pickled in the salt of a sucking fish, there is power to pick up gold which has fallen into the deepest wells"; there were "mountains of such stones and they draw to them and break ships that are nailed with iron"; the stone could be used as a "love potion" and also had "the power to reconcile husbands to their wives, and to recall brides to their husbands."

mandrake

The plant was formerly known as *mandragora*, which is still its scientific name. Five or six hundred years ago, however, although actually of Greek source, this name was thought to be a combination of *man* and *dragon*. But at that time a dragon was commonly known as *drake*; so *mandragora* became *mandrake* in common speech. Because the plant is poisonous and because the root sometimes bears an uncanny resemblance to a diminutive man, all sorts of fantastic beliefs have been associated with the plant from remote times. Thus in the Bible (Genesis 30) we find that the plant was anciently thought to be able to cure barrenness in women; nevertheless, as Josephus records (*History of the Jewish War*, Book vii, chapter 6), it was exceedingly dangerous to dig up the root. The safest way, he says, was to remove most of the soil about the root, taking care to avoid touching it, then with a cord tied with one end about the stalk of the plant and the other to a dog, the dog could be lured to drag the root from the ground. The dog would die, but thereafter anyone could handle the plant harmlessly. Josephus called the plant *baaras*, but probably referred to the mandrake. He thought that its chief virtue lay in the power that it possessed to cast out demons from sick persons. The plant, even in the times of Shakespeare, was supposed to shriek when drawn out of the ground, and to cause madness, or sometimes death, to any who might taste of it. Sometimes the roots were thought to have a female form. Such were supposed to have especial potency when concocted into a love philter for men.

manure

This was originally a verb, its origin the Old French verb *manouvrer*. Thus, in the fourteenth century, it meant "to work by hand; especially, to work the soil by hand; to cultivate the soil." From that came the noun, which at first meant "that which may be worked by hand; the action of cultivating the soil." Our present meaning was a later extension.

March

This, the name of the third month in our calendar, denoted the first month in the Roman year before the reforms made under Julius Caesar. (See JANUARY.) We commonly think of the Roman god *Mars*, for whom the month was named, as their god of war, equivalent to the Greek god Ares, and think it peculiar to associate his name with the advent of spring. But in remote times Mars, who bore the surname of Silvanus, was worshiped by early Italians of the tribe of Sabines as the god of agriculture; sacrifices were offered to him for the success of crops and herds. The later Romans considered Mars to be the father of their race and the god of war as well as the patron of agriculture. As the latter they worshiped him under the name *Mars Silvanus*, but under the name *Mars Gradivus* as the god of war. The Roman calendar, however, was supposed to have been established by Numa, the second legendary king; and, because Numa was a Sabine, he would have thought of Mars as Silvanus, the god of forests, fields, and crops. It was for that reason that the advent of spring was dedicated to this god.

marmalade

In theory, at least, this delicacy should always be made of or contain quince, for such is implied by the name. Or to be even more exact, if the fruit were available, it should be a "honey-apple," which was anciently obtained through grafting some kind of apple upon the quince stalk. The Greek name for the resulting fruit was *melimelon*, literally "honey-apple." It was known in Latin as *melimelum*. From the latter the Portuguese name for "quince" became *marmelo*, and the preserve made from it they called *marmelado*. English housewives later discovered that other fruits, especially the orange, could be used for making a similar preserve, and this, regardless of the inherent meaning of the word, they proceeded to call by the already familiar term *marmalade*.

marshal

Just as in the Roman Empire of the East the master of the stable, *comes stabuli*, became count of the stable, his title eventually altered to *constable*, so in the West was the history of our word *marshal.* Under the kings of the Franks the *mariscalcus*, to use the Latin form of the old Teutonic title, was no more than a groom of the stable. (Even after the term became altered to *marshal*, this was still one of its meanings in England.) But the term gradually assumed greater importance. Cavalry, in the eighth century, again became of great value in the armies of Europe after a long period of decline, and both the offices of constable and of marshal, the lesser functionary, rose in dignity. In England, the two officers also served as judges in the Court of Chivalry, the marshal serving alone after the office of constable was virtually abolished in 1521. In warfare he was the esquire of the king and commanded the vanguard. From this his functions became extended to embrace full command of the armed forces. The *field marshal*, a title that arose in Germany, was originally a subordinate of the marshal. In warfare he was one of several officials who selected the camping sites and assigned locations to the knights and lords. In France the field marshal is still subordinate to the marshal in rank, though above all others, but in England the title denotes the highest military rank. In the United States, where a *marshal* is an officer of the civil court, the title has descended from one of the duties attending the office in thirteenth-century England. At that time, and thereafter until the eighteenth century, the marshal was an officer of the civil court and had custody of prisoners. In certain ceremonial functions the title is borne by the man in charge of the proceedings, reminiscent of the *marshal* of the Age of Chivalry.

martinet

When the young king of France, Louis XIV, decided to take the reins of government into his own hands in 1660, after the death of Mazarin, the former minister, he appointed as his war minister a youthful military genius, François Michel le Tellier Louvain. The young minister—he was only nineteen at the time—promptly set about to reorganize the army. Previously, in time of war, a nation hired most of its army, a regiment being in the employ of its colonel and a company in the employ of its captain. The units of an army had thus been independent, and discipline was lacking. Louvain decided to change this, to have an army in the employ of the state and constantly available for duty. The Royal Regiment, commanded by Colonel Jean Martinet, exhibited the kind of infantry training which, he thought, would be needed for such an army; so Louvain gave Colonel Martinet the responsibility for devising the system of drill which was to be used. Voltaire, in his *Siècle de Louis XIV*, says of the result, "The exact discipline which was kept up in the army made it appear in a different light from any that had yet been seen." Eventually all the nations of Europe adopted Louvain's scheme of a standing army, and eventually they copied or modified the drills and discipline invented by Martinet. But in England the matter of discipline was at first ridiculed. Few could see any point in an exacting discipline. The result was that *Martinet* became an epithet, in England, applied to any officer who was a stickler for military precision or a stern disciplinarian. In France, the name never acquired that connotation; the French still attach more importance to the small copper boats or pontoons that this officer invented than to the military drill that he established.

match

It isn't a certainty, but it is the belief that *match*, referring to the article with which we make fire, is a descendant from the Greek word *myxa*, which meant mucus from the nostril. This may seem far-fetched, but the course is reasonably straight. Greek *myxa* gave rise to Latin *myxus*, which by metonymy was used as the name for the nozzle of a lamp, the ancient lamp, the flame of which came from a wick projecting from the spout or nozzle. It is highly probable that the Italian *miccia*, a lampwick, came from either the Latin or the Greek word, getting its meaning through association of ideas, the lampwick from the spout suggesting mucus from the nose. Our word *match*, formerly written *macche*, comes from the Italian word by way of several altered French forms. Originally it, too, meant lampwick. Our present meaning developed after guns were invented, from the use of lampwicks for igniting the gunpowder. The wicks, or similar cords, were impregnated with saltpeter and sections were cut to the length desired. Guns fired by such slow-burning *matches* were called "matchlocks." It was a natural step to apply the name "matchwood" to splinters of resinous wood that burned slowly or evenly, and thus to give the name *match* its present application.

matinee (noon)

"Noon" did not always refer to the middle of the day, as we always understand it now to mean. It formerly meant three o'clock. That is, in the Roman system of reckoning, the day began at sunrise, or six o'clock, as the average time of sunrise. The principal meal of the day—dinner—was served at the ninth hour—*nona hora*—from sunrise, which would be at three o'clock in our present reckoning. Certain ecclesiastical services held at the ninth hour in Christian churches were also called *nona hora*, a term corrupted to *nones* in English usage. This latter term, *nones*, became not only the name of the services held at the ninth hour (subsequently observed earlier in the day), but also the name of the dinner hour. The spelling later became altered to "noon." "Noon"—that is, three o'clock—continued to be the dinner hour in England and France until the fourteenth century. "Morning," which is *matin* in French, was thus understood to extend from sunrise until three o'clock. The noon meals in most of the baronial halls of the period were bountiful, and the lords of the manors usually had guests whom they delighted to entertain for an hour or two before dinner. Therefore, strolling troubadours, jongleurs, jugglers, and other entertainers were careful to plan their journeys so as to arrive in ample time to delight the lord and his guests with their tricks and accomplishments before they sat at table, sometimes during the meal as well. Such a show, thus held in the "morning" of that period, was known as a *matinee*. When customs decreed that dinner should be served at six o'clock and that "noon," no longer either the ninth hour or the dinner hour, should denote midday, social usage still permitted "morning" to embrace all the period before dinner. This usage is still reflected in the names "morning coat" and "morning dress." The term *matinee* is a similar holdover, but is usually still applied to a show or entertainment that begins before three o'clock.

maudlin

The search for word origins takes us into some strange places. Here, we look into the miracle plays, as they are called, of Old England, and we must learn something about their production. These crude plays flourished for about three hundred years, from the late thirteenth century to the late sixteenth century at least. They were based on some miracle described in the Bible or that had occurred in the life of some saint. And originally they were produced by one or another of the religious houses of England. By the late thirteenth century, however, the productions were taken over by the various craft guilds of a city, though still with religious sanction.

Each play was actually a series of pageants in regular sequence, and each pageant was staged by one or another of the guilds of the city. For the performance, a pageant somewhat resembled a scene from a play, mounted upon a platform or stage on four wheels. The first pageant (or scene) was played before the doors of the abbey, and was then hauled off to its next position in the city. The second pageant then succeeded the first—and so on, until all the pageants, in due order, had traversed the appointed settings throughout the city. Thus all the people were given an opportunity to see each play. These plays did not vary from year to year and they were shown annually at least. Consequently, the townspeople became very familiar with all the plays and with the characters in them.

Favorite among the subjects were those plays that presented the life of Christ. In all of these one of the chief characters was Mary Magdalen. And when we recall that Mary Magdalen, at that period, was supposed to be the same person as Mary, the sister of Lazarus, and as the sinner who washed the feet of Jesus with her tears, it is evident that she appeared in a number of the pageants. Thanks to the pronunciation of the French name, *Madelaine*, the English "Magdalen" was formerly always pronounced and frequently spelled "Maudlin"—Magdalen College, Oxford, and Magdalene College, Cambridge, are still so pronounced. So when we bear in mind that in almost every pageant in which Mary Magdalen appeared—at the death of her brother, Lazarus; when washing the feet of Jesus, and during the scenes of the Crucifixion and Resurrection—she was in tears, and when we remember that each of these pageants went from one street to another and that, therefore, all day long the actors who played that part had to be shown constantly in a state of tearful affection, it is not at all amazing that, during the course of many years, *maudlin* was taken into the language to signify a state of sentimental and tearful affection.

maundy

The Christian Church early laid stress upon humility. There were various instances in the New Testament to show that this was a basic precept. Perhaps chief of these was the washing of the feet of His disciples by Jesus before the Feast of the Passover. This, because of the example of great condescension, is observed to this day by Christian churches, celebrated the evening before Good Friday. The ceremony itself was formerly solemnly observed in all churches. In England, until the time of James II, it was the custom that the king also receive on that evening as many poor men as he was years old and personally wash their feet, after which money, food, or clothing was distributed among them. The charitable gift became known as *maundy*, for a curious reason, and the day, which of course fell on Thursday, is still known as *Maundy Thursday*. This came about from the fact that, in church, the celebration of the washing of feet was always followed by a discourse which opened with the words of the thirty-fourth verse of the thirteenth chapter of the Gospel according to John: "A new commandment I give unto you." In the French spoken by the clergy of England after the conquest of that country by the Normans, *mandé* was the word used for "commandment." Its pronunciation at that period sounded to the English as *maundy*, and this later became the recognized English spelling. Thus the day before Good Friday became known as *Maundy Thursday*, for it was the day upon which *maundies* were said and the day upon which *maundy money* or *maundy gifts* were distributed.

mausoleum

There was once, in Asia Minor, a small kingdom known as Caria. In the fourth century B.C., its inhabitants were mostly Persians, although those dwelling in the two principal cities, Halicarnassus and Rhodes, were mainly Greeks. The Persian king at that time was not outstanding and had done nothing that would particularly commend him, but he was greatly adored by his wife, Artemisia, who, in the peculiar customs of the time, was also his sister. The king's name was *Mausolus*. When he died in 353 B.C., his wife was inconsolable. She was said to have had his ashes collected and to have added a portion of them to her daily drink until she died of grief two years later. But Artemisia also gathered together the best architects and sculptors before her death and caused them to begin to erect at Halicarnassus a sepulchral monument to her husband. This sepulcher was called *mausoleum* in memory of his name. It was completed after her own death and was long regarded as one of the seven wonders of the world. Ruins of the building were excavated in 1857 which showed that the area of its base had been about 230 by 250 feet and that it was cased with marble. Fragments of numerous statues were found, including a statue of Mausolus, now in the British Museum. The edifice was standing at the time of the Crusades, but was left in ruins by the knights of St. John of Jerusalem, who occupied Halicarnassus in 1402 and used much of the material from the tomb in building their castle.

May

The month of May is believed to have been named in honor of a goddess *Maia*, but it is not certain which goddess was thus honored. Among the Greeks the divinity so named was regarded as the mother of Hermes, whose father was Zeus. It would have been strange, however, for the Romans to have placed the name of a Greek goddess in their calendar. Late Roman writers, who may have been right, explained that *Maia* was the ancient name of Fauna, daughter or sister of Faunus, and that she was therefore the goddess of spring. The Roman months were presumably named by Numa who was traditionally the successor of Romulus and who aided him in the founding of Rome. Numa was a member of the neighboring tribe of the Sabini, and he may have used the old Sabine name, *Maia*, later called *Fauna* by the Romans. Some think that the ancient name was one of the various appellations of the great goddess whom the Romans usually referred to as *Bona Dea*, "the good goddess."

meander

There is a river in the western part of Turkey, Asia Minor, now called Menderes, known in ancient times as Mæander. The nature of the stream has greatly changed in the centuries since it was described by Herodotas, Xenophon, and other writers. In those days, however, although the river was not remarkable for length or width, it was especially notable for the number of twists and turns it pursued through low, flat country on its way to the sea. Perhaps such windings amazed the Greeks because, living in a mountainous country, they were accustomed to streams that flowed rapidly and directly to the sea. But the extremely tortuous *Mæander* was so unusual to them that its name became a term which they applied to anything that deviated frequently in its course or pursued a labyrinthine pattern. The altered spelling *meander* is a variant that has now become generally accepted.

meerschaum

Because of its whiteness and softness, and because it was often cast up along the shores of the sea, the ancients thought this light, soft mineral actually to be the foam of the sea turned into stone. Hence in all languages it was named "sea foam." Little practical use was found for the mineral until German artisans began to carve it into pipe bowls and cigar holders, seeing that it would readily absorb nicotine from the tobacco and acquire a beautiful, warm brown color. Thanks to this German application we have accepted the German name, from *meer*, sea, and *schaum*, foam. The scientific name is "sepiolite," from Greek *sepia*, cuttlefish, and *lithos*, stone, because the mineral resembles the bone obtained from those animals. A more appropriate name for us to use than German *meerschaum* would have been "aphrodite," from Greek *aphros*, foam. This would have honored the goddess Aphrodite, supposed to have been created from sea foam. Unfortunately, however, the name is now applied to another mineral of similar composition.

mentor

When Odysseus left Ithaca to participate in the siege and capture of Troy, according to Homer's *Odyssey*, he entrusted the care of his wife, Penelope, and his infant son, Telemachus, to his great friend, *Mentor*. Homer does not develop the character of the loyal friend to any extent, but twenty years later the young Telemachus, we are told, started out to try to find his father, accompanied, as he thought, by his old tutor. Actually, however, the form of *Mentor* had been assumed by Athena, goddess of wisdom, who gave the young man the benefit of her counsel and advice. The story was taken by the French author, Fénelon, archbishop of Cambrai, as the basis for the political novel, *Télémaque*, which he published in 1699. In this he assigns the role of adviser and counselor of the young hero entirely to the aged tutor, *Mentor*, and makes him second only in importance to the chief character. The book received great acclaim. Voltaire called it "a Greek poem in French prose." From the wisdom and counsel displayed by this fictional companion, *mentor* became one of our common words for any person who serves as a counselor to another.

mercerize

John Mercer was born in Lancashire, England, in 1791. He became a calico printer. When he was fifty-three years old he discovered a chemical process by which cotton fabric became thicker and softer and its affinity for dyes greatly increased. He patented the process in 1855, but no practical use came of the discovery for another forty-five years. The difficulty was that the fabric shrunk from 20 to 25 per cent in the process. This loss, plus the cost, was then considered prohibitive for the results obtained. But in 1895, taking advantage of intermediate discoveries, Messrs. Thomas and Prevost found that the shrinkage could be almost eliminated by treating the material under tension and that, at the same time, a permanent silky luster was imparted to the fabric. Mercer, who had died in 1866, had merely spoken of his process as "sodaizing," with reference to the caustic soda that he used. But in view of the original discovery made by him, the revised process became known as *mercerization*, and the operator is said to *mercerize* the cloth.

mesmerism

In 1766 a young Austrian physician of 32, Friedrich Anton Mesmer, published a thesis in which he argued that, through the diffusion of some invisible vapor, the heavenly bodies affect the nervous systems of all living beings. The argument did not receive the attention which the young physician had hoped, so he went to Vienna to extend his theory. There he identified his invisible force with magnetism, and began to attempt to cure patients by stroking them with magnets. When he learned that a rival practitioner was effecting cures by manipulation alone, however, he discarded his magnets and proclaimed his ability to cure disease by what he called "animal magnetism." This claim he began to demonstrate in Paris in 1778. There he made many converts and made a fortune for himself through gifts from grateful patients. His methods were spectacular. In a dimly lit room Mesmer, garbed in the robes of an astrologer, would receive a group of patients. He formed them into a circle, with joined hands, and then to the accompaniment of soft music he passed from one to another, fixing his eyes upon and touching each one in turn. Many cures were alleged, and there were some reputable physicians who supported his claims. Upon the demand of others, nevertheless, a government commission was appointed to investigate. The commission, which included Benjamin Franklin among its members, rendered an unfavorable report, deriding Mesmer as a charlatan and an imposter. He removed himself then to Switzerland, where he died in 1815. His process, subsequently called *mesmerism*, after its claimant, was later identified as a form of hypnotism.

milliner

From early in the sixteenth century traders from Milan flocked into England with the products of their city and of Lombardy. Steel work was a large part of the manufactures they brought, but their chief articles of commerce were textile fabrics. Milan bonnets, Milan gloves, Milan lace, Milan ribbons were in great demand. The English pronunciation of the name of that foreign city, however, was not that which we use today; they rimed it then with "villain." In fact, the English often spelled the name "Millain." Merchants from Milan were naturally called Milaners, pronounced as if spelled *milliners*, and thus *Milliner* actually became the general spelling. Hence, subsequently, any person dealing with products similar to those that had once come from Milan became known as a *milliner*. Restriction of the term to women's headgear and the like is recent.

miniature

Important writings or manuscripts in the Middle Ages were often decorated or illuminated with "minium." This was the name then used for the color that we now call vermilion, taking the name of the Latin *minium*, red lead. Thus the monks or scribes who illuminated those manuscripts were said to "miniate" the parchment, because the decorative color was chiefly red. Sometimes the decorator was called upon to illuminate a manuscript further with a picture. This required fine workmanship because of the small space allotted to the artist. The picture thus obtained was term a *miniature* because it was done by "miniating." Strictly speaking, it could have been of any size and would still have been a *miniature* if done by that process, but owing to the fact that there was invariably a *minimum* of space for the picture, *miniature* acquired by association a significance of a picture on a small scale.

miscreant

Through its origin, *miscreant* was at first used only in a theological sense. Its source was the Old French prefix, *mes*, badly or wrongly, and *creant*, believing. Hence a *miscreant* in olden times was a heretic, an unbeliever. But through the fact that an unbeliever is one who is likely to violate the code of morals set up by believers, the term *miscreant* lost its original limited sense long ago and was applied instead to any such depraved person as a robber, a thief, or evil-doer of any sort.

mob

It used to be called a rabble. Then some Latin scholar of the seventeenth century recalled that the Latin phrase for a "fickle rabble" was *mobile vulgus*. This was picked up by others who shortened it to the one word, *mobile* (pronounced "mobilly" at that time). But even this was too long, and before the end of the century, much to the disgust of the purists of the period, it had been further shortened to *mob*.

money, monetary (mint)

According to legend, during a war when the Romans were hard pressed for the means to carry on their campaign they appealed to the goddess Juno for aid. They were told that their cause was just and therefore that their resources would be replenished and made ample for their needs. In grateful appreciation for the victory that followed, we are told, the Romans then erected a temple to Juno, giving it the name *Moneta*, "the advisor." It was in this temple, according to historical records, that in the year 269 B.C., silver coins were first produced by the Romans. These coins, from their place of coinage, were henceforth commonly given the name *moneta*, to distinguish them from the earlier copper coins. And it is from this word, through corruptions in sound and spelling in Old French, that we have obtained both our terms *money* and *mint*. From the uncorrupted Latin *moneta* came the Latin *monetarius*, "pertaining to the mint," from which we have derived our word *monetary*.

monster (demonstrate) (prodigy)

Any sign thought to have been given by the old Roman gods, that is, any strange incident or wonderful appearance, was taken as a warning, a belief that the gods were provoked. The sign prophesied the approach of a calamity or misfortune, of public nature or to the nation as a whole, rather than to an individual. Such a foreboding omen or portent was variously called. The term most frequently used was *prodigium*, though this might also denote, rarely, a favorable portent. This, when borrowed into English use in the form *prodigy*, continued at first to mean something of extraordinary nature taken as an omen, but is now applied especially to a person or animal above the ordinary in some skill or talent or mentality. Another term was *monstrum*, which always, from the nature of the strange incident, denoted the approach of some catastrophe. The term was derived from the verb *monstro*, to show, point out, familiar to us in the derivative, *demonstrate*. But through the dread inspired by the term *monstrum*, that word also came to be applied to whatever was the fearful thing, the strange appearance of unusual and frightening form, that had been taken as an omen of evil. Thus, even among the Romans, *monstrum*, which became *monster* in English, was used also for anything abnormally large, or of unusual or frightening appearance.

morphine (somnolent)

The Roman poet Ovid found a need for a new god while writing the poem, *Metamorphoses*, a series of stories written by him a few years before his banishment in A.D. 8. This series is devoted largely to the adventures of the gods in their amatory pursuits of nymphs and the daughters of mortals. While writing, the poet's fancy took him into the realms of dreams, which he felt to be apart from sleep. There was a god of sleep, the Greek Somnus, from whom "somnolent" and related words were derived, but there was no god of dreams. So, taking the Greek word *morphe*, "shape" or "form," he coined the name *Morpheus*, whom he described as being the god of such dreams as include human shapes or forms. Later poets accepted the name as if there had actually been such a god among those of the Greeks or Romans. In more recent times, however, the god of dreams has been confused with the god of sleep, and *Morpheus* is popularly supposed to have been the name of the latter. The result has been that some of our modern terms, such as *morphine*, which actually pertain to sleep, rather than to dreams, have received their names from Ovid's fictional god.

mortgage

Literally this Old French expression, introduced into the law courts of England after the Norman Conquest, meant a "dead pledge," from *mort*, dead, and *gage*, pledge. The reason for calling the legal instrument a "dead pledge" was given by the great English jurist of the seventeenth century, Sir Edward Coke, in these terms:

It seemeth that the cause why it is called mortgage is, for that it is doubtful whether the Feoffor will pay at the day limited such summe [sum] or not, & if he doth not pay, then the Land which is put in pledge vpon [upon] condition for the payment of the money, is taken from him for euer [ever], and so dead to him vpon condition, &c. And if he doth pay the money, then the pledge is dead as to the Tenant, &c.

mountebank

Much of the business of Italian cities of the Middle Ages was conducted upon benches placed in the streets or public squares, especially in Venice. The Italian word for bench, *banca*, accounts for our English word "bank." Usually the business thus conducted in public was of the ordinary serious nature, but there were also itinerant quacks in those days, just as there are today. Such men knew, as others had known from the beginning of time, that the best way to get folks to buy their wares was to attract a crowd, and the best way to attract a crowd was to put on a show. Juggling was the favorite performance, but in order to be seen to better advantage, the juggler would, of course, step up upon a bench if one were nearby, perhaps at the shouted request of someone in his audience. The Italian for such a request is "*Monta in banco* (Climb upon a bench)." Quacks soon realized that it was to their advantage to have a bench nearby upon which to mount, and even to get on it before being asked. Hence they came to be known as *montimbancos*, altered to *mountebank* in England. Sometimes the quack was assisted by a professional clown, or by a rope-dancer, or an acrobat, or a ballad singer, and sometimes in their wanderings the mountebanks would accumulate a considerable show, somewhat on the order of a traveling vaudeville. The majority, however, traveled alone or with one or two assistants. Some English writers in the seventeenth century tried to bring the Italian term *saltimbanco* into the language. This, from the Italian *saltare*, to leap, was applied especially to the charlatans who performed upon their platforms or benches by dancing, leaping, or tumbling.

mugwump

John Eliot, so-called "apostle to the Indians," had many difficulties when, in the middle of the seventeenth century, he was translating the Bible into the Indian language. There were so many words for which the Indians had no equivalent. Hence, when he came to the thirty-sixth chapter of Genesis, he lacked a word for "duke," which occurs forty-three times in that chapter. He decided upon *mukquomp*, an Algonquian term sometimes used to mean a chief or great man. Perhaps other New Englanders picked the word up at that time and used it jokingly of someone who thought himself a great man. We do not know, but we do know that it had already been modified to *mugwump* and was so used in the early nineteenth century, especially of those who thought themselves rather superior. So in 1884, when quite a number of Republicans bolted from the party and supported Cleveland for the presidency, rather than Blaine, the New York *Evening Post* derided them as *mugwumps*, people who thought themselves too good or too superior to vote for Blaine. But the men who were thus sneered at turned the tables and adopted the term themselves, saying that they were independent voters and were therefore proud to call themselves *mugwumps* or "great men."

muscle (mussel)

Our ancestors had a good sense of humor. With one accord, no matter in what part of Europe they lived, they agreed that the Romans had properly described a muscle by the name given to it. All, with variations arising from language of course, adopted that name. It is *muscle* also in French, *muscolo* in Italian, *músculo* in Spanish, and *muskel* in German, Dutch, Danish, and Swedish. The Romans named it "a little mouse"—Latin, *musculus*. Perhaps they were thinking of the biceps of some Casper Milquetoast of ancient Rome, or the muscles of the arms and legs of most of us. It is more likely, however, that the intent was just the opposite. The Romans were great lovers of beauty and great admirers of physical perfection. Some poet among them, seeing the smooth rippling play of muscle in the arms, shoulders, back, or thigh of a well-developed athlete, may have seen how the muscles resembled little mice appearing and disappearing in their play. His whimsy may have taken the popular fancy and may have thus been perpetuated to this day. Similarly, the marine bivalve, though we spell it *mussel*, was also known to the Romans as a "little mouse" or *musculus*, but that was doubtless because of the size and color.

museum

Today it seems rather far-fetched to associate this word with the nine Muses of ancient Greece, for we do not usually think of these beautiful nymphs in connection with collections of paintings, furniture, insects, curios, or the like. Nor do we connect the term with any one of them, nor with the art over which each presided— Clio, history; Calliope, epic poetry; Polyhymnia, sacred music; Euterpe, the music of the flute; Terpsichore, the dance; Erato, love poetry; Melpomene, tragedy; Thalia, comedy; Urania, astronomy.

But shrines to the Muses were common among the cities influenced by Hellenic culture. Such a shrine was known as a *mouseion*, or, in Latin, a *museum*. Hence about 285 B.C., when Ptolemy Soter erected his widely famed temple of learning at Alexandria, which was dedicated to the Muses, it became properly known as the *Museum* at Alexandria. Under that name it flourished for about seven hundred years and was the forerunner of our present universities. When it was destroyed by fire in the fourth century, however, the name became merely a memory and the word dropped almost completely out of use.

Then about three hundred years ago some scholar dug the word out of the dusty past and thought that *museum* would apply to any room or building which provided a "home for the Muses," such as the library or study of a learned man. From this careless use, *museum* came to be thought of as a home for anything pertaining to learning; hence, to collections of scientific curios or of antiquities. The first of these latter *museums* was the Ashmolean Museum, a collection of scientific material presented by Elias Ashmole to Oxford University in 1683. It is thus seen that the Muses do preside over our modern museums.

musket

Early types of artillery developed in the fifteenth and sixteenth centuries were usually named after the venomous serpent or swift bird of prey to which they were likened. Most of these names are now archaic, along with the artillery, and we are no longer familiar with the names of some of the animals. There was the *basilisk*, a fabulous serpent whose name was applied to a large brass cannon; the *culverin*, originally a small handgun, named for a snake called *coulevrine* in French; the *falconet*, a small cannon named from the falcon, a bird of prey; the *saker*, slightly larger than the falconet, named for the saker, a species of falcon, and the *musket*. This was originally a matchlock weapon, fired from a rest which the *musketeer* stuck into the ground before him. The French, who named the weapon, called it *mousquet* from the sparrow hawk, known to them by that name.

mystery

Ancient nations, like fraternal orders of our day, always kept some of their religious rites and ceremonials hidden from the eyes of the multitude or from those not yet initiated. To preserve that secrecy the rites were sometimes observed at night or within some sanctuary. These were the secret parts of the worship, in which the participants had undergone some form of initiation and were sworn never to disclose them to others. The Greek term for such a secret rite, ceremony, or sacrifice was *mysterion*. The *mysterion*, or *mystery*, often consisted in the recital of legends, and sometimes this was accompanied by a dramatic representation in which certain holy things, including symbols and relics, were revealed. In many cases a symbol—very like a fraternal button, pin, or token in our times—was openly displayed, but the meaning of the symbol was known only to those initiated.

nabob (nawab)

The great Tamerlane invaded India in 1398, looting its treasures at will, but making no attempt to add it to his empire. But, in 1526, Baber, the fifth in descent in this illustrious line of eastern rulers, led another expedition southward. From this invasion India came under the rule of a long line of Mogul emperors, lasting until the country came under the British crown in 1858. Among the customs during the Mogul Empire was the delegation of authority in the various subdivisions of India to men who acted as governors or vice-regents. The native title of these men was *nawwab*, or Arabic *na'ib*, meaning "deputy." In theory, the provinces or districts under a *nawwab*, corrupted by Europeans into *nabob*, continued to pay tribute to the central government in Delhi, but some of these districts grew so wealthy and powerful that the tribute did not pass beyond the nabob. Thus they grew fabulously wealthy and, with the further decline of central government, the office became hereditary. Through the wealth of these officials, Europeans acquired the habit of referring to any wealthy man as a *nabob*, especially such a person as had obtained his wealth in India. The custom spread to England, and we now use the term to include any influential person of great wealth.

namby-pamby

In 1725-26 the English poet, Ambrose Philips, chiefly noted for his pastoral poems, published some simple pieces addressed to the infant children of his friends, Lord John Carteret and Daniel Pulteny. These little poems, though charming, would probably have attracted little attention had it not been for Alexander Pope. Some years earlier Pope and Philips had become bitter enemies, and Pope, with his gift for satire, lost no opportunity to hold Philips up to ridicule. On this occasion, however, it was a friend of Pope's, the poet Henry Carey, who opened the attack. Philips' poems were, perhaps, somewhat sentimental. Carey seized upon that feature and wrote a parody upon the verses that he thought most insipid. His title, "*Namby Pamby*," he took from "Amby," the diminutive of Ambrose, with the initial of Philips suggesting the alliterative. Pope carried the name further into the language when he republished his *Dunciad* in 1733. Through the wide popularity of the latter, *namby-pamby* came to denote anything, especially of a literary nature, that was sweetly sentimental.

narcissus, narcotic

After the nymph Echo was permitted to speak only when she heard another voice and could then repeat only what she heard, (See ECHO.) it was her further misfortune to fall in love with the youth, Narcissus. This young man, according to Greek mythology, was exceptionally handsome. There are several stories that account for his ultimate fate. In one it is said that he was wholly untouched by the feeling of love, and when Echo pined away in grief over her unrequited love she prayed that he might fall in love with himself. And this, when Narcissus chanced to see his own beautiful face reflected from a pool, is what he did. As he was unable to approach his own image, he in turn perished with love. One account says that he melted away into the pool in which he saw his reflection. In another tale, in which Echo plays no part, it is said that Narcissus had a twin sister as fair as himself and with identical features. His love for her was so great that, to recall her image to him after her death, he sat and gazed constantly at his own reflection in a pool until he himself died with grief. In all the stories it is further related that after the death of Narcissus his body was changed by the gods into the flower that bears his name. The Greeks considered the *narcissus* to be sacred to Hades and a symbol of death. Varieties of the plant contain properties that induce sleep; hence, *narcotic* and other derivatives are based upon the same term.

necklace

In the sixteenth century, when this word was introduced, its meaning was exactly that indicated by its two components, lace for the neck. But lace was not then what we usually consider it today. (See LACE.) Its meaning had expanded from a string or cord (still preserved in our word "shoelace") and, in the sixteenth century, had come to include ornamental braid of gold or silver. Such gold lace or silver lace, made of wire, was usually sewn on garments, but was sometimes further ornamented with precious stones and worn about the neck and was then called *necklace*.

neighbor

In the early days of our language, in the times that we call Old English, this was a compound word, made up of the two elements, *neah* and *gebur*. These separately have descended to us as "nigh" and "boor," and that is exactly what *neighbor* originally meant—a nearby rustic or peasant, a husbandman dwelling nearby. From the origin it would appear, therefore, that the term applies only to countryfolk and to small villages, but it was early taken into the towns and cities and applied to anyone who lived nearby.

nemesis

Not all of the Greek gods were kindly. There was one, according to mythology, whose duty it was to sit in judgment upon men. Her name was *Nemesis*, thought to have been the daughter of Night. She measured out happiness and unhappiness, and saw to it that any who were too greatly or too frequently blessed by fortune were visited in equal measure by loss or suffering. From this last she became looked upon as the goddess of retribution, as a goddess of vengeance and punishment.

nepenthe

When Paris abducted Helen from the home of her husband, Menelaus, in Sparta and fled with her to Troy, he wanted her to forget her family and former home. To that end, according to Homer, he gave to her an Egyptian drug, believed to allay grief and induce forgetfulness. This drug was known as *nepenthe* or *nepenthes*, and was probably some form of opium. We use its name now to indicate any agency that may bring about freedom from mental pain, but we owe the name to Homer's story.

nepotism

One after the other of the popes of the fifteenth and sixteenth centuries, upon ascending the papal throne, used its great power to further his own ambitions. To do so it was first advantageous to have important offices filled by men who would be tied to him. There were none better for that than members of his own family. Best of all were his own illegitimate sons who, by courtesy, were referred to as "nephews." Perhaps the most notorious of these political popes was the Spaniard, Rodrigo Borgia, who, as Alexander VI, reigned at the turn of the century. His son Giovanni became duke of Gandia; his son Cesare was created an archbishop at 16 and was elected cardinal at 17; his nephew Giovanni also received a cardinal's hat, and other members of the family received similar important honors. Such favors as these to nephews by courtesy and nephews in fact, as well as to other relatives, all accompanied by great gifts of land and wealth from the resources of the Church, brought a new word into the languages of Europe. In English, it was *nepotism*. The original source was the Latin *nepos*, which meant "a descendant," such as a grandson, or, especially, a nephew. The detractors of the popes of that period gave the new term a slightly larger range, including not only nephews and descendants, but also all members of the family who received undue preferment over other qualified persons.

newt (eft)

Solvers of cross-word puzzles may sometimes wonder why *newt* and *eft*, such different words in appearance and sound, are apparently used interchangeably. When is a newt an eft, they may ask. The answer is that a newt is an eft in the United States, sometimes, and in some sections of England, but the usual name of this curious little relative of the salamander is newt in both countries. Actually even the names are one and the same. The ancient word was *efeta*, in which the *f* was sometimes voiced and sometimes voiceless. When voiced, the spelling became changed to *eveta*. Then, because the letters *v* and *u* were used interchangeably in writing, this word was often written *eueta*. The next change to *ewte* probably came about after the introduction of the letter *w* and through the fact that the combination *ue* (such as *due*) was usually pronounced like *ew* (*dew*). At about that time also, just as with "nickname," the *n* of *an* (in *an ewte*) was transferred in common speech to the word that followed, producing *a newte*, which eventually gave us *newt*. While these changes were going on there were other lesser sections of England in which the original word was undergoing another modification. These were the sections in which the *f* of *efeta* was voiceless. (In *of* the *f* is voiced; in *often*, voiceless.) In this speech the form of the word gradually changed into *eft*. For many years both *newt* and *eft* were used according to whim, many writers using both words to make sure that the reader would understand. But gradually *newt* has become the more common form, *eft* becoming obsolescent.

nickel

German miners looking for copper were often baffled by an ore which, though it had an appearance of copper, yielded none whatsoever when it was tediously excavated, brought to the surface, and treated. Time and time again they were fooled by this stuff. They thought it must be that a demon or sprite had entered into ore that had been copper and had changed it into worthless stuff. For that reason they called it *kupfernickel*, copper nickel, in which *nickel* was an old Teutonic name for demon. But in 1751 the Swedish mineralogist, Axel F. Cronstedt, succeeded in treating the ore and in isolating the metal from it, although in an impure form. To name the metal thus obtained he went to the name given to the ore in disgust by German miners and called it *nickel*. (Compare COBALT.)

nickname

From early times men have been in the custom of giving to their acquaintances some name considered to be more fitting than the name given by the parents. It is an added name, one in addition to the name already borne. In olden England, when *eke* meant to "add," such an added name became known as *an ekename*. Many words which began with a vowel became altered at that period through the transference of the *n* from the indefinite article *an*, thus producing "a nox" for "an ox," "a negge" for "an egg," "a napple" for "an apple," and so on. Most of these alterations were temporary. But *ekename* when altered to *nekename*, like "eft" when altered to "newt," also speedily suffered a change in pronunciation which served to disguise the earlier form. Thus *nekename* changed in sound to *nickname*, and the original *ekename* dropped from memory. (Compare APRON.)

nicotine

The French ambassador to Lisbon in 1560, Jean Nicot, became curious about some seeds that he saw. They had been brought from the new continent of America a year or two earlier and were said to be seeds from the curious plant that the Spaniards called "tobacco." Some of the seeds were courteously presented to Nicot, who then sent them back to his queen, Catherine de' Medici. The seeds were planted and thus produced the first tobacco, it is said, to be raised in Europe. Through the services of Nicot in obtaining the seed, the scientific name of the plant became *Nicotiana*, and, many years later, the oily liquid contained in its leaves became known as *nicotine*.

Nimrod

Now these are the generations of the sons of Noah, Ham, Shem, and Japheth . . . And the sons of Ham; Cush and Mizraim, and Phut and Canaan . . . And Cush begat Nimrod: he began to be a mighty one in the earth. He was a mighty hunter before the Lord: wherefore it is said, Even as Nimrod the mighty hunter before the Lord.

Thus, from the tenth chapter of Genesis, *Nimrod* has come to be a nickname for anyone noted as a hunter.

nostrum

The plague that beset England in 1563-64 terrified the populace. A thousand people were reported to have died from it each week in London alone, while everyone feared that it might reach the terrific toll of the Black Plague of the fourteenth century when two-thirds or more of the population of the entire country was wiped out. The later plague was not so devastating, but there were several sporadic recurrences, probably new epidemics, which developed in London and elsewhere through the remainder of the century and into the following, with great loss of life. The culmination was the Great Plague of 1665-66, with a death total during 1665 alone of about sixty-nine thousand persons in London only. Medical science was helpless during that period, either to prevent infection or to cure the victim. The result was an influx of quacks from Holland, charlatans from France, mountebanks from Italy. Each proclaimed loudly the virtues of the secret concoction that he alone could produce. This, to make his claim the more impressive, he labeled *Nostrum*, thereby displaying his learning in the Latin tongue. The term thus became a general name for any quack medicine or, in later years, for a patent medicine. But the Latin meaning of *nostrum*, however, is merely "Our own"—that is, "our own preparation."

omelet

Oddly enough, *omelet* comes to us from the Latin word *lamina*, a plate, by virtue of several modifications in passing through French. The Romans had earlier created *lamella* to denote "a small plate." This became *la lemelle*, the thin plate, in French, and—in manner very similar to the alteration of English *an ekename* to *a nickname*—the *a* of *la* was prefixed to the word that followed, thus *la lemelle* became *l'alemelle*. Early French cooks must have prepared eggs in some manner by which, when whipped, seasoned, and fried, the resulting dish resembled a thin plate. At least it was this dish which they called *alemelle*. The next change in the word was the alteration of the ending *-elle* into *-ette*, in accord with the usual diminutive suffix, a change which produced *alemette*, as well as *alumette*. Next came a simple transposition of *l* and *m*, resulting in *amelette*. Possibly each of these alterations came about through the speech of illiterate cooks and were put down upon parchment by literate writers who, knowing nothing about cooking, wrote what they heard. This last form was thence introduced into England, and was in turn variously written. From the sound of the French speech the more common form was *omelet*, which ultimately became preferred. And this in turn has been accepted in France in the form *omelette*.

one

Here we have a curious pronunciation. As seen from the words *alone* and *atone*, which are really compounds formed from *all one* and *at one*, an early sound of *one* was identical with our present word "own." Our word "only," once written "onely," still preserves the old pronunciation. There were variances, of course, but that remained the standard sound until the eighteenth century. In certain dialects, however, there became a tendency in the fifteenth century to sound an initial *w* before some words beginning with *o*. Thus "oats" was sounded and sometimes spelled "wotes"; "oath," "wothe"; "oak," "woke"; "old," "wold." This tendency, occurring only when the initial vowel was long, was not general and did not persist. But in the words *one* and *once*, which were sometimes spelled *won* or *wone* and *wons* or *wonus*, the tendency was persistent. Apparently this tendency toward sounding these words as if spelled with initial *w*, and in which they were then pronounced *wun* and *wunce*, became increasingly common. Grammarians did not recognize them, but they had become so generally used by the seventeenth century as to be the only pronunciations of the two words (except, perhaps, the colloquial "*un*," as in "He's a good un,") to be brought to America. They were standard pronunciations in England by the eighteenth century.

oracle

The ancients would not think of entering upon any important undertaking without first consulting the will of the gods. (See also AUGUR.) Perhaps this was partly curiosity as to the outcome of future events, but more probably it arose from a deep reverence for their gods and a belief that nothing should be undertaken without their approval. Although Zeus was regarded as the father of all gods and men, they did not often approach him directly, because he was believed to be too remote from mortals to be concerned with their individual actions. Instead they made their usual supplications to the lesser gods and goddesses. The questions, accompanied by prescribed gifts or sacrifices, were asked of the priests of the god whose favor was sought, and it was through these priests that the will of the god was then revealed. The replies or prophecies that finally came from the lips of the priests, often in verse form, were usually of so obscure a nature that the supplicant could interpret them as he chose. Sometimes, however, the replies showed great judgment. The temple or place where prophecies were sought, as well as the answer that was received, was known in Greece as *manteion* or *chresterion*. In Rome, where the gods were consulted in similar manner, the more simple term was *oraculum*, from *oro*, pray, which has come to us as *oracle*.

ordeal

To this day in parts of the world, as among some African tribes, persons suspected of a crime are tested with a red-hot iron. He who can have it pressed against his flesh without a blister forming is adjudged innocent; he upon whom a blister forms is guilty. Such a test, or one of similar nature, has been known among primitive races from early ages. Among Teutonic tribes an accused person might be compelled to walk barefooted and blindfolded among a number of red-hot plowshares. He was declared innocent if, by chance, he did not step against one. Or the test might be that he was compelled to step on each of the plowshares, or to carry a glowing iron bar a certain distance; his innocence was thought to be clearly proved if he were uninjured. Sometimes an accused person was tested by having his arm thrust into boiling water. Or the test might be with cold water; a guilty person would float, rejected by the water; the innocent would sink. Among the Germans of old, any such test was called *urdeli*. The Saxon term became *ordel* in Old English, and ultimately *ordeal*. Many of these ordeals were carried into Christian times and adopted by the clergy. Persons accused of witchcraft were sometimes compelled to undergo the ordeal of cold water. She thus adjudged was first stripped, rendered powerless by having her right thumb tied to her left toe and the left thumb to the right toe, and was then tossed into the water. If a witch, she floated. In the ordeal of the bier, known in England until the seventeenth century, a person suspected of murder was obliged to approach or touch the body of the victim. If the wounds bled at his touch, or if foam appeared at the mouth, or if the body altered its position, the accused was declared guilty.

ostracism

When Athens adopted the constitution, in 508 B.C., that was intended
to make it an ideal democratic state, unique provision was made that
no one should again be able to exert his wealth or power and seize
the reins of government. Each year, at a stated assembly of the
populace, the question was asked whether anyone had reason to
suspect that such an attempt was being made, or that a citizen was
acquiring dangerous power. No one was named, and there might be
several persons under suspicion, so if an affirmative answer was
given, the senate gave notice that the matter would be voted on at
a special meeting of all the citizens two months later. Each citizen
came to this second meeting with his ballot prepared. If he thought
that the charge was well founded and that some man (or men)
was endangering the state, the name of that man (or those men) was
written upon his ballot, but if he did not think so, he cast a blank
ballot. He was expected to be very conscientious, because if a
majority of the ballots named one person, it meant that that person
would be banished from the state for the next ten years. The man
thus sent into exile would not lose his property and would regain
full rights of citizenship upon his return, though his other losses
might be great. On the other hand, the state sometimes lost the
services of some of its wisest counselors, as when such men as Aris-
tides, Themistocles, and Thucydides were banished.

Ordinary voting, in Athens, was by show of hands or by other
device in which a simple affirmative or negative opinion could be
expressed. The vote of banishment, however, had to be written,
but because paper, or papyrus, was rare and costly, the ballot was
written upon the most common article to be found about any household of that period—broken pieces of pottery or pieces of tile. Any
such piece of baked clay was called *ostrakon*, a name first applied
to the shell of an oyster, which it somewhat resembled. Thus, because
a vote to send a man into exile was commonly written upon a piece
of broken pottery, the Greeks gave the name *ostrakismos* to the
banishment itself. Our word *ostracism* is taken directly from this,
but we use the term more frequently now to denote social banishment, such as the barring of a person from one's social contact, and

the decision is reached by common agreement, rather than by ballot.

oscillate

Perhaps to frighten birds away, or perhaps to propitiate the gods, it was the custom of ancient Roman vintners to hang little images of the face of Bacchus upon their vines, to be swung by the breeze and turned in all directions. The supposition was that in whatever direction the faces were turned about, the crops would increase in fruitfulness in that portion of the vineyard. Now the Latin word for face is *os*; for a little face this becomes *oscillum*, and it is true that little masks such as these were used as described. Some of the older etymologists concluded, therefore, that the Latin verb *oscillo*, which means to swing, was derived from the motion imparted to these *oscilla* by the breeze. However, the majority of present-day scholars doubt this explanation, and prefer to say merely that our word *oscillate* is derived from *oscillo*, without attempting to decide the source of the Latin verb.

ottoman

In the last half of the thirteenth century a small band of Moslems moved eastward out of Persia into western Asia Minor. Their leader took them into the service of a local ruler, but after the death of that leader his son took the remnants of the band into territory still further to the west. There he set up an independent nation. The name of that young leader was Othman, sometimes spelled Osman. The nation that he established is known to us as Turkey, but is also known, from the name of its founder, as the *Ottoman* Empire, and its citizens call themselves *Osmanli*. In time it prospered, and in time it became noted for the luxurious fittings of its court and its palaces. Some of these Oriental fittings and comforts were greatly admired by visitors from western lands, and astute merchants saw to it that western markets then became supplied. Velvets, silks, and carpets were in greatest demand, but when it became the fashion in France under the Bourbons to invest an apartment with couches and divans from Turkey, another article of Turkish source was also introduced. This was a smaller couch than the divan, and, although backless, was intended primarily as a seat for one or two persons. The Oriental name was not brought to the western market, but, coming from the Ottoman Empire, the French dubbed it *ottomane*. The English, first calling it *ottoman sofa*, also finally settled on *ottoman*.

pagan (heathen)

The story of *pagan* and *heathen* can best be told in the words of Archbishop Trench (1807-86) in his *Study of Words*:

You are aware that *pagani*, derived from (Latin) *pagus*, a village, had at first no religious significance, but designated the dwellers in hamlets and villages, as distinguished from the inhabitants of towns and cities. It was, indeed, often applied to all civilians, as contradistinguished from the military caste; and this fact may have had a certain influence when the idea of the faithful as soldiers of Christ was strongly realized in the minds of men. But it was mainly in the following way that it became a name for those alien from the faith of Christ. The Church fixed itself first in the seats and centers of intelligence, in the towns and cities of the Roman Empire; in them its earliest triumphs were won; while, long after these had accepted the truth, heathen superstitions and idolatries lingered on in the obscure hamlets and villages; so that *pagans*, or villagers, came to be applied to all the remaining votaries of the old and decayed superstitions. . . . Heathen has run a course curiously similar. When the Christian faith was first introduced into Germany, it was the wild dwellers on the heaths who were the last to accept it, the last probably whom it reached.

palace

Chief among the famous seven hills upon which Rome was built, and most central of the seven, was the Palatine Hill—*Mons Palatinus*, as it was known, named for the Sabine goddess, Pales. According to tradition, this hill, selected by Romulus upon which to build the city, was ever the seat of government, and upon it Augustus Cæsar caused a large residence to be built for him when he became emperor, in 27 B.C. This edifice, occupied by his successors as well, was not only of great size, but was also of great magnificence, fitting for the emperors of Rome. Because of its location upon the Palatine Hill, the building was referred to as the *Palatium*; and when other wealthy Romans later built similar grand structures in and about Rome or her dominions, each strove to follow the elegance of the emperor's residence and termed his own also a *palatium*. This word degenerated into the Old French form *palais*, and was introduced into English speech in that form. Our present spelling, *palace*, was an alteration from that.

palaver (parable)

The Greek term for "parable" was *parabole*; literally, "a throwing beside," from *para*, beside, and *ballo*, to throw. But the Greek meaning of the compound word was "a placing beside"; hence, "a comparison," and this is, of course, what we mean by parable—a comparison, in the form of an allegorical story, by which some moral is taught. The recorded teachings of Jesus were often in the form of parables, for it was a favorite Hebrew device; the Book of Proverbs contains other examples. The term passed into Latin as *parabola*, and thence into the languages of the West. Its Portuguese form was *palavra*, but when Portuguese traders carried the term to Africa in the fifteenth or sixteenth century, they extended its meaning to include the lengthy powwows with the chieftains that the native conventions required. It was there, in the eighteenth century, that English traders encountered the word, though they understood it to be *palaver*. We continue to use it with the meaning it acquired in Africa.

pale

Originally, *pale*, from the Latin *palus*, stake, meant just that, a stake to be driven into the ground. It had an especial meaning, also—a stake to be driven into the ground along with others, so as to form a fence. From the latter it came to mean a definite limit or boundary, and this was further extended so as to signify a territory outside the area of, but under the control of a nation. Thus the *English pale* once denoted an area in France on either side of Calais which, until 1558, was under English jurisdiction. Most notably, however, the *English pale* was that portion of Ireland—the present counties of Dublin, Kildare, Louth, and Meath—which was under English domination from the twelfth century until the subjugation of the entire island in the reign of Elizabeth. The name *pale* was not applied to it, however, until the fourteenth century. (The adjective "pale," of whitish appearance, is from Latin *pallidus*, pallid.)

Pall Mall

Although now the name of a popular cigarette and of a street in London, the names were both derived from an old outdoor game. The original game and its name were of French origin, literally a game of ball, *palle*, and mallet, *maille*. The game was popular in France in the sixteenth century and, when introduced in the reign of Charles I (1625-49), became popular in England. The boxwood ball used in the game was about the size of the modern croquet ball, and the mallet, also of wood, was similar to the croquet mallet, except that the head was curved and the two faces sloped toward the shaft. The game was played on an alley of considerable length, from the starting point at one end to an iron ring suspended at some height at the other end. The player was winner who took the fewest strokes to drive his ball through the ring. The most noted alley in London in which the game was played was that near St. James's, now bearing the name of the game. The French name was long retained, but because of its pronunciation the spelling was altered by some to *pell-mell*. Others, however, recalled that the Latin sources of the French words were respectively *palla* and *malleus*, and therefore insisted upon the spelling *pall-mall*, which, nevertheless, is still pronounced in England either as if spelled "pell-mell" or like the first syllables of "pallet" and "mallet" respectively.

pamphlet

In the thirteenth century there appeared in France a few leaves containing a poem of love with the title *Pamphilus, seu de Amore.* The story became very popular, so popular that the small work became familiarly known as *Pamphilet*, just like the small book of Aesop's Fables had been familiarly named *Esopet.* Hence, the English, because French was still the court language, also referred to the poem as *Pamphilet*, although later spelling it *Pamflet, Pamfilet,* or eventually *Pamphlet.* Because of the few pages which were required to hold this old poem, any other treatise that occupied approximately the same few pages came also to be known as a *pamphlet* even by the fourteenth century. It became an extremely popular term during the period of the Reformation in the sixteenth century, when numerous religious tracts were circulated as *pamphlets*, their writers designated as *pamphleteers*.

pandemonium

When writing *Paradise Lost* Milton's imagination led him to suppose a place that would serve as the capital of Hell, a place that would be inhabited only by the demons and which would be the meeting place and council chambers of all the evil spirits. He coined a name for this imaginary place and called it *Pandemonium*, from the Greek *pan*, all, and *daimon*, demon. The name passed later into general use as a polite substitute for "hell," and through the popular notion that hell is a place of great noise and wild confusion, *pandemonium* now denotes also any scene of great tumult and uproar.

pander

English readers of the fourteenth century were treated to a great story told by two different great writers. It was the story of the love of the Trojan prince, Troilus, for the beautiful Chryseis or Cressida. Boccaccio told the story, in Italian, in his *Filostrato*, basing it upon two legendary accounts of the siege of Troy written by men who were reported to have then lived within the city. Chaucer retold the story in English later in the century in greater detail, using all of the earlier writings and adding to them his own vivid imagination. English readers thus became acquainted with the plight of the brave and handsome Troilus and how, in his desperation, he called upon his great friend Pandarus, kinsman of Chryseis, to aid him in his suit for her love. The story thereafter is chiefly filled with the plots devised by Pandarus to arouse the interest of Chryseis (called Criseyde, by Chaucer) in the Trojan prince and to stimulate that interest into affection. Thus Pandarus became a familiar character to the readers of these two romances, and because the name, for the purpose of rime, was often written Pandare by Chaucer, later writers adopted the designation *Pandare* for anyone who acted as a go-between in love affairs. This was later corrupted to *pander*.

panic

The Greeks ascribed many things to their demigod Pan; among them, the power to inspire great fear or terror in one who saw or heard him—"*Panic* fear," it was called. Through such unreasoning fear, it was said, the Persians were put to flight at the battle of Marathon, when Pan took up the cause of the Athenians. And the same terror affected men who, hunting in the forests of the mountains, heard fearsome noises which, they thought, were produced by Pan. It is not strange that the superstitious Greeks were frightened by this god and derived the word *panic* from him, for they pictured him in a terrifying form. As described by ancient Greek writers, he was a monster, half man and half beast. His head and torso were those of a man, except that such of his face as could be seen was fiery red. His nose was flat, two short horns grew from his head, and his face and body were covered with thick hair. He had the legs, thighs, tail, and feet of a goat. He was said to have been the son of Hermes and a nymph, and his appearance at birth was so frightening that his nurse fled in terror. He dwelt, it was believed, among the mountains or in the forests. One good thing, however, has been accredited to Pan—the invention of a musical instrument, the so-called "pipes of Pan," or panpipes, hollow reeds of graduated length, bound together side by side, to be played on by the mouth, like a harmonica.

panjandrum

The Irish actor, Charles Macklin, retired from the London stage in 1753 at the age of fifty-four and opened a tavern near the Drury Lane theater, the scene of many of his successes. It became his custom, in his new role of innkeeper, to serve dinner personally. Then afterward he would deliver a lecture to such as would listen. A debate invariably followed. Macklin was rather pompous, and the younger actors who frequented the place loved to lead him into making the assertion that he had so trained his memory that he could repeat anything after he had once heard it. Upon one such occasion the witty young actor, Samuel Foote, thereupon composed the following nonsense lines to expose the old man's folly:

So she went into the garden to cut a cabbage leaf to make an apple pie; and at the same time a great she-bear, coming up the street, pops its head into the shop, "What! no soap?" So he died, and she very imprudently married the barber; and there were present the picninnies, and the Joblillies, and the Garyulies, and the Grand Panjandrum himself, with the little round button at top, and they all fell to playing the game of catch as catch can, till the gunpowder ran out at the heel of their boots.

The lines became a grand test for anyone's memory, but were no more than that until Edward Fitzgerald, best known for his translation of the *Rubaiyat*, took *panjandrum* a hundred years later and applied it humorously to a self-important local official, whom he designated "the Grand Panjandrum." Since then, it has become a term of disparagement applied to any pompous individual.

pannier

When introduced from France in the thirteenth century, *pannier* denoted nothing more than a basket, originally for the carrying of bread—whence its name, from the Latin *panarius*, bread basket. But it had also come to mean a fish basket or, if of larger size, a basket for the carrying of provisions of any kind. When someone in later centuries conceived the brilliant notion of balancing two of these larger baskets across the back of a donkey, these too became *panniers*. It was but a step, then, to transfer the name to the basketlike frames which, at the demand of fashion, women affix beneath skirts to extend the size of the hips.

panorama (cyclorama)

In 1788 a Scottish portrait painter, Robert Barker, succeeded in carrying out in practical form an idea that had previously been suggested by a German architect named Breissig. This was to produce and exhibit on canvas the effect of the continuous scene that is open to anyone who turns himself completely around at one spot. To achieve the desired effect, he erected a rotunda, about sixty feet in diameter and reached by stairway, with a continuous painting mounted upon its cylindrical inner wall. Ceiling and floor were blended into the painting to suggest sky and ground. At first Barker called his invention, "*La Nature à coup d'Œil* (Nature at a Glance)," but later he coined the more euphonious name, *panorama*, from Greek *pan*, all, and *orama*, view. Robert Fulton, more noted then as artist than as engineer, was one of those greatly attracted by Barker's invention, and introduced the *panorama* into Paris, where he was staying, in 1799. Nowadays *panorama* also embraces a complete natural view in all directions, and the term *cyclorama*, from Greek *kyklos*, circle, and *orama*, view, is used for the artificial scene.

pants, pantaloons

A hundred years ago the witty poet, Oliver Wendell Holmes, wrote the delightfully humorous *Rhymed Lesson*, in which he sought to correct various bad habits. Among them was the use of the word *pants*, which, he wrote, was "A word not made for gentlemen, but 'gents.' " There are still some people who agree with him, but most Americans think its use is now as legitimate as the well established "cab," for "cabriolet," or "bus," for "omnibus." *Pants* is, of course, a contraction of *pantaloons*, a contraction that sprang up in America almost as soon as the garment itself reached our shores in the last years of the eighteenth century. So our story must be of *pantaloons*. This takes us back to a character in fifteenth-century Italian comedy, to a part that was always played by a lean and silly old man, always representing a foolish old Venetian and always wearing spectacles and slippers. The most characteristic part of his attire, however, was his nether garment, a pair of trousers that, skin-tight about the thin shanks, flared out above the knees like a petticoat. This character, in the comedy, always bore the name, *Pantaleone*, possibly because of some allusion to an early Christian martyr of that name especially honored by Venetians. The comedy, played as a pantomime, was popular throughout Italy and was played by strolling bands of actors in many other countries. Always *Pantaleone* —*Pantalon* in France, *Pantaloon* in England—appeared in his extravagant trousers. From that Italian character, then, any unusual kind of trousers, especially one covering both the upper and lower legs, was immediately described as *Pantaloon*. But it was in France, during the Revolution at the close of the eighteenth century, that the *pantalon* became popular. In the early days of that terrible struggle the Revolutionary army was composed chiefly of poor and ill-clad volunteers. The aristocrats called them *sans-culottes*, "without breeches," because the trousers which they wore were so tattered as almost to be no clothing at all. Later, however, when the Revolution had succeeded, the Revolutionaries took this as a term of honor, and repudiating the aristocratic knee breeches, adopted the *pantalon* as the masculine garb of republicanism. The well-cut, stylish garment of the period following the Revolution, the garment first imported to England and the United States in the earliest years of the nineteenth century, fitted tightly from thighs to ankles, with buttons or laces below the calves of the legs to assure a snug fit. Almost from the first, in America, they were popularly called *pants*, and, regardless of change in cut, style, length, and purpose, the abbreviated name has persisted despite all efforts of purists and pedagogs.

paraphernalia

In ancient Greece, as well as in some modern countries, a bride-groom received some gift or dowry—money, cattle, or other prop-erty—along with his bride, usually from her parents. This dowry then became his, to dispose of as he might wish. But the bride might also bring with her certain personal property, such as slaves or jewels, for example. These, under Greek law, her husband could not touch. They were distinctly her own possessions, and were known as *parapherna*, from *para*, beyond, and *phero*, bring; that is, belongings brought beyond those specified in the marriage contract. In present-day legal usage the Latinized term, *paraphernalia*, carries the same general interpretation, varying somewhat in our different States. The term is also used more broadly to designate any sort of miscellaneous equipment possessed by any individual or group.

parasite

Originally, in ancient Greece, there was nothing derogatory in referring to a man as a *parasite* (Greek *parasitos*, from *para*, beside, and *sitos*, food). It then referred to a class of priests, probably, who feasted together after a sacrifice. At an early date, however, it was applied to one who, as a guest, ate at the table of a friend. But, just as today a perfect guest does not insult a host, in those far-off times it was then customary for the perfect guest to choose his words even more carefully and to make nothing but complimentary remarks to his host. The more complimentary the remarks, the greater the chance that invitations would be repeated, for human nature hasn't changed very much in that respect. In time, therefore, a *parasite* came to be known contemptuously as one who lived entirely at the expense of another, feeding him with servile flattery in return for food and drink for one's own stomach.

pariah

In prehistorical times much of southern India was occupied, apparently, by a black-skinned race of primitive people. Some time after the Aryan invasion, which may have been as early as 2000 B.C., these people were subjugated and forced into menial positions. Gradually, after the caste system was introduced, they became separated into different lowly classes. Among these people was one class known as *Pariah*, which, from the name, indicates that at one time they were the hereditary beaters of the drum (*parai*) at various festivals. Eventually they became agricultural laborers and, among the British, household servants. They are not the lowest caste, but are regarded by the Brahmans as "untouchable." Among the British, therefore, *pariah* became a general term for anyone of low caste, but especially for the lowest of the low, or for those of no caste at all. Hence, although the application is not strictly correct, any person (or animal) who is an outcast among his kind has become known as a *pariah*.

pasquinade

In the year 1501 a mutilated old statue was dug up in Rome near the palace of Cardinal Caraffa. The statue was not identified, but the Cardinal, nevertheless, had it set up in the roadway at the corner of the palace. Opposite the spot where the statue had been found there had lived an old man with a sharp wit, said to have been either a tailor, a cobbler, or a schoolmaster, whose name had been Pasquino. Accordingly, as soon as it had been set up on its pedestal, the statue was promptly dubbed "Pasquino." Thereafter, on St. Mark's Day, it became the custom for the young men of a nearby school to dress "Pasquino" in various garments and to salute him with mock solemnity in passing and ask him for advice. It was not long before such requests were put into writing and posted or hung upon the statue. Then the written matter took the form of witty and satirical lampoons upon prominent persons and especially upon the papal government. The citizens of Rome began to enjoy these squibs, referring to them as *Pasquinata*, from the name given to the statue. A printed collection of them appeared in 1509. The name became *Pasquinade* in English, because the fame of these sharp little squibs had spread throughout Europe. Popular enjoyment was enhanced when another old statue was discovered and placed near "Pasquino." This was given the name "Marforio," because it came *a Martis foro* (from the forum of Mars). The lampoons then often took the form of dialog, with "Marforio" propounding questions for the caustic "Pasquino" to answer. The authors were numerous and their identities were never revealed, although the successive popes, against whose private and public conduct the lampoons were generally directed, would have taken harsh measures against them. The statue "Marforio," the recumbent figure of a man, was removed to the Capitoline Museum in 1784, but by that time the former pungency of the pasquinade had largely disappeared and these lampoons had become infrequent.

patrol

The Old French source of the verb was *patouiller*, and it then meant "to dabble in the mud." The supposition is that French soldiers detailed to guard a camp at night found that their duty seemed to consist of nothing but tramping interminably back and forth in the mud, and thus adopted this word to express in a slang sense the nature of the duty. The spelling was altered to *patrouiller* in modern French, and it had then become an accepted military term, meaning, "to go the rounds, as the guard of a camp." England, which adopted many French military practices, took over this term also, but further altered it to *patrol*.

patter

The Lord's Prayer was recited in the Middle Ages in very much the fashion that one often hears it today, especially by children—with great rapidity and with no shadow of understanding of the words. The difference is that in the Middle Ages the recitation was in Latin, so that few people knew what they were saying. Instead of opening with the words, "Our Father," therefore, it opened with *"Pater noster"*—thus giving rise to the word *paternoster* as a general name for the Lord's Prayer. It was because of this glib and indistinct utterance, then so commonly heard in church, that the slang word *patter* was formed, taken from the first word of the prayer.

pavilion (tavern, tabernacle)

The Roman military tent was often called *taberna*, a term that usually denoted a shop, because, like the shop, it was generally constructed of boards. (This word was also the source of *tavern*, since many Roman shops sold wine and served as inns. It is also the source of *tabernacle*, which, as Latin *tabernaculum*, meant a little tent, a hut.) But for non-military purposes in which a structure of less permanent nature was needed for protection against sun or rain, the Romans were accustomed to stretch a many-hued cloth, somewhat like an awning, over upright poles. Under it, in hot weather, they sometimes ate the morning or midday meal. This brilliant cloth structure, when fully spread, looked not unlike a mammoth butterfly with outspread wings; so they named it *papilio*, the Latin name of that pretty creature. Through later centuries such temporary structures found increasing use in France; its name was corrupted to *pavilon*, however, and in this form it passed into England. Our present spelling, *pavilion*, arose in the seventeenth century.

peculiar

From the same source as *pecuniary*, the Romans coined the adjective *peculiaris*, which, though originally referring to one's property in cattle, acquired a broader reference to personal property in general. From this, even in Roman days, *peculiaris* took on the more specific meaning, "one's own; belonging particularly to one's self." Thus, a Roman slave, although the absolute property of his master, was sometimes able to save some money in one way or another. This the master could not legally touch; it was *peculiares servi*, strictly belonging to the slave. Hence, without taking into consideration the shades of meaning that *peculiar* has acquired in English, its general sense pertains to character, qualities, abilities, or the like that are unshared with any other person, that are distinctly one's own.

pecuniary (impecunious)

Back in olden times, just as in many rural regions today, a man's wealth was measured, not by the money he might have in the bank nor the land that he held, but by the cattle that he owned; that is, the number of sheep, cows, or goats that he had. Now the Latin word for such a general collection of farm animals was *pecus*. Therefore, it followed that *pecus* also came to mean personal wealth or riches. But in later times, when property began to consist of other forms of wealth, the Romans altered the term slightly into *pecunia*, a word broad enough in meaning to include money as well as other riches, but which ultimately meant money in particular. From this was formed our adjective *pecuniary*, which we use to mean pertaining to money or wealth. The prefix *im-* "without" or "lacking," gives us *impecunious*, without or lacking wealth —or, in the older Roman meaning, pertaining to a person who has no cattle.

pedagog

In the Grecian family there was one slave, especially selected for his prudence, whose duty it was to attend the sons of the family during boyhood. One of these duties was to accompany his charges when they went upon the public roads, to and from the gymnasium, or elsewhere. From the nature of his duties such a slave was known, in Greek, as a *paidagogos*, literally a leader of boys, from *pais*, boy, and *agogos*, leader. Sometimes the *pedagog*, as the term became in English, was himself a man of high learning, unfortunate enough to have been captured in warfare and subsequently sold as a slave. In such instances he also served as a tutor to the boys of the family. It is from the latter that the term has come to signify a schoolteacher.

pedigree

This is a distorted spelling of the French words from which it is said to have originated, *pied de grue*. Some of the many English forms the word has taken since its introduction into the language in the early fifteenth century, were *pee de grew, petiegrew, pytagru, peti degree, pedicru*, to show just a few of them. The French phrase means "foot of a crane," and the reason for giving this peculiar name to the genealogical table that shows one's line of descent is explained thus:

Back in the Middle Ages, people were just as proud of their ancestry as many are today; in fact, numerous instances in the Bible, especially the First Book of Chronicles, show that such pride is very ancient. It exists among all races. But in England, the study of genealogy began to assume undue importance in the fourteenth century when, after the Norman Conquest, matters of inherited rights came into question. Scholars, usually monks, were employed to trace back the lines of descent claimed by noblemen, or to prove that some remote relative was the legitimate heir to an estate or title after all the direct descendants had died or been killed in battle. Hence, just as among scholars of our day certain signs or symbols have acquired particular significance—as the asterisk (*), the dagger (†), the double dagger (‡)—so did the genealogists of the Middle Ages also employ certain conventional significant symbols. Thus, it appears, the line of descent that one was engaged in tracing was marked by a symbol that was easy to make—a caret or inverted V having a straight line extending from slightly above the apex down through it to the base (λ). Some monk, probably, knowing the tracks that birds make in mud or snow, must have seen the resemblance between this symbol and the track made by a crane and, French being the court language, called it *pied de grue*. The name of the mark was retained, and, marking the lines of descent, the line itself came to be called *pied de grue*, eventually corrupted into the English spelling, *pedigree*, under the influence of the French pronunciation.

pen, pencil, penicillin

In spite of the fact that these names apply to writing instruments which, nowadays, look something alike, and despite the fact that the three letters of one form the first syllable of the other, the sources of the two words are unrelated. *Pen* is derived from the Latin *penna*, a quill, feather, because, until the invention of steel pens late in the eighteenth century—and long thereafter, until the quality was improved and the price cheapened—sharpened quills had been in use since about the eighth century A.D. As the point became dulled with use a new point could be made with a sharp knife; hence the term *penknife*. Before the unknown inventor discovered that a *penna*, or goose quill, could be sharpened for use, the chief writing implement had been the *calamus* or sharpened reed, dating back to classic Greek use.

The term *pencil*, however, was first employed by artists and referred especially to the finely sharpened brushes that they used. Its source was the Latin *peniculus*, meaning "a little tail," because painters' brushes were first made from hairs from the tails of oxen or horses. The name was borrowed for the lead pencil when the latter device was invented, about the middle of the sixteenth century A.D., probably because of the softness of the graphite that was first used in them and the resemblance thereby to the soft little brush of the artist. The medicinal drug, *penicillin*, was so named because the mold from which it was first obtained resembled numerous tiny brushes.

person

Greek and Roman actors almost invariably wore masks in every dramatic appearance. Such a mask covered the entire face and was made with highly exaggerated features so as to be readily distinguished by the remote spectator. Thus, an actor, donning the proper mask, could assume any character that the drama called for. In a Greek tragedy, for example, a pale mask with hollow cheeks and floating fair hair invariably denoted a sick young man, whereas if the hair were black, mixed with gray, and the mask were pale, the character would be recognized as a man of about forty who was suffering from sickness or wounds. The gods, who appeared in most tragedies, were each also represented by a particular mask. Every character could thus be recognized from the mask. Now the Roman name for "mask" was *persona*, and *persona* thus came to signify a particular character in a play. From that, *persona* came to mean the player who wore the mask, and eventually a human being. The old senses, along with the new, still prevailed when Old French *persone* was first brought into England and altered to the present *person*.

petticoat

The early *petticoat*, or "little coat," was worn by men. In fact, men continued to wear petticoats until the eighteenth century, although the garments were then usually called waistcoats. But the small coats worn by men of the fourteenth and fifteenth centuries were actually coats, not skirts, and were worn under the doublet.

phaeton

Helios, in Greek mythology, had charge of the chariot of the sun. It was his duty to drive it each day from the ocean of the farthest east across the heavens and to the ocean of the farthest west. (Thence, it was believed, Helios, his chariot, and the four horses that drew it were wafted in a golden boat during the night along the northern rim of the earth back to the east again.) Helios had a young son, it was said, whose name was Phaëton. The lad, as boys will, tremendously admired the shining chariot and the wonderfully speedy horses, and constantly begged the privilege of driving it. His pleas fell on deaf ears, until, finally, he persuaded his mother, Clymene, to add her petitions. Thus, one day, Helios yielded against his better judgment, and the young lad set forth proudly. But as the morning wore on young Phaëton's arms grew weary from the strain of controlling the four dashing steeds, and he became unable to keep them upon the straight course. The chariot was sometimes pulled high into the sky, when, exerting all his strength, the lad brought it back so close to the earth that the ground scorched. Zeus, watching the erratic course of the chariot through the sky, feared that both heaven and earth would be set afire. To stop it he drew a thunderbolt from his shaft and hurled it at the boy, whose lifeless body then fell into the Eridanus, a mythical river subsequently thought to be the Oder or the Vistula. His weeping sisters rushed to the spot, mourning his death. There the sympathetic gods transformed them into poplars, their tears into amber, a formation later found abundantly at the mouths of those two rivers. It was to this ancient legend that the British alluded in the sixteenth century when they called any reckless young driver dashing along the roads a *Phaeton*. The sound of the word was pleasing, so the name was transferred later to the vehicle which, drawn by two horses, became fashionable in the eighteenth century.

phantasmagoria

Today we have television. Before that we had motion pictures, or cinema. Earlier was the stereopticon, and before that the magic lantern. But in 1802 a man by the name of Philipstal introduced a device that was considered a great improvement upon the older magic lantern. In part the difference was that the figures to be projected, instead of being on transparent glass, were themselves painted in transparent colors, the rest of the glass slide opaque. Thus it was the image only that was projected upon the screen. Such slides were later adopted in all magic lanterns. But the chief feature of the new invention was the means that Philipstal devised for creating optical illusions. His screen, of thin silk, was mounted between the lantern and the spectators and could be moved imperceptibly forward or back. Thus the images appeared to advance or recede, and, by separate device, could be made to fade from one into another or disappear entirely. These are common illusions in the motion picture of today, but were then considered marvelous. Philipstal coined a mouth-filling name for his invention and named it *phantasmagoria*, probably devising it from the Greek *phantasma*, phantasm, and *agora*, assembly. We now apply his term to any dreamlike fancy in which figures fade or shift into others.

philopena (fillipeen)

How old the German custom might be, no one knows. It was probably brought to America in the early eighteenth century, but that is entirely a guess because the earliest written record is not until a century later. The custom was that if, in the eating of almonds, hazelnuts, or other like nut, one were to find twin kernels within the shell, the contents were shared—a lady sharing with a gentleman, a gentleman with a lady. The next time these two persons met, the one who was first to say, "*Guten Morgen, Vielliebchen* (Good morning, sweetheart)," would receive a present, perhaps previously agreed upon, from the other. American youth, ignorant of German but almost catching the pronunciation, appreciated the custom, especially if the reward were a kiss, but corrupted the German *Vielliebchen* into the sound *fillipeen*. But because that was not a known word, it was often altered in print to *philippine*. Both game and name have been varied, but the name is now usually written either *philopena* or *fillipeen*.

photography

Cameras and the production of pictures upon paper or glass had been made before the nineteenth century, but the first to produce permanent pictures by these means was Joseph Niepce of France, with the cooperation of his fellow countryman, Louis Daguerre. The process was first called *héliographie*, later dropped in favor of *daguerreotype* when the process was further improved. In January of 1839, however, an Englishman, W. H. Fox Talbot, described a further improvement made by him which he called *photogenic drawing*. This has been called the first of the processes for printing pictures. A few months later, in March of the same year, Sir John Herschel announced yet another advance in the rapidly expanding new field, and brought us the name that has now become standard, *photography*, which, it is supposed, he coined from the first element of Talbot's *photogenic* and the last element of Niepce's *héliographie*.

piano

Unknown to each other, several men were working simultaneously upon the same problem in the early years of the eighteenth century. The harpsichord had been developed two centuries earlier from the older clavichord, a distinct improvement; but the instrument, with its tones produced by the action of quills plucking the strings, was still too soft for concert work; it could be heard only in a small room, and composers were demanding a greater volume of sound. The first to reach the goal was Bartolomeo Christoforo, a maker of harpsichords in Florence, Italy. In 1709 he produced the instrument that he called *piano e forte*; that is, in Italian, "soft and loud," because the instrument, with hammers striking its strings, could be played with great volume or, by damping the strings, with the softest of tones. The name was promptly contracted to *pianoforte*, and this is still the correct name technically, though it is commonly further abridged to *piano*. England had its claimant for the invention in the person of Father Wood, who made a similar *pianoforte* in 1711. A German claimant, Christoph Gottlieb Schroter, delivered a differing device to the Elector of Saxony in 1717.

pompadour

Jeanne Antoinette Poisson was born in Paris in 1721 of poor parents, but was early taken into the home of a wealthy financier and educated as if she were his daughter. She was extremely beautiful and received every social advantage. At the age of twenty she married the nephew of her benefactor, Lenormant d'Etoiles, and became the queen of fashionable Paris. Three years after her marriage, however, she met the king of France, Louis XV. From that time until her death in 1764 her life was devoted to the king, who was equally attached to her. In 1745 he established her in the court of Versailles and, a few years later, bought for her the estate of Pompadour, giving her the title "Marquise," later "Duchesse" de Pompadour. She became a person of great power in the court, where she retained her leadership of Parisian fashion. Various innovations of style and costume were attributed to her. One in particular was a mode of hairdressing that she affected in which the hair was swept upward high above the forehead. That style, somewhat modified, is still known as *pompadour* after the famous mistress of Louis XV.

poplin

From 1309 to 1376 the papal see was located at Avignon in France. Clement V, pope from 1305 to 1314 never entered the Vatican in Rome. He was French, and so were the five popes who directly followed him. After Gregory XI transferred the seat of papal power again to Rome, Avignon continued in importance because first one and then a second antipope assumed the papacy and resided in the city until expelled in 1408. Avignon was also noted at that period for a certain textile fabric made by its weavers. Made with a silk warp and a weft of worsted yarn, it was in demand both as a dress material and for upholstery. Fabrics at that period were usually identified in some unmistakable manner with the place at which they were made. Thus, because Avignon, sold to the papacy in 1348, remained a papal town until 1791, the term *papeline*, papal, was applied to it. English merchants, attempting the French pronunciation, reduced the name of the material to *poplin*.

post, posthaste

Marco Polo is responsible for our use of *post* in connection with mail. It was after his return from his long sojourn in China in the thirteenth century, when he described the Great Khan's system for receiving and sending messages from and to all parts of his vast empire. Large stations, housing many horses and men, were placed at twenty-five-mile intervals along all the great roads, and messages were thus quickly relayed to their destinations. The system was not unknown in Europe; Augustus Caesar had such a system, and so had the Persian king, Darius the Great. But in describing the Khan's system, Polo used the term *poste* (from the Latin *positus*, placed) for the "station" at which each of the relays of men and horses were kept. Hence, when European traders established a similar system, in later centuries, for sending messages to and from their agents, Polo's term was adopted. In England, the station for men and horses became a *post*house; the rider, a *post*boy, and we still recall the speed of horse and rider in *posthaste*.

potato

Shortly after the West Indies were discovered, Spanish navigators must have learned of the plant, new to them, with its tuberous roots which the natives used as a food. But the first mention of these plants in European accounts appears to have been in 1526. The name, in Haiti, was *batata*, and it was under this name that the plant was first known in Europe. This plant, however, was what we now call the sweet potato. It was cultivated only as a curiosity for some time after its introduction into Europe; its edible qualities were viewed with suspicion. When the Spaniards reached Peru and began to explore its resources, they found another tuberous plant with white tubers which the natives of that region also ate. Although the local name appeared to be *papas*, the Spaniards took it to be another variety of the West Indian plant and called it *batata* also, though the two are unrelated. The latter plant, described in 1553, may have been brought to Spain before 1580, but that is the earliest recorded date. It was then independently cultivated in Italy, France, and in Germany before the end of the century. And, although the plant is not a native of Virginia and Sir Walter Raleigh was never in that colony, it was stated that Raleigh introduced the plant from Virginia into England in 1596. The early *batata* was corrupted in Spain to *patata* and was altered to *potato* when first described in England. They also called it the Virginia or common potato to distinguish it from the earlier sweet or Spanish potato. Except in Ireland, such cultivation as it had was as a food for cattle, rather than for human consumption. There, from early in the seventeenth century, it became so staple an article of food and was so largely cultivated that the common name of the white potato has become "Irish potato," or, humorously, "Murphy." The colloquial American name "spud" arises from the narrow, spadelike tool of that name used in digging potatoes.

precipitate, precipice

The Latin source of both is *præcipito* which, in early use, meant "to cast down or fall headlong," as if from a high place. It is from *præ*, before, and *caput*, head; hence, literally, "headforemost." The term was used many times by Roman writers when referring to criminals executed by being cast from the Tarpeian Rock in Rome, or to those who, by similar means, committed suicide, and *præcipitium* (English *precipice*) was applied to such a place or such a fall. Later writers extended the meaning of *præcipito* to have it mean "to rush headlong," as if down a steep grade, and thus *precipitate* has come to mean to take hasty action of some sort, action so hurried as to appear rash.

precocious

Were we to reserve this for its ancient Latin meaning, we would use it now instead of "precooked," for that was the original literal sense. It was derived from *præ*, before, and *coquo*, cook or boil. But *præcoquo* came early to mean "to ripen fully," and from that sense its participle, *præcoquus* or *præcox*, was applied to fruit "ripening before its time; prematurely." We continue to use *precocious* in this latter sense, but we also apply it especially to children who develop prematurely, either mentally or physically.

preposterous

When the Romans had occasion to express the notion that we have in mind when we use "putting the cart before the horse," they did it by the compound word *præposterus*. Freely translated, that means "the before coming after," from *præ*, before, and *posterus*, following. The exact meaning of our *preposterous* is, therefore, "inverted; in a reversed order"; but because things reversed or turned upside down are contrary to the natural order, *preposterous* has also taken the meaning "nonsensical, utterly absurd."

pretext

The principal outer garment of the Roman citizen, in olden days, was the toga. This outer cloak was variously marked to distinguish the rank of its wearer. That worn by various high magistrates, and by freeborn children until the age of puberty, was marked in front by a border of purple. It was known as a *toga prætexta*, or more commonly as *prætexta*, the name being derived from *præ*, before, and *texo*, weave. But, just as our word "cloak" has come to mean a cover or shield which conceals one's real purpose, so did the Romans use *prætexta* in precisely the same figurative sense. Hence, when in the form *pretext* the term came into English, it was the figurative meaning only that persisted.

prevaricator

If a cowboy had been seen in the streets of Rome in the days of Caesar it is likely that a spectator, seeing his bowed legs, would have called him a *prævaricator*. That is what the term meant—a bandy-legged person, a straddler with crooked legs, one who, because of his distorted legs, cannot walk in a straight line. The term was used especially in the Roman law courts where it was applied to a prosecutor who, though supposed to represent one party, made a secret agreement with the opposite party and betrayed his own client. He did not walk straight; he straddled the issue. It was, therefore, a false defense (or a false accusation) that was formerly meant by *prevarication*, and it was that type of crookedness and falsehood which marked a *prevaricator*.

procrastination

We have a saying, "Never put off till tomorrow what can be done today." The ancient Romans condensed such an action into a single word—*procrastinatio*. Its literal meaning is "a putting off to the morrow." It was formed by joining the preposition *pro*, for the benefit of, to the adverb *crastinus*, tomorrow.

Procrustean

According to Greek legend, there lived in the days of Theseus a highwayman named Procrustes who dwelt on the road toward

Eleusis. Travelers, it was said, seeing his house by the roadside, sometimes stopped to seek accommodation for the night. Procrustes never turned any away. But he had two beds, one a short one and the other quite long. If the traveler was tall, Procrustes showed him into the room having only the short bed, a short traveler saw only the long bed. But Procrustes always had a remedy. He chopped off the feet or legs of the tall guest or stretched the bones of the short one. In either case the traveler died, and the bandit stole his wealth. According to another account of the legend, Procrustes, who was also known as Damastes or Polypemon, used but one bed, but fitted his guests to that in the same manner. In either story the villain was eventually slain by Theseus. His method of fitting something by arbitrary methods to a condition which it does not meet is called *Procrustean*, often in the phrase, "*Procrustean* bed."

profane

In certain rites of the ancient religions of the Greeks and Romans none but men who were fully initiated into the mysteries were permitted to participate. Those sacred ceremonies and sacrifices, the objects of worship, and the traditions, with the interpretations of all of these, were disclosed only to those admitted into the body of the initiates. All others were, as the Romans put it, *profane*, that is, not admitted into the innermost secrets of the temple. The word is from Latin *pro*, which here means "outside," and *fanum*, temple. Such was also the original sense of *profane* when it was brought into English use, but it was applied particularly to persons or things not belonging to the Christian religion. Then, because of the contempt held by nonbelievers, *profane* came to be associated with irreverence and blasphemy.

Promethean

Among the traditions of the Greeks was one of an ancient hero whose name, Prometheus, signified "forethought," and his brother Epimetheus, whose name meant "afterthought." It was Prometheus who stole fire from Zeus and brought it to mortals, and who taught them in all the useful arts and sciences. It was Epimetheus who, against the advice of his wiser brother, became flattered by the charms of Pandora and prevailed upon her to open the box from which then escaped all the evils that have since plagued mankind. But the tradition chiefly relates the punishment inflicted by Zeus upon Prometheus for stealing the divine fire. He was caused to be chained to a rock upon the side of a mountain, and there, defenseless, he was attacked every day by a huge bird, an eagle or a vulture, which feasted upon his liver. Each night his wounds were healed, only to be subjected to the attack of the evil bird the following day. This continued until after eons of torture, Zeus relented and permitted Heracles to kill the bird and break the chains of Prometheus. Our adjective *Promethean* may thus be connected with recurring ills, reminiscent of the punishment of this mythical hero, or with any of the many skills and arts credited to his beneficence.

purple

Hundreds of years before the Christian Era the Phoenicians who dwelt along the coast of the Mediterranean Sea near Tyre discovered a curious shellfish attached to the adjacent rocks. This shellfish or mussel was found to yield a minute quantity of fluid which imparted a dark crimson color to cloth. It is said that the stain was first observed about the mouth of a dog which had crushed and eaten one of the mussels. The Greeks called this shellfish *porphyros*, because the color it yielded resembled the red volcanic rock, that we call porphyry, then quarried in Egypt. The name was altered to *purpura*, in Latin, further corrupted in English to *purple*. The dye that was thus discovered became greatly desired because of its scarcity. The mussels were found only along shores nearby Tyre, and there was but a tiny amount in each mussel. None but emperors or men of great wealth could afford "Tyrian *purple*," as it was called. The dye, used only in the finest cloths, became the distinguishing mark of the dress of emperors and kings. Thus, the expression, "born to the *purple*," still denotes a person of royal birth.

pygmy

Travelers in southern Egypt brought tales to ancient Greece of a fabulous race of dwarfs who lived along the upper Nile. These dwarfs, it was said, were so small that they were in constant battle with the cranes, constantly on guard against being seized and swallowed. Greek historians, at a loss for a name for such a dwarf, invented the descriptive name *pygmaios*. This was because the people were said to be no taller than the length of a man's arm from the elbow to the knuckles, and *pygme* was the term for that unit of length, the English ell. The form of the word was gradually altered to *pygmy* after its introduction into our language.

python

The oracle of Apollo at Delphi was the most celebrated of all the places in ancient Greece where the will of the gods was sought. But, by some traditions, this oracle had not always been sacred to Apollo. Its chasm, from which mysterious smoke arose, was believed to have first been an oracle of the goddess Gea and to have been guarded by a fearsome dragon known as *Python*. This dragon was said to have pursued Leto, mother of Apollo, when she arrived at Delos in search of a resting place to give birth to her son. Four days after his birth, the infant Apollo pursued the dragon and slew it in revenge, and thus acquired the oracle for himself. The large snake of India and Africa which we now call *python* received the name of this mythical monster only a hundred years ago, when zoologists determined that it was a separate genus of the family of boas.

quack

The duck makes the same sound regardless of the country she is in and, with her waddle, she reminds one always of a pompous person, strutting along, and eternally quack-quacking to himself. That is what the Dutch thought of the charlatans and mountebanks parading around through plague-ridden Europe in the sixteenth century, each proclaiming loudly the virtues of his salve or nostrum. Accordingly the Dutch named them *quacksalvers*, ducks quacking over their salves. Neighboring countries thought the term so apt that it was borrowed by Germany, Sweden, and England. The English, however, soon shortened it to *quack*, and applied it to any pretender of medical learning and skill.

Quaker

The members of the Society of Friends sometimes use the name *Quaker*, but have never officially adopted it. The term is said to have been first applied to the founder of the Society, George Fox, according to Fox himself, in 1650 by Justice Bennet of Derby. Fox was being arraigned before two justices in Derbyshire and was exhorting them to "tremble at the word of God." This Judge Bennet sarcastically interpreted as "quaking," and thus sneeringly referred to those who practiced it as *quakers*. The term was picked up as a humorous appellation for the new sect, although it was later the belief of many that the name had reference to some practices thought to be a result of the religion. Thus a writer in the late seventeenth century, referring to the Friends, said that they "do not now quake, and howl, and foam with their mouths, as they did formerly."

quarry

Hunting dogs of the Middle Ages were as well trained as those of today and held their prey at bay until the hunters had arrived for the kill. As a reward for this restraint it was the custom to give the dogs certain parts of the animal, which was usually a stag. These parts were placed on the skin of the animal, and it was this which gave the feast its name. "Skin," in Old French, was *cuiree*. This became *quirre* in Middle English and was ultimately converted into *quarry*. But that which had originally denoted the skin of the animal and then the part of the animal placed upon that skin as a reward to the dogs, became in turn the entire live animal which the dogs sought as their prey, and was then applied also to any animal or human chased by hunters. (The term *quarry* which designates an excavation for stone blocks is from the Latin *quadratus*, square.)

quisling

Perhaps the term will not survive; few other names of traitors to their country have become part of the language of their owner, let alone being adopted into our speech. But the circumstances that made *quisling* a synonym for "traitor," and *quisle* to mean "to betray one's

country," have warranted the inclusion of both terms into several recent English dictionaries. These were the circumstances: Vidkun
Abraham Quisling was born in Norway, July 18, 1887. He received a
military education and entered the Norwegian army in 1911, taking
the oath of allegiance both to country and king. Seven years later
he served as military attaché to his country's embassy at Leningrad,
and from 1919 to 1921 in the same capacity at Helsingfors. Through
promotions he was commissioned a major in the Norwegian army in
1931. But two years later, within four months after Adolf Hitler
became chancellor of Germany, Quisling organized a Fascist Party
in Norway, imitating the German organization of Hitler and becoming an ardent admirer of that leader. Hence, when word was
received in the winter of 1939-40 that the German army, already
having overrun most of western Europe in the first few months of
World War II, was contemplating an invasion of Norway, Quisling,
then on the retired list, and his small party of Fascists got themselves in readiness. The invasion surprised all Norway and Europe;
it occurred, partly by sea and partly by air, on the night of April 8-9,
1940. The government refused to yield to German demands for surrender, and ordered a full mobilization of its army. But Quisling
and his followers seized control of the Oslo radio station and coun-
termanded the orders. King Haakon and his loyal ministers fled
northward and eventually escaped by sea to England, where a
government-in-exile was set up. After the king's flight, Quisling
was named the head of government by the German commander, a
position that he occupied briefly. But in the following September
he was again given the title, and thereafter carried out all the orders
of his German overlords until the German military collapse in
April, 1945. Immediately, then, Quisling was placed under arrest by
orders of the legal government, charged with treason, murder, and
theft. The murder charge was based upon his responsibility for the
deaths of a thousand Jewish and a hundred other Norwegian civilians. He was convicted on all counts in September, 1945. The
verdict, a sentence of death, was the first of such extreme penalties
given by a Norwegian court in many years, for criminal execution
had long been abolished under the laws of the country. However,
the Supreme Court promptly upheld an act passed in October, 1941,
by the government-in-exile re-establishing that penalty for con-

victed traitors, and Quisling was shot by a firing squad at the Akershus fortress in the early hours of October 24, 1945. Because of the great contempt in which his actions were held by the peoples of all nations fighting against Germany, his name became a hateful byword applied, especially during the war, to anyone whose actions were traitorous.

quixotic

Cervantes, in writing his most famous work, *The History of Don Quixote*, in 1605, stated that its "fabulous extravagances" should be interpreted as "only an invective against the books of chivalry" which had been riotously produced in Spain. There is reason to doubt the sincerity of that statement, however, because the books he referred to had already been out of fashion for fifty years. But he created the characters of the decayed nobleman, Don Quixote, and of his stout serving-man, Sancho Panza, in burlesque imitation of the valiant knights and faithful squires of earlier writers. He made the elderly Don on his ignoble steed the very epitome of chivalry in its purest form, inspired by high ideals and filled with enthusiasm, but pitifully and ludicrously unaware of the false and visionary nature of his dreams. The book became immensely popular and, though Cervantes died in great poverty a dozen years later, it was translated into most of the languages of Europe. It added the word *quixotic* to our language, expressive of lofty but impractical sentiments resembling those of the foolishly romantic hero, Don Quixote.

quorum

The literal meaning of this Latin word is "of whom." But, like other of our words, such as "patter" and "omnibus," *quorum* was once part of a Latin phrase—in this instance, a legal phrase. Originally, that is, it was a custom, among English justices of the peace, to name one, or perhaps two or three, of especial knowledge or prudence and without whose presence the other justices would be unwilling or unable to proceed with the business of the court. Thus the wording of the commissions naming such a justice or justices, contained the Latin expression, "*quorum vos*, William Jones, (or *vestrum*, William Jones, John Smith, etc.) *unum* (*duos, tres,* etc.)

esse volumus, of whom we will that you, William Jones (or you, William Jones, John Smith, etc.), be one (two, three, etc.)." The abbreviation, *quorum,* was thus first applied to specified persons who were required to be present before a session could be opened, and it ultimately developed the meaning in which we now employ it, a prescribed number of the members of a group whose presence is necessary before business may be transacted.

raffle

Raffle was a game of chance in Chaucer's time, played with three dice. Every player in turn strove to throw a triplet, but if no one made that lucky cast, the winner was he who threw the highest pair. The game and its name were of French origin.

rake

The dissolute man whom we now speak of as a *rake* was said to be a *rakehell* four hundred years ago, and we still sometimes use the older word. The original term was cynical and figurative. It came from the thought that one would have to *rake hell* to find a person so vile as the dissolute scoundrel whose character was under consideration.

rapt, rapture

In its earliest use, *rapture* meant "an abduction," especially the forcible kidnaping of a woman. It was formed, in analogy with "capture," from *rapt,* at a time when *rapt* meant "abducted." The Latin source was *rapio,* to snatch, seize, which became *rape* in English, and the Latin participle *raptus,* seized, was shortened to *rapt.* The latter word, however, acquired a theological usage; it was applied to such personages as Elijah, Elisha, Enoch, and others who were said to have been *rapt*—that is, snatched—into heaven. From this theological use it acquired further extension into the senses now current, "carried into realms of emotion or deep thought." The course of *rapture* was similar, from "abduction" to "transportation into heaven," hence "mental or emotional transport."

recalcitrant (refractory)

Sometimes a stubborn horse or mule is content to let fly a few kicks without doing much damage, and let it go at that, but at other times he does not stop until he has broken up the cart to which he is hitched or has injured the driver. On the first occasion the animal is most fittingly described as *recalcitrant*, which literally means "kicking back," from Latin *re*, back, and *calcitro* (from *calx*, heel), to kick. He may, of course, do damage. A *refractory* animal or person, however, if the word is taken literally, is not content with being obstinate or stubborn; he breaks something. The word, from Latin *refractarius*, is derived from *refringo*, to break up.

record

In the days when few could read and fewer still could write, *record* was used in its literal sense, "to get by heart; fix in the memory." Its remote Latin source was *re*, back, and *cor*, heart, thus denoting that anything back in the heart was fixed in the memory. The more immediate Latin was the verb *recordor*. With the increase of knowledge of reading and writing, things that theretofore had been repeated from memory or fixed in the mind through repetition were reduced to writing, and *record* thus took on its present meanings.

reefer (peajacket)

Midshipmen, in the sailing vessels of a century ago, were often familiarly called "reefers," because, to quote an authority of that period, "they have to attend in the tops during the operation of taking in reefs." That duty, especially in cold weather, would prevent the midshipman from wearing the long topcoat of an officer, but as the midshipman was next in line to the lowest commissioned officer it was beneath his dignity to wear a sailor's peajacket. Accordingly he wore a close-fitting, heavy woolen coat. It was properly described as a "reefing jacket," but, because worn by a "reefer," it too was dubbed a *reefer*, and this became the common term for the garment of similar cut adopted by landlubbers. The "peajacket" of the sailor, incidentally, took its name, not from the garden vegetable, but from the Dutch word for "woolen," *pij*, identical with "pea" in sound.

remora

This strange fish, which attaches itself to moving objects by a curious sucking-disk along the top of its head, was known to ancient

Roman navigators. The fish would attach itself to the bottoms or sides of their slow-moving sailing vessels, and it was believed that they acted as a drag to the vessel, holding it back or even stopping its progress. It was for that reason that the Romans gave it the name *remora*, which means that which holds back, a delayer.

remorse

Our own language once contained an exact synonym of this—*ayenbite*, "again bite." There was a fourteenth-century English book under the title, *Ayenbite of Inwit*, literally, "Again-bite of Inner Wit," but which we would understand better if translated, "Remorse of Conscience." *Remorse* came to us, through French, from the Latin *remordeo*, and its literal meaning was exactly that of Old English *ayenbite*, "to bite again." Its use, however, was generally figurative, expressive of the inner bitings of one's mind, just as we use it now.

requiem

To many persons this term merely denotes a dirge played or sung at a funeral service. Its source, however, is found in the opening word of the solemn mass sung, in Latin, in Roman Catholic churches for the repose of the dead. The first line is, *Requiem æternam dona eis, Domine* (Give eternal rest to them, O Lord), in which *requiem* means "rest."

retaliate

This, in its Latin form, *retalio*, might be said to have been the equivalent of the English response, "And the same to you!" after an uncomplimentary remark. The source was *re*, back, and *talis*, such. *Retalio* thus meant "to give tit for tat, to return like for like." In legal usage it meant "to inflict punishment similar and equal to the injury that had been sustained." When introduced into the English language in the seventeenth century as *retaliate*, a new meaning was added, "to return good for good." That meaning is still recorded, but in general the verb has returned to the Latin sense.

reynard (renard, bruin, chanticleer, monkey)

Some time—probably in the tenth century, but that is not certain—
there began to develop in France or Flanders a series of stories about
animals. They were somewhat like the Uncle Remus stories of our
present age, but the chief character was a fox, instead of a rabbit.
The name given to the fox was *Renard* or *Renart*, in Old French,
usually altered to *Reynard* in English. The tales became exceedingly
popular and traveled by word of mouth all over western Europe,
translated into the common speech of all races. Probably gifted
story-tellers added new episodes to the narrative, for it became
eventually a lengthy epic and the versions of one country did not
wholly agree in detail with those of others. This folk tale dealt
chiefly with the adventures of "Reynard the Fox" and the sly tricks
that he played on separate occasions upon the other beasts. Like
the fox, each of the beasts had its nickname. Several of the names
thus bestowed became so familiar that they have since become
synonymous names for the animals to whom they were applied.
Thus our word *bruin* came from the tale which concerned "Bruin
the Bear," *chanticleer* from "Chanticleer the Cock," and of course,
reynard from "Reynard the Fox." Other names were "Noble the
Lion," "Tybert (or Tibert) the Cat," "Isengrim the Wolf," "Ky-
ward the Hare," etc. Our word *monkey* may also have originated
in this epic, but that is not certain. It does not occur in the first
printed English version, published by Caxton in 1481, but it does
appear in a Low-German version of the same period in which the son
of "Martin the Ape" is called *Moneke*. A similar version may already
have been known in England, because the epic was familiar long
before Caxton's time, or it may be that *moneke* was carried to England by German showmen. The ultimate sources of these nicknames
is not known; they may have been inventions of the unknown "Uncle
Remus" of a thousand years ago.

rhubarb

The plant was known to the ancient Greeks, and it was they
who named it. The general theory explaining its source is that the
plant was native to the regions along the river Volga, then known
as the Rha. This, of course, was territory foreign to the Greeks,

and was therefore classed as "barbarian." The plant, then, was described as *rha barbaron*, "from the barbarian (foreign) Rha." Its later Latin name was *rhabarbarum*, which, by elision, corruption, and partial restoration, passed into English *rubarbe* and, with Greek characteristics partly restored, *rhubarb*.

rigmarole

The reason is not known, but back in the fourteenth century a list or roll of names was called a *rageman*. Later this was altered to *ragman*, and the list itself was generally called *ragman roll*. Perhaps because, like in a dictionary, the subject matter in a list or roll changes frequently, *ragman roll* became equivalent to a series of disconnected statements. In the process its own name became altered, by the eighteenth century, to *rigmarole*.

rival

The Latin *rivalis*, whence our *rival*, referred to one who lives on the same stream with another—it came from *rivus*, a brook. That would make any such two persons neighbors, of course. But the ancients had many things in common with men of today. Two people who share the same stream are inevitably at odds. Each wishes to use the water in his own way, and is constantly contending with the other. If one uses the stream for irrigation, the other has no water for his cattle. In such fashion, *rival* came to mean one who contends with another for the same object.

road (raid, inroad)

In the early days of the English language, *road* meant the act of riding, a journey upon a horse. The horseback journey itself was made upon a "highway," if upon the principal way between two cities, or upon a "way," if a lesser path were used. At that time *road* had a sinister meaning also. Because of the fact that a group of mounted men often betokened a hostile intent, *road* sometimes signified a foray by mounted men, an attack upon some person or district. The Scottish word *raid*, which Sir Walter Scott brought into English usage, is now often used to convey that meaning, and the old sense is still present in our word *inroad*. In reality *road* and *raid* are merely different spellings of the Old English *rad*, but the Scottish

development went no further than the hostile foray. Through association of ideas, probably, the act of riding a horse was carried over
to the act of riding the waves; hence, *road* also came to mean a
place where ships may anchor with safety, a roadstead. This sense,
wherein space and security were implied, seems to have affected
the development of *road* into its present chief use, a public thorough-
fare. Strangely enough, this use which is now so common to us, was
unknown much before the time of Shakespeare.

roam

It is traditional that *roam* was derived from *Rome*, and that it referred
originally to the roundabout course taken by English pilgrims of the
Middle Ages to that holy city. Language experts through the past
hundred years, however, have searched for proof of that tradition
and have been unable to find it. All that can thus far be said is,
"source doubtful." The tradition is strengthened, however, by the
fact that other countries, from which pilgrimages were also made
to Rome, had similar words. Thus, in France, *romier* meant a pilgrim
to Rome; in Spain, *romero*, a wanderer; in Italy, *romeo*, a wayfarer,
wanderer.

robe

Some notion of the extreme poverty of the common people of
Europe in the Middle Ages may be obtained from a treatise written
by Sir John Fortescue. Though written (in Latin) in the latter
part of the fifteenth century, his description would have served
equally well in the preceding three or four hundred years. He says,
in part, to quote from a translation made in the following century,
that the French common people

be so impoverishid and distroyyd, that they may unneth lyve [barely
live]. Thay drink water, thay eate apples, with bred right brown made
of rye. Thay eate no fleshe, but if it be a litill larde, or of the entrails or
heds of bests sclayne for the nobles and merchants of the land. They
weryn no wollyn, but if it be a pore cote under their uttermost garment,
made of grete convass, and cal it a frok. Their hosyn be of like canvas,
and passen not their knee, wherfor they be gartrid and their thyghs
bare. Their wifs and children gone bare fote.

Under conditions such as these the common people, little better than beasts, were reduced to treachery, thievery, and every sort of rascality. Footpads abounded. The readiest victims were wayfarers, especially such as traveled with few or no servants in inclement weather. The servants were usually dispersed easily by a gang of footpads, and it took but a quick hand to throw the traveler's cloak over his head and thus blindfold him. Lucky the traveler who was able to slip out of his cloak, or cape, and take to his heels (see ESCAPE). But the victim's cloak was almost as greatly prized as his purse, for it provided protection and warmth. It was through this latter association—of the cloak with the robber—that the cloak came to be called a *robe*, the thing "robbed."

rostrum

In this word we commemorate an event in Roman history dating back to 338 B.C. It happened off the coast of Antium, a spot of Italy that will again be long remembered under its present historic name, Anzio. The inhabitants of the region in those days had long been guilty of acts of piracy against Roman traders and of direct acts of aggression against the Roman people. It was determined, therefore to suppress them conclusively, and the consul, Mænius, was sent against them. He was wholly victorious, and brought back with him to Rome the bronze prows or beaks of six of the ships that he captured. These prows were attached to a platform, previously erected in the Forum, which was used by orators. That platform then became known as *rostra*, or "the beaks." The singular, *rostrum*, has become preferred in English use, although the plural, *rostra*, is historically correct.

rubber

The material which we call rubber was not known in Europe before the voyages of Columbus. The first probable mention occurs in the account written by that discoverer after his second trip, in which he tells of the "bouncing balls" with which the people of Haiti amuse themselves. But, although the Spaniards of the seventeenth century attempted to use the gummy substance to produce a water-proof canvas, no really satisfactory use had been found for "elastic gum," as it was then called, until near the end of the eighteenth century. The chemist, Joseph Priestley, then found that it possessed one useful quality—it did serve as an extremely satisfactory medium for rubbing out pencil marks. Because of that quality, the name "elastic gum" was dropped and the material has been called *rubber*, or *India rubber*, ever since.

sabotage

Nobody knows just when the French began to use the word *sabotage*. Probably it was formed a number of years ago when children found to their delight that, clattering together in their clumsy wooden sabots, they could drive their teachers or their parents to distraction. At least, in some such manner, *sabotage* came to signify any kind of nuisance that might or would bring about a desired end. But in 1887 it acquired a more sinister meaning. In that year the French General Confederation of Labor adopted *sabotage* as an instrument of industrial warfare. It was to include any kind of malicious damage that would injure an employer in any way—the disablement of machinery by dropping sand in its bearings, the destruction of tools, destruction of belting, spoilage of raw material—anything at all that was calculated to force an employer to yield to a demand by labor. The term came into English use by journalists in describing a long and disastrous strike upon the railway lines of France, at which time all the principles of *sabotage* were put into practice.

sacrament

All Roman soldiers, at the beginning of any military campaign, took an oath of allegiance. The usual method was that one soldier in each legion was called forward by its tribune and asked if he would swear that he would obey the commands of his generals and execute them promptly, that he would not desert, and that, in battle, he would not leave the ranks except to save the life of a Roman citizen. After that oath was taken, each of the other soldiers, in answering to his name, then said, "*Idem in me* (The same for me)." This oath was termed *sacramentum*, literally, an action of sacred nature. Its violation by any soldier was sufficient cause for the general to order his death without trial. The term was also used in courts of law, applying to the sum of money deposited by the contestants of a suit. But perhaps because of the formal nature attending the ceremony of *sacramentum*, the term was taken by Christian writers of the third and later centuries to be the equivalent of the Greek *mysterion*, a term originally applied to the secret rites attending the worship of Greek gods, but in Christian use applied to the rites connected with Christian worship. The term *sacrament* continues to apply to those rites observed in Roman Catholic and Protestant churches, whereas *mystery* is the term for similar rites in the Greek Orthodox Church. (Compare MYSTERY.)

sacrifice

Among most early religions based upon the worship of supernatural beings, the thought persisted that evil might be averted or some purpose achieved if something treasured were offered in exchange. The greater the treasure or the more it was cherished, it was thought, the greater the chance that the desired end might be obtained. When the religions became formalized, as they did in Egypt, Greece, and Rome, it was customary for the priests to indicate the treasure that would be most acceptable to the god for the particular occasion. Usually the offering was something that might be eaten, such as fruit, cakes, or farm animals, which were thought to be pleasing to the gods. When the offering had been determined, the person offering it first washed his hands and then, with clean hands to avoid pollution, carried or led it to the temple. Then, if the priest found the offering to be without blemish, for only such things were acceptable, it was declared sacred. Such an offering thus became, in Latin, *sacrificium*, literally, a thing made sacred, from *sacer*, sacred, and *facio*, make. The term, which became *sacrifice* in English, although chiefly retaining a religious sense, has also become loosely used for a surrender of anything that is valued, with or without a gain that may offset the loss.

sacrilege

Because it was the custom in ancient Rome to offer cakes, or fruits, or even pots of cooked beans upon the altars of the gods as tokens of gratitude, there was an always present temptation before the poor people of the city to steal and eat of these when no priest was in sight, or to conceal them in their clothing and make off with them.

Or if an animal had been offered up in sacrifice, bits of its charred flesh might sometimes be found clinging to a bone. But whatever the temptation to steal these or any other of the things that had been consecrated to the gods, the penalty exacted of any who were caught in such a crime was expected to deter all but the most daring or the most desperate. Such theft was called *sacrilegium*, literally, from *sacer*, sacred, and *lego*, to pick, the picking up of a sacred thing. If committed by a member of the lower classes, the penalty was always death. The victim might then be thrown to the wild beasts of the circus, or crucified, or burned alive as a public spectacle. Or under certain conditions his life might be permitted to drag out a few years longer by work in the mines. If the criminal were a person of higher class, he was deported. In later times, as recorded by Cicero, *sacrilege*, to use the English form, embraced not only the crime of stealing sacred objects, but also the act of profaning anything held sacred.

salary

The ancients knew that of all the things required for the support of human life salt was the most essential. The Romans called this element *sal*, and whenever the Roman soldier was sent to a foreign land he was given, over and above his regular pay, an amount of money for the purchase of salt. This was called his *salarium*, salt money. The amount varied, because salt might be hard to get and expensive in one country, but cheap and plentiful in another. Later, after the days of Augustus, *salarium* denoted the sum of money which a military officer or a governor of a province or a like official received at intervals, in addition to various supplies in kind. And still later, by the end of the third century A.D., all connection with the original notion of salt money had passed away and *salarium*, or *salary*, carried no more than the present meaning, "monetary payment at stated intervals."

saltcellar

This container for salt has nothing in common with the cellar of a house, except its spelling. And the spelling is a mistake. It should be, and originally was, *saler*. If we returned to that spelling, however, it would be redundant to leave *salt* in front of it, because *saler* itself denoted a saltcellar. The old word, used in the fourteenth and fifteenth centuries in England, was derived from the Latin adjective *salarius*, "pertaining to salt." The early English container was commonly of pewter, but was made of gold or silver for noble or wealthy persons. In the houses of the great, the position of the *saler* on the table separated the honored guests from those unhonored. Those whom the host honored, he placed "above the salt," or toward the end that he graced. All others sat "below the salt."

salver

Poison was the favored medium for getting rid of one's enemies in olden times, and was especially popular in the Middle Ages. Placed in the wine cup or the food, the victim had it swallowed before its presence was detected, and cook or servitor could be bribed to put the poison into the plate or cup. The real murderer might thus remain undetected—perhaps a near relative or, ostensibly, a friend. Because of the constant danger, wealthy men or men of high position kept a servant standing by his place at table whose duty it was to drink of the goblet and partake of the meat before his master touched them. After a due interval, if the servant were not taken sick, the master thought it safe for him to drink and eat. The Spanish term for such precautionary measures—for such attempted murders were especially frequent in Spain—was *salva*, derived from the Latin *salvo*, to save, protect. Then, eventually, because the master's food was invariably served and tested upon a separate tray, the term *salva* included the tray, as well as the victuals to be tasted. Under stricter laws, the need for this protection subsided. The tray, however, continued to retain the name. In England, perhaps in analogy with "platter" from "plate," or from resemblance to "silver," of which the tray was usually composed, *salva* was altered to *salver*. (See also CREDENCE.)

sandwich

For the entire duration of the American Revolution, or until March of 1782, the first lord of the British admiralty was John Montague, 4th Earl of Sandwich. He was exceedingly unpopular, and the period of his tenure of office was notorious for graft, bribery, and general mismanagement. The personal life of the Earl was also corrupt. Although married, he kept as his mistress a Miss Margaret or Marth Reay, by whom he had four children. (She was murdered by a rejected suitor in 1779.) And he was an inveterate gambler. It was in his honor, because he was first lord of the admiralty at the time of their discovery, that the Hawaiian Islands were first called and long known as the Sandwich Islands. But the misdemeanors of the Earl have now been forgotten and he is remembered only for his introduction of the convenient quick lunch composed of two slices of bread with a slice of meat or other filling between them. It is said that this repast, called a *sandwich* in his honor, was devised at his direction during an exciting all-night session at cards when he did not wish to leave the gaming table for a full meal. But, unfortunately, no record has been found of the date of the occasion. The sandwich cannot be said to have been invented by the Earl, however, because the Romans had a similar slight repast, called *offula*, many centuries before his time.

sarcasm

The Greeks loved metaphor. They loved to compare human emotions and human tendencies with the actions or traits exhibited by animals. And, because dogs were ever at hand for purposes of comparison, the ways of the dog served as convenient and well-understood metaphor. Thus they took the word *sarkazo* and gave it a figurative meaning. Literally it meant "to tear flesh" after the manner of dogs, to snap and rip. The physical effect upon the animal or person thus attacked by a fierce dog was so similar to the mental effect resulting from a sharp and stinging taunt or gibe that *sarkazo* seemed perfectly fitted to the latter meaning also. The caustic remark became *sarkasmos*. Altered by Latin *sarcasmus*, this ultimately became English *sarcasm*.

sarcophagus

Generally the ancient Greeks disposed of their dead very much as do we of the present age, either by burial or by cremation. But there were some who adopted a burial custom found in Egypt. In place of the ordinary coffin of baked clay or the elaborately carved stone tomb, a stone coffin was procured from a special region in Asia Minor. The stone of that region was almost pure lime and, according to Pliny, a coffin made of it had the power to completely destroy a body interred in it within forty days. Because of its properties, such a coffin was called *sarcophagus*, the name being derived from Greek *sarx*, flesh, and *phagos*, eating.

sardonic, sardonyx

There grew on the island of Sardinia, according to ancient Grecian folklore, a plant that was to be shunned above all others. It had a fearful effect upon anyone so unfortunate as to eat it. The mouth and face became horribly drawn up as if in scornful laughter. The victim was fortunate if he did not die. Because the Greek name of Sardinia was Sardo, this appearance of laughter was called *Sardonios gelos*, Sardinian laughter. This then led to the transfer of *Sardonios* to any laughter that was scornful or mocking, and, hence, to any scorn or mockery. The Greek *Sardonios* was first altered in English to *Sardonian*, but French development had led to *sardonique* which, altered to *sardonic* in English, eventually replaced the earlier form. The name of the semiprecious stone, *sardonyx*, bears only an accidental resemblance. Its name is really composed of the two elements, *sard* and *onyx*, because the stone itself consists of layers of onyx alternating with layers of sard.

Saturday

Egyptian astronomers believed that there were only seven planets and that these all revolved about the earth. From the most remote they were successively Saturn, Jupiter, Mars, the Sun, Venus, Mercury, and the Moon, using our present names. These planets were held to preside in the same order over the twenty-four hours of the day, and the day of the week was accordingly named after the name of the planet which presided over its first hour. As Saturday (the day of Saturn) began the Egyptian week, its first hour and each successive seventh hour—the eighth, fifteenth, and twenty-second hour, respectively—was presided over by the planet Saturn. The twenty-third hour was then governed by Jupiter, and the twenty-fourth by Mars. The first hour of the next day was therefore presided over by the Sun, the next in order, and the second day of the Egyptian week received the name of that planet. In the same manner of reckoning, the Moon presided over the third day, Mars over the fourth, Mercury over the fifth, Jupiter over the sixth, and Venus over the seventh, when Saturn again took over the first hour of the beginning of the next week. Although the Egyptians regarded the week as beginning with the day of Saturn, the Hebrews regarded that day as the last day of the week, because, it is said, of their hatred toward their Egyptian oppressors when they fled from the country. The week of seven days was not adopted in Rome until the reign of Constantine, A.D. 324-37. For lack of a better system of nomenclature, probably, the days continued to be named after the planets, following the ancient pagan Egyptian system, though with Saturday (*dies Saturni*, the day of Saturn) as the seventh day. Teutonic mythology did not embrace a god equivalent to the Roman god, Saturn, god of harvests, after whom the planet was named, so, in Old English, a partial translation of the Latin *dies Saturni* became *Sæternesdæg*, which has descended through many shifts into our present *Saturday*.

savage

Most plants and animals growing or living in forested country are wild. For this reason the Romans spoke of all such things as *silvaticus*. The term was really equivalent to our word "sylvan," of or pertaining to forests, being derived from *silva*, forest, but was transferred to mean the plants and animals found in such places, especially the animals. Thus *silvaticus* acquired the meaning, "wild." The popular sound of the word was *salvaticus*, and this, through the general alteration of Latin words occurring in France, became *salvage* in Old French and *sauvage* in later French, in which form it was carried to England. Gradual change brought it to the present form, *savage*, and its use to apply especially to persons or animals thought originally to dwell in forests, hence of ferocious nature.

scapegoat

And he (Aaron) shall take the two goats, and present them before the Lord . . . And Aaron shall cast lots upon the two goats; one lot for the Lord, and the other lot for the *scapegoat*. And Aaron shall bring the goat upon which the Lord's lot fell, and offer him for a sin offering. But the goat, on which the lot fell to be the *scapegoat*, shall be presented alive before the Lord, to make an atonement with him, and to let him go for a *scapegoat* into the wilderness . . . And Aaron shall lay both his hands upon the head of the live goat, and confess over him all the iniquities of the children of Israel, and all their transgressions in all their sins, putting them upon the head of the goat, and shall send him away by the hand of a fit man into the wilderness.

The quotation is from the sixteenth chapter of Leviticus, in the King James Version of the Bible. Thus, *scapegoat* entered the language and has become applied to one chosen arbitrarily or at random to receive the punishment merited by a group.

scavenger

It was the custom in London and some of the other cities of England, during the late Middle Ages especially, to inspect the wares and collect a fee or toll from foreign merchants who might exhibit their wares for sale. The Old English law called such a toll a *sceawung*, "showing," but after the Norman invasion the Anglo-French form *scawage*, later *scavage*, was adopted. The man authorized by the city officials to collect these tolls was, of course, a *scavager*, which later became modern *scavenger*. (Similar alterations are found in "messenger" from "message," "passenger" from "passage," "porringer" from "porridge," etc.) But the duties of the scavenger as inspector and collector of tariffs in the early days could not have occupied his full time, because as early as the fifteenth century we find that he was also expected to keep the streets clean. This latter duty the *scavenger* has retained, even though his original office, showing the source of the name, has long been abolished.

scepter

The *skeptron* of the Homeric period of Greece was a walking-stick, a cane or staff for the aged or infirm. But such a staff was also carried by foot travelers as a weapon of defense, or perhaps of offense. Either as cane or weapon, however, it received ornamentation and embellishment, and was handed down from father to son in token of transfer of authority. It became enriched with gold or silver studs, and perhaps adorned with gems for persons of high rank or leadership. In time this simple staff, transformed into a jeweled rod of gold and known to us as *scepter*, became a symbol of the authority of the leader of an empire, a monarch.

school

The Greek *scholē* which was the original source of *school*, once meant just the opposite from what the schoolboy of today thinks of that institution. It meant vacation, leisure, rest. The education of a Greek boy was by private teachers in reading, writing, arithmetic, singing, and gymnastics. But no man ever considered his education to be completed. His leisure time was spent in listening to the discussions of learned men, and thus this product of leisure, this use of one's spare time came also to be called *scholē*. Eventually the Greeks used the term for the lectures or discussions themselves, and ultimately it included as well the place wherein the instruction was given. It was the latter sense which descended to English use.

schooner

Captain Andrew Robinson, of Gloucester, Massachusetts, is credited with being the builder of the first vessel of this type. It was completed in 1713, according to evidence, and attracted a good deal of notice. Its launching was attended with much interest. When the blocks were knocked away and the vessel slid gracefully into the water, an excited bystander, according to the story often told, is said to have exclaimed, "Oh, how she *scoons!*" Captain Robinson overheard the remark and, not having decided what to call the new type of vessel, spoke up and said, "A *scooner* let her be." The subsequent spelling, *schooner*, was probably due to the influence of "school." The source of the bystander's *scoon* may have been the Scottish word *scon*, "to make flat stones skip over the water."

scot-free

In olden times, although the source is uncertain, a *scot* was the amount that one owed for entertainment, usually the amount of one's share in that entertainment, as for the drinks in a tavern. *Scot-free* thus described one whose debt was assumed by others or whose drink was "on the house." From that beginning, the meaning of *scot-free* came to be freedom from other kinds of payment, as taxes or tolls, and from that it became extended to freedom from punishment.

scruple

Anyone whose shoe has worn thin enough for a nail to press through into the foot can have some sympathy for the sufferings constantly threatening the old Romans. They were not troubled with nails coming through the soles of their sandals, but there was every likelihood of picking up a sharp pebble—and no stocking even to protect the tender foot. The word for such a pebble or pointed bit of stone was *scrupulus*, from which our *scruple* developed. It is easy to see how the uneasiness one would feel from a pebble in the sandal gave rise to the figurative use of *scrupulus* for an uneasiness of the mind. The small apothecaries' weight, *scruple*, came from the same Latin source. And our adjective, *scrupulous*, which denotes extreme caution and carefulness, suggests the care that the old Romans would take in traversing a road described as *scrupulosus*, "full of tiny sharp pebbles."

senate

In the republics of Greece and Rome the government was divided between the popular assembly and a group of men selected for their wisdom. But because it was considered that full wisdom came only with advanced years, all members of the latter group were persons of advanced age, old men. For this reason the Roman group was *senatus*, a council of old men, from *senex*, old. Thus, to be literal, a member of our own *senate* should be an old man, an age set by our Constitution, however, as not less than thirty.

Septuagint

There were really seventy-two of these men, according to the story, although the Latin *septuaginta* means "seventy" only. The story was supposed to have been told by a man of Cyprus, Aristeas by name, in a letter to his brother Philocrates, some time during the reign of Ptolemy II, 285 to 247 B.C. It relates that the king had been requested to have a copy of the laws of the Jews translated into Greek. The king agreed, and the chief priest of the Jews was asked to appoint six learned men from each of the twelve tribes to perform the task. These seventy-two men were lodged in a house on the island of Pharos, the letter went on to say, and there they completed their difficult task within the space of seventy-two days. Modern scholars do not wholly accept this story. They agree, however, that the Jewish laws were translated into Greek in Alexandria and at the time stated, but do not believe that it was done at the request of Ptolemy. Nor by seventy-two men in seventy-two days. They think it more likely that the translation was made solely for the benefit of the Greek-speaking Jews who lived in Alexandria. The remainder of the Old Testament was later translated. Nevertheless, this earliest Greek version of the Old Testament, traditionally ascribed to seventy-two (or, in round numbers, seventy) Jewish scholars, has become known as the Septuagint, often expressed by the Roman numeral, "LXX."

shagreen (chagrin)

The skill of the metal workers of Damascus and Arabia was gradually acquired by European artisans after the Crusades. Along with that skill the new workmen also copied many of the practices which the Orientals had learned through long centuries of experience. Thus it had long been known that nothing was better for rubbing and polishing fine metal than the hard and rough leather from the rump of a horse or ass. The Arabian term for such leather was *saghri*. Both the practice and the name were borrowed by Europeans, but to the Venetian worker it became *sahgrin*. The French, taking it from the Venetians, called it *chagrin*. Some English workers may then have retained the French spelling, but the majority, influenced by the sound of the French word, called and spelled it *shagreen*. The leather that we now know by this name may derive from any one of several land or marine animals. It is generally dyed green, probably after the color the old-time leather assumed after long use in polishing gold, silver, or copper. The French term, *chagrin*, also acquired a later figurative meaning, and was borrowed in this sense by the English. Because of the rough surface of the leather, which gently abraded the metal, *chagrin* came to be applied to cares and worries which fret the mind. From this our present sense arose, a feeling of disappointment, vexation, or humiliation which frets the spirit.

shambles

In its earliest sense in our language a *shamble*, although then spelled *scomul*, meant a stool. (By a roundabout course it had come from the Latin *scamellum*, a little bench.) From stool, *shamble* became the name of the bench, table, or stall where meat was sold. Then, although after the fifteenth century always spelled in plural form, through the constant association of *shambles* with the blood of meat, the meaning was extended to cover the place where animals were slaughtered for meat. From this its meaning was further extended figuratively to any place of bloody slaughter, especially a place of widespread carnage, such as a battlefield. But, because battles are usually accompanied by wholesale destruction, the word *shambles* acquired a still further figurative sense in World War II, when it was often used to designate the scenes of destruction brought about by the bombing of cities. In the latter application blood or bloodshed is no longer essentially attached to the word, as it was for many centuries.

shibboleth

This Hebrew word actually means "ear of grain" but, because of the odd use to which the word was put on one occasion, it has taken on an altogether different meaning. This meaning arises from a bit of history told in the Bible, in the twelfth chapter of the Book of Judges. It is related, in this chapter, how the men of Ephraim rose against Jephthah and his army, but the latter were victorious in the fight that followed. In their victory they seized the passages over the river Jordan where the fleeing Ephraimites must cross to save their lives. But Jephthah had posted guards at the fords and had given them a catchword by which they could tell friend from foe. That word was *shibboleth*. Jephthah knew that an Ephraimite "could not frame to pronounce it right," but would say, "Sibboleth." All the Ephraimites were thus detected and slain, to the number of "forty and two thousand." Hence, *shibboleth*, regardless of its original meaning, has come to refer to any catchword or slogan or pet phrase, such as one used by a political party.

shrapnel

The inventor, for whom this missile was named, was Henry Shrapnel. He was born in Wiltshire, England, in 1761, entered the army when a young man, and began the study of hollow projectiles as a young officer of twenty-three. He was a colonel, however, before the most notable invention resulting from his studies was accepted by the army. The official name of the invention at the time of its adoption was "*Shrapnel's* shot" or "*Shrapnel's* shell," and it was not long before *Shrapnel* had become the customary abridgment. The first actual test of the new shell in combat came in 1803 when the British seized a portion of Surinam from the Dutch and established British Guiana. In the Peninsular War of 1808 to 1814, in which England fought against Napoleon to free Portugal and Spain from French domination, the *shrapnel* was proved to have high military value. The inventor died in 1842, and had then attained the rank of lieutenant general.

shrew, shrewd

Many centuries ago in Old England the name *shrew* (Old English *screawa*) was applied to a common small animal about the size and appearance of a mouse, though having a long sharp snout. The source of the name is unknown. The animals, living chiefly in the woods and feeding upon insects, grubs, and the like, were not destructive, and for some peculiar reason the name by which they were once known dropped into disuse for five or six hundred years. But the little animals had one characteristic and were thought to possess another which seem to have caused their name to be used in another manner. They were found to be exceedingly pugnacious. Two would fight over a morsel of food until one was killed; the fallen would then be eaten by the victor. They were also thought to be venomous, and, in popular superstition, if one were to run over the leg or body of a farm animal, that animal was then believed to be poisoned. It might be cured if a live shrew were imprisoned in a hole bored into an ash tree, and then twigs of that ash gently brushed over the affected parts of the animal. Because of the pugnacity and suspected venomosity, the term *shrew* was transferred to either a man or woman whose character was evil or malignant, especially to one, usually a woman (now always a woman), whose disposition was to nag, scold, or rail. This led to the formation of the verb *to shrew*. Its past participle was *shrewd*, and this, in its early sense, meant evil-disposed, vicious, dangerous, but has passed into sharp or acute, or into astute or keen-witted.

silhouette

France was ill prepared when, at the outbreak of the Seven Years' War in 1756, Louis XV plunged his government into the conflict. Under the domination of his mistress, Madame de Pompadour, the government had become completely corrupt and on the verge of bankruptcy. Both Canada and India, partly French possessions at the time, speedily fell to the British through lack of competent generals and adequate support. In 1759, hoping for a miracle, Madame de Pompadour induced the king to replace the French minister of finance with a man of her own choice, a man of fifty who had made a small name for himself by the publication of studies on governmental finance. His name was Étienne de Silhouette. Immediately upon assuming office the new minister imposed systems calling for the most rigorous economy. These appeared to be directed especially against the nobility, whose members found the restrictions placed upon them extremely irritating. They might endure the conversion of their table plate into currency, but they poked fun at regulations calling for coats without folds and snuffboxes made of wood. At this time, by chance, there had also been revived the ancient art of profile drawing; that is, drawings made by tracing the outlines of shadows cast by a light—an art said to have been invented by the daughter of Dibutades, in ancient Corinth, who traced the outline of her lover's face as thrown in shadow on the wall. The revival became popular. But, because they replaced costly painted portraits, these drawings too, along with the snuffboxes, the coats, and other petty economies, were sneeringly referred to as "*à la Silhouette*, according to Silhouette." Through popular clamor, perhaps also because of incompetence, Étienne de Silhouette was obliged to relinquish his post after nine months. His name, however, had become permanently attached to the profiles which are so easily drawn.

simony

In the eighth chapter of Acts in the New Testament, we are told of the conversion of a magician to Christianity by the Apostles. That is, the magician professed to be converted, but it soon turned out that he was not. He had himself been skilled, and was able to perform marvelous tricks. Hence, when he saw the miraculous cures effected by Peter and Philip simply through the laying on of hands, he thought it to be a new kind of sorcery, one that he could use to advantage. So he sought out the Apostles and offered them money to teach him these tricks. "But Peter said unto him, Thy money perish with thee, because thou hast thought that the gift of God may be purchased with money." The name of this sorcerer was Simon—sometimes referred to as "Simon *Magus*," that is, "Simon the magician." From his name and the sin that he committed, the purchase or sale of ecclesiastical position is now described by the word *simony*.

sincere

It has been often said that *sincere* came from two Latin words *sine*, without, and *cera*, wax. This fanciful source was explained as arising from the alleged practice by Roman artisans of using wax for filling cracks or holes in furniture, whence *sine cera* would mean "without flaw; pure; clean." Modern scholars, however, do not accept that dubious account. The present belief is that the Latin *sincerus*, which became *sincere* in English, came from *sine*, without, and some lost word that was akin to *caries*, decay. It would thus be synonymous with the Greek *akeratos*, without taint.

sinecure

This began as a church term, part of the Latin phrase *beneficium sine cura*, a benefice without care (of souls). It was a practice of the Church of England, developing in the seventeenth century, upon occasion to reward a deserving rector by alloting to him a parish in which he did not reside and for whose parishioners he had no responsibility. Such a benefice was highly desirable, for it entailed no work in return for the good living that it brought. The actual work of the parish was performed by a vicar, though his absent superior got the better pay. The ecclesiastical practice was abolished in 1840, but the expression—at first *sine-cura*, eventually *sinecure*—had long since become a term for any office or position which the incumbent might fill with a minimum of labor, or none at all, in return for a fixed income.

sinister

Roman augurs, when studying the heavens for signs which, it was believed, would indicate the will of the gods, faced toward the south. The eastern heavens from which favorable omens were expected, were therefore upon the left; unfavorable omens in the west or toward the right. Thus among the Romans, *sinister*, which means left or left-hand, meant lucky, favorable, or auspicious, and *dexter*, which means right or right-hand, meant unlucky or inauspicious. But Greek augurs faced the north when looking for signs from the heavens. The eastern or favorable omens, accordingly, appeared on the right side, and the unfavorable ones upon the left. Roman poets, who almost invariably aped Greek customs, followed the Greek thought in this field as well. Hence, because the writings of the Roman poets were popular in the literary world of England in the sixteenth and seventeenth centuries, *sinister*, although a Latin word, has come down to us in the sense ascribed by the Greek augurs to the left or western side of the heavens; hence, of evil aspect.

siren

When Odysseus was nearing the end of his long homeward journey after the Trojan War, according to Homer, he was told one evening by the sorceress Circe of some of the perils that yet awaited him. The first would be the sweet-voiced sea nymphs, the *Sirens*. These, she told him sang the most beguiling songs of all the world. But woe betide any passing sailor who heard them. In his enchantment he would leap into the sea to join the nymphs, and nevermore see his home and loved ones again. Circe counseled Odysseus to seal the ears of all his companions with wax before passing that shore, and have himself bound most securely to the mast, his men warned to tie him even more tightly if he signaled them to unbind him. Thus

Odysseus and his crew safely passed this danger, but it is because of the dulcet lure anciently thought to have come from the throats of those beautiful nymphs that the name *siren* has been applied to various warning signals of penetrating tone.

sirloin

The story is told of various British monarchs. Henry VIII was the first to receive credit. That would be some time between 1509 and 1547, although he did not receive the credit until 1655. Next, in 1732, Jonathan Swift bestowed the credit upon James I, who reigned from 1603 to 1625. The last to be credited, in 1822, was Charles II, ruler between 1660 and 1685. In each tale the monarch was supposed to have been so delighted with the quality of a roasted upper portion of a loin of beef, upon some special occasion, that he drew out his sword, touched the beef with it, and said, "Hereafter thou shalt be dubbed 'Sir Loin.'" Aside from the profusion of "dubbers," the only trouble with the tale is that it is utterly fictitious. The only story in the word is that some time about 1600 it began to be misspelled. For many years this cut of meat had been known as *surloin*, which, from *sur*, over or above, meant nothing more than the cut over the loin. This correct spelling persisted, but after the foregoing stories began to be taken seriously, everyone began to shift to *sirloin*.

size (assize)

Here we have a word passing through a great shift in meaning. The parent word, which became *assize*, was borrowed from France after the Norman Conquest and meant "a sitting," as of a legislative body or court, a meaning that it still retains. *Assize* also began to embrace the regulations established at such sittings, specifically those relating to weights and measures and, thus, to quantity and dimension. In all these senses, however, the word *assize* was taken by many people, especially by those untrained in law, to be merely "*a size*." And because it was the common people who were most affected by quantity and dimensions, *size* became the common term for all standards of measurement or specified quantities and, ultimately, for dimensions or magnitude of any sort.

skeptic (sceptic)

Schools of philosophy in ancient Greece were almost as plentiful as the philosophers. Thus, in the third century B.C., came the philosopher Pyrrho who carried some of the earlier theories a stage further and thereby provided a new name for his followers. His thesis, in the main, was that human judgment is liable to uncertainty, for no one can be absolutely certain that that which seems to be is exactly what it seems. This thesis he extended into ten topics of argument, as recorded by one of his disciples. His followers came to be called the *skeptikoi*, the hesitants, or philosophers who would assert nothing positively, but only thought. Through later extensions of this philosophy, *skeptic* reached its present senses.

slave

Prior to the Christian Era little was known of the people living north of the Carpathian Mountains, in the vast regions now embracing, in particular, Poland and adjacent areas. The names of a few tribes had been mentioned by some Roman and Greek historians, but few travelers or even military expeditions had penetrated those lands. By the sixth century A.D., however, the northern tribes along the Baltic began pressing to the west against their more warlike neighbors, the Germans, along the banks of the Elbe. The Germans called them *Sclavs*. In the inevitable conflicts that followed, the fierce Germans found these people no match for their arms and were able to take many captives. Some were sold into serfdom to willing Roman and Greek buyers of the south, and others were held in bondage by their captors. In time the entire population of parts of their land were reduced to servility by their Teutonic neighbors, and *Sclav* or *Sclave* became a term of contempt applied to anyone of servile character or actually in bondage. Later it became a synonym for the latter condition only. When it came into English use, the term retained the initial *scl-* until the sixteenth century, then our present form, *slave*, began to appear.

smog

London has been troubled throughout its history by occasional blankets of fog, so dense that traffic becomes dangerous. The condition is aggravated, especially during the heating season, by the vast volumes of black smoke rising from the soft coal used by householders and industries and in public buildings. The result is almost total darkness at those times. Many other cities suffer from similar combinations of smoke and fog, although possibly none to the same extent as London. In 1905, according to the London *Globe* in its issue of July 27 of that year, "at a meeting of the Public Health Congress Dr. Des Voeux did a public service in coining a new word for the London fog, which was referred to as *smog*, a compound of 'smoke' and 'fog.'" Adoption of this portmanteau word has been slow, although it is recognized in all the dictionaries.

snob

No one knows the origin. It may be related to an Old Norse word that means "dolt," but in the late eighteenth century *snob* was a British slang term for a shoemaker. Students at Cambridge took up the term and applied it somewhat more broadly to any townsman, to one not attending the university. Perhaps some Cambridge citizens, to impress their acquaintances, began to ape the speech and mannerisms of students or lecturers at the university. It is not known. But for some such cause, *snob* became applied to one who affects to be what he is not, in birth, wealth, or breeding, or to one who seeks unduly the society of persons possessing those qualities.

sock

The professional comedian of ancient Rome, he who acted in comedy, took every precaution when he stepped upon the stage to have no one mistake him for other than a comic actor. Of course he wore the grinning mask which, by its hair or beard, complexion or wrinkles, or other well-known markings would indicate whether the character he was portraying was old or young, sick or well. (See PERSON.) But in addition he wore upon his feet a pair of loose leather slippers, slippers of a type that, in Rome, were worn only by women or by effeminate men. These were in sharp distinction from the *cothurnus*, worn by actors in tragedy, which laced high up the calf of the leg. The soft, low slipper—*soccus*, it was called—of comedy was shaped somewhat like the modern pump, but loosely covered little more than the toes and heel. These light shoes were the forerunners of our *socks*. Romans carried the name *soccus* to Germany, whence, abridged to *soc*, it traveled to England. There, even until recent times, the name—*sock*, by that time—still meant a light slipper. But, many years ago, *sock* also came to be applied to any soft covering for the foot, worn inside of a boot or shoe. Neither hose nor stocking then covered the foot, for these were coverings for the leg. Eventually foot and leg covering were attached, and *sock* then became the term for a short stocking, extending to the calf of the leg.

solecism

There was anciently a colony in the province of Cilicia, Asia Minor, known as Soli. The colony had been settled by Grecians, and the inhabitants thought they spoke Greek. But the ears of fastidious Athenians were greatly offended by the barbarous, uncouth speech of these outlanders. Words were mispronounced; speech was slurred, but most prominent were the terrific mistakes in grammar. To the Athenian, such speech was an unpardonable offense. He called it *soloikismos*, the speech of *Soli*; hence, incorrectness. Through the Latin, this has become *solecism* in English.

soldier, solidus

It may be that the members of the far-flung legions of the Roman Empire sometimes wearied of waiting for their pay. That may have been the reason, we do not know; but at some time during the first or second century A.D., they began to refer to the *aurum,* the gold coin used in paying them, as "solid," perhaps because it was better than promises. The term they used, of course, was *solidus*, and this term was later generally employed when speaking of military pay. The *solidus* was a fractional part of the silver pound, *libra*, and was further divided into other fractional coins called *denarii*. (These names were subsequently adopted for British currency, thus giving rise to the initials, £, *s*, *d*, now referred to as pound, shilling, pence.) Among members of the Roman military outposts, where Latin was mingled with native speech, *solidus* became corrupted in France to *solde* or *soude* or similar variant, and the person who received military pay became a *soldior* or *soudiour* or the like. The name had many other spellings when it passed into English, but ultimately became *soldier*.

spinnaker

The facts are not ascertainable. Apparently no one kept a record. But from such evidence as there is it would appear that some yacht owner in the 1860's devised a new sail for his racing vessel. It was rigged at right angles from the vessel's side and extended from the masthead to the deck, ballooning far out to get full advantage of all the breeze. The name of the vessel carrying this unusual sail is said to have been *Sphinx*. Its crew had great difficulty in pronouncing that name. "Spinnicks," was as near as they could make it. They spoke of the new great sail devised for this yacht as "Spinnicker's sail," and, so the story goes, *spinnaker* the name became.

spoonerism

The Reverend William A. Spooner of New College, Oxford, England, who was born in 1844 and died in 1930, was one of many of us who, when speaking, accidentally transpose the initial sounds of two or more words, sometimes to one's own great embarrassment and the hilarity of one's audience. Such slips are usually the result of nervousness, sometimes from too great an effort on the part of a speaker to say a difficult combination of words correctly. Such transposition of letters or sounds is known in rhetoric as "metathesis." To their horror, radio announcers have been known to make some that were extremely amusing to their listeners. But the Reverend Mr. Spooner constantly made these unintentional transpositions. Thus, upon one occasion, when he intended to say that something was "a half-formed wish," he convulsed his listeners with "a half-warmed fish." Upon another he was heard to refer to "our queer old dean," when he meant to say, "our dear old queen." He is said to have chided a student who had "hissed my mystery lecture." But perhaps the most notable of his numerous slips was the hymn that he announced: "When Kinkering Congs Their Titles Take." From his affliction, this type of metathesis is now often called *spoonerism*.

spruce

Anything from Prussia or native to that region was said to be *Pruce*, in England of the Middle Ages. Thus there was "Pruce beer" from the "Pruce tree," and "Pruce leather," and the country itself was

"Pruceland." Gradually, through the fourteenth and later centuries, *Pruce* absorbed an initial "s" and became *Spruce*. This in turn was applied to the products of Prussia—or "Sprucia," as it was now sometimes called. There was then "Spruce beer" from the "Spruce tree," "Spruce leather," and so on. Then, during the sixteenth century especially, men of fashion began to ape, in their dress, the manners of particular countries. Thus in the reign of Henry VIII and for some time thereafter it was the style for courtiers to affect the garb of the nobles of Prussia, in doublets of crimson velvet, cloaks of satin, silver chains hanging from the neck, large, broad-brimmed hats with flowing feathers, and other fanciful attire. Men thus gaily and smartly appareled were said to be *spruce*.

staple

The term that now means the chief commodity of a place, once had a quite different meaning. The German word *stapol*, which had once meant a post or pillar, developed into the English word *staple* which came to mean a U-shaped pin or rod to be driven into a post or pillar or the like as a fastener. We still attach such a meaning to the word. But through another line of development the German term came also to designate a place, specifically the place where the judgment of a king was administered. Thence, borrowed by the French in the form *estaple* (modern *étape*), its meaning was altered to specify a market place, emporium. By the thirteenth or fourteenth century, the French *estaple*, transformed to *staple* in English, especially designated a town appointed by the king in which the merchants had a monopoly on the purchase of certain goods for export. Thus, for example, as long as the port of Calais was an English possession, that is from about 1390 to 1558, that city was the *staple* for the export of all English wool. Its merchants had the exclusive right to purchase wool for export. Other important cities enjoyed similar privileges. Gradually the meaning of *staple* underwent reversal. From the place where certain wares could be bought, it came to have the present meaning of the chief wares to be found at a certain place.

steelyard

Royal permission was granted, in the thirteenth century, to merchants of Hamburg, Lübeck, and Cologne to set up a trading association, a hanse or branch of the Hanseatic League, in the city of London. These merchants took a place of business near London Bridge on the north bank of the Thames, and designated it, *Stalhof*. The name merely signifies a "courtyard" (*Hof*) in which a "sample" (*Stal*) may be inspected or tested. Suspended in the courtyard there was one of the old-style Roman balances for the weighing of goods, a balance with a short arm or beam from which an object is hung at the end, and its weight determined from a counterpoise slid along the opposite and much longer beam. But the German *Stal*, sample, has exactly the same sound as the German *Stahl*, steel, and the latter word was much more familiar to Londoners. Hence, *Stalhof* began to be translated, "Steel yard," as if the German name were "*Stahl-hof*," and this locality was long known thereafter as "Steel yard." At the same time it became customary to refer to the old Roman balance in the courtyard as the "*Steel-yard* beam," a name shortened later to *steelyard*.

stentorian

Among the Greeks at the siege of Troy, as recorded in Homer's *Iliad*, was a herald named *Stentor*. Homer described him as having "a voice of bronze" and with a cry "as loud as the cry of fifty men." His name passed into a Greek saying, "to shout louder than *Stentor*," whence *stentorian* became an English synonym for "extremely loud-voiced." Greek legend says that *Stentor* died, however, as the result of a vocal contest with Hermes, herald of the gods.

stigma

Greek slaves, on the whole, were treated leniently. But they were usually captives taken as a result of warfare, and it was but natural that escape was eagerly sought. If they did not succeed, however, they were returned to their owners and, to make further attempts to escape more difficult, they were branded upon the forehead, usually by a hot iron, but sometimes with a tattooed mark. Such brand or mark was called *stigma*, a word borrowed by the Romans for a similar mark. The Greeks used the letter "phi" (ϕ), initial of *pheutikos*, fugitive; the Roman mark was the letter "F," which might designate either *fur*, for a slave branded as a "thief," or *fugitivus*, for a "fugitive." Sometimes a black coloring substance was put in the wound to make the mark more prominent. In Rome, a person so marked was said to be *literatus*, that is, "lettered," a term that later designated a person well educated. From the practice of branding slaves the meaning of *stigma* extended to embrace any mark or sign of shame or disgrace.

stoic

About three centuries before Christ, the Greek philosopher Zeno founded a new sect. Various principles were expounded by the founder, but the supreme duty of the wise man, he maintained, was complete and serene submission to divine will. The doctrines were taught by Zeno in the corridor on the north side of the market place in Athens, a place usually referred to as *Stoa Poikile*, "the Painted Porch," from the frescoes representing scenes of the Trojan War which adorned it. (See also INK.) Consequently, from the place where lectures on the new philosophy were given—the "Stoa"—the followers of this school became known as *Stoics*. And through the fact that the most notable of the doctrines was that true wisdom is superior to passion, joy, or grief, both *stoic* and *stoicism* came to be regarded as indifference to feelings of pleasure and pain.

succinct

The Roman tunic, like the Greek chiton, was a simple garment worn by all classes of people. In its early form it was a wide woolen sheet, folded across the body and pinned over one shoulder, sometimes with a hole on the opposite side for the other arm. This garment was thus sleeveless and entirely open down one side. A girdle or *cinctura* just below the chest held it in place, however. But the later tunic was made very much like a long shirt, and usually with short sleeves. It extended just above the knees, and was also kept in place by a *cinctura*. For freedom of movement, it was common practice to loosen the garment above the *cinctura*, thus having a fold of the tunic over the girdle. And for still greater freedom, as when one was at work, the tunic was shortened still more, tucked still higher under the girdle. Thus from the two words *sub*, under, and *cingo*, to gird, was developed *succingo*, to tuck up; hence, to shorten. The participle, *succinctus*, shortened, produced our adjective, *succinct*.

supercilious

Actually the Latin source, *supercilium*, means the eyebrow, from *super*, above, and *cilium*, eyelid. But the haughty man who looks contemptuously at those whom he regards as inferiors, inevitably looks at them with his eyebrows raised. The old Romans were aware of this characteristic lifting of the brows in expression of scorn, and even with them *superciliosus* denoted an air of disdain.

superman

The German philosopher of the nineteenth century, F. W. Nietzsche, used the German term, *übermensch*, to describe his notion of the ideal man evolved from the present type. This, by literal translation, would produce the English "overman" or perhaps "beyondman," but neither of these terms seemed agreeable to the ear of George Bernard Shaw when, in 1903, he sought to extend the earlier philosophy. Hence, using the Latin prefix for "over," he coined *superman*, when writing his work, *Man and Superman.*

surplice

The age of this liturgical vestment is not precisely known, but it dates at least from the eleventh century. At that time and probably earlier, but certainly for a number of centuries after, lack of heat in the churches necessitated that the clergy wear warm garments as a protection from the cold dampness of those stone buildings. Hence it was the custom to wear a robe of fur. But this necessitated an overgarment of white. Its name is therefore derived from its function —*surplice*, corrupted through Old French from the Latin *super*, over, and *pellicia*, fur garment.

sybarite

In the eighth century B.C., some people from Thessaly in central Greece crossed the Ionian Sea and established a colony on the shores of the Gulf of Tarantum in southern Italy. They named the colony Sybaris. The land was found to be very fertile and it was not long before the city that sprang up became large and prosperous, with citizens from all quarters. But its opulence proved to be the undoing of the colony; its people turned toward greater and greater luxury and effeminacy. Thus its name became a byword among the Greeks, a *Sybarite* denoting any person given over to luxurious living or sensuality, a meaning retained to the present day. The life of Sybaris was short, however. Its inhabitants became so soft and pleasure loving that, when attacked by the army of the nearby city of Crotona in 510 B.C., the city fell an easy prey. Its enemies razed the city to the ground and diverted the river Crathis to engulf the ruins.

sycophant

Various attempts have been made to explain the original intent of this word. Its source is the Greek *sykophantes*, which came from the two words, *sykon*, a fig, and *phaino*, to show. Because the Greeks themselves used *sykophantes* to mean "an informer," the general supposition is that the early "one who shows figs" was one who informed against persons who were attempting to export figs from Attica. A person against whom such an accusation was made was subject to a stiff penalty. The Greeks also used *sykophantes* to mean "a false accuser," so it is probable that many a false accusation was made against an unpopular person. English usage originally followed the Greek sense, "an informer," after the term was introduced into the language in the sixteenth century, but the object of the informer was soon inverted. From being a person who bore tales against a person in high position, it came to designate one who bore tales to that person and otherwise fawned upon him.

sylph

The great German alchemist of the early sixteenth century, best known under his assumed name, Paracelsus, collected a vast amount of information and made many important contributions to medical and chemical knowledge. The science of the times, however, compelled him to sail some uncharted seas, and we might today laugh at some of his theories. Thus the title of one of his writings is *Liber de Nymphis, Sylphis, Pygmæis, et Salamandris et Cæteris Spiritibus* (Book concerning Nymphs, Sylphs, Pygmies, and Salamanders and Other Spirits). His intent was to account for and describe the four elements of the alchemists, water, air, earth, and fire. The *nymphs*, in his system, were the spirits of water (later disciples called them *Undines*); *sylphs* were spirits of the air; *pygmies* (later called *gnomes*) were spirits of the earth, and *salamanders* were spirits of fire. The term *sylph* was coined by Paracelsus. He regarded these elemental spirits of the air as being in all respects like man, though able to move with greater agility and speed, and having bodies more diaphanous than man. Probably through the influence of Pope's *Rape of the Lock*, in which the term appeared, the concept of *sylph* became altered to apply only to a girl or woman of graceful form and movement.

symposium

Greeks of old did not customarily drink with their meals. Instead, after a dinner was finished, the host and his guests—and perhaps some guests who had not attended the dinner—were served wine to the extent that might be desired. This drinking party was called *symposion* (taken into Latin as *symposium*), derived from *syn*, together, and *poton*, drink. These occasions, enjoyed by men only, were accompanied by music, dancing, games, or other amusements, or sometimes merely by agreeable conversation. It is through the latter diversion that, nowadays, we regard a *symposium* as a discussion by several persons upon a given topic, often in writing. But drink, although the essence of the original word, is no longer necessarily an accompanying feature.

tabloid

In 1884 a British manufacturer of medical and pharmacal supplies, Messrs. Burroughs, Wellcome & Co., registered a trade-mark for a name that the Company applied to certain of its products. These were, generally, chemical drugs compressed into tablets. The name which the Company had devised was *Tabloid*, a name which, by process of registry, was then legally restricted to the preparations made by that firm. But the Company succeeded better than it had supposed in acquainting the public with its trade-mark. *Tabloid*, instead of denoting only the compressed tablets of Messrs. Burroughs, Wellcome & Co., came to be applied to various things other than drugs which appeared to be compressed or concentrated. The Company made many efforts in the law courts of both England and America to stop other use of the term, but is now protected only to the extent that the name may not be legally applied to products which interfere with its trade rights.

talent

In the biblical parable of the man who, before going on an extensive journey, left certain amounts of money with three of the servants whom he wished to test, the amount in each instance is referred to as *talents*. The source of the word is the Greek *talanton* which, like the English word "pound," was used both as the name of a weight and as the name of an amount of silver of that weight. The weight varied among different peoples and at different times, so it cannot be determined how great was the value of the talent in the biblical story. If it were the Roman talent, the value might have been no more than $500 of our money; if the Attic talent, about $1,200, but if the Babylonian talent, the equivalent value might have been $2,000. The point of the parable, however, lies in the passage that the amount received by each servant was allotted "according to his several ability." Consequently the theologians of the later Middle Ages began to give *talent* a figurative meaning, to use it as if it meant "natural ability." The figurative usage became predominant, and has so extended that the original ancient sense, "a weight," is forgotten.

tally

For a number of centuries the British Exchequer kept its accounts by a system that now seems fantastic. A stick of willow or hazel, about one inch square and twelve inches long, represented each transaction, the nature of which was written on two opposite faces of the stick. The sum of money involved, as, for example, a loan to the royal crown, was indicated by notches cut across the other two faces, the character, size, and depth of the cuts accurately representing the amount of the transaction in pounds, shillings, and pence. After the account was thus marked by characteristic notches, the stick was then split in half lengthwise across the cuts, each half thus having the entire series of notches. One half was given as a form of receipt to the person making the loan and the other was retained by the Exchequer. Each party thus had a record of the transaction. The stick was called a *tally*—*talea* being the Latin for "stick." The system was completely abandoned in 1826 and the great accumulation of the wooden tallies was then used as fuel for the stoves in the houses of Parliament. In October of 1834 so much of this dried wood was piled into the stoves that they became overheated, thus setting fire to and burning down the houses of Parliament.

tantalize

One story accounting for the severe punishment administered to Tantalus was that he had stolen nectar and ambrosia from the table of the gods to give to his friends. Another was that, receiving a golden dog, stolen by someone else from the temple to Zeus, he later denied that he had received the dog. And another was that, seeking to test the wisdom of the gods, he had cut his own son Pelops into pieces, boiled them, and served them to the gods with their meal. The crime was discovered, however, and Pelops was restored to life. But the most popular account was that Tantalus, a great favorite of the gods, betrayed some confidences which Zeus had entrusted to him. Whatever the crime he was punished by being placed in the lower world in the midst of a lake with clusters of fruit hanging over his head. Whenever he stooped to drink of the lake, however, the waters receded, and whenever he stretched up his hand for the fruit, the branches drew away. Thus, though water and fruit were apparently plentiful to relieve thirst and hunger, he was forever in torment by the withdrawal of that which he desired. *Tantalize*, formed from his name, commemorates the nature of his punishment.

tarantula, tarantism, tarantella (St. Vitus's dance)

Along about 708 B.C., a body of Greeks from Sparta moved across the Adriatic Sea and established a colony on a favorable spot upon a seacoast in southern Italy. Under the ancient name, *Tarentum*, the colony prospered, vying briefly with Rome for greatness in the third century B.C. The present city, its name altered to Taranto, is now an important naval base. But the region about ancient Tarentum harbored a species of fearsome-looking, hairy spiders capable of inflicting a painful, if not dangerous, bite. This spider, from the place of its discovery, was called *tarantula*. Sometime during the Middle Ages, a strange disease broke out in various parts of Europe. It manifested itself by a twitching or jerking of the limbs of the person afflicted, and was accompanied by an almost uncontrollable impulse to dance. In Italy, the superstition grew that the disease was caused by the bite of the tarantula. From that erroneous belief, the disease became known as *tarantism*, though it is now called "chorea," from Greek *choreia*, dance. Through the spread of the epidemic, accompanied by a form of hysteria, and perhaps religious mania, a dancing mania seized much of Europe, recorded in Germany first in 1374. In southern Italy the dance, if done in rapid measure, was thought to be beneficial to victims of the disease and, by the fifteenth century or earlier, such a dance had been developed and standardized. It, too, was named from the supposed source of the disease—*tarantella*. Children afflicted with tarantism were taught, in olden days, to offer up their prayers to the child martyr, Saint Vitus. This young saint, martyred under Diocletian in the fourth century, was firmly believed to be able to cure them. It is for that reason that chorea among children, especially, is still called "Saint Vitus's dance."

tariff

Some books that may still be in circulation account for this word in an interesting fashion. The story is plausible, but unfortunately is not true. It runs thus: For many centuries the Moors had strongholds on either side of the Strait of Gibraltar. Thus their vessels were able to intercept all merchant craft sailing into or out of the Mediterranean and exact tribute. On the European side, the Moorish pirates had their quarters in a town nestling at the foot of the Rock of Gibraltar, the name of which was Tarifa. That much of the story is true. There was such a Moorish town, named in the eighth century from the Moorish invader, Tarif, and the Moors did use it for piratical raids until the end of the thirteenth century. But, although our word *tariff* is Arabian in source, it was not derived from the name of the Moorish village, Tarifa, as the story concludes. The real source is humdrum by comparison. The Arabic term for "inventory" is *ta'rif*. This became *tarifa* in Spanish and *tariffe* in French, from which it became English *tariff*.

tartar

Chief among the Mongols ruled over by Genghis Khan were the people known as Ta-ta Mongols. Through their warlike qualities they had extended his dominions, before his death in 1227, to embrace all China, had successfully invaded northern India and Persia, and had crossed the Caucasus Mountains, penetrating as far westward as the Volga and Dnieper rivers. But it was under the successors of "the Great Khan" that these fierce warriors left their memory upon European countries for all time. Known as *Tartars* (later more correctly spelled *Tatars*), these bloodthirsty hordes of the thirteenth century swept as far westward as Poland and Hungary, and into Palestine to the south. They massacred all who opposed, leaving smoking ruins behind them. (See also HORDE.) From their early name *tartar* became synonymous with "savage," and is still applied to any person of violent temper, or, if to a woman, to one who is notably shrewish.

tattoo

Various military and naval expressions made their way into our language through the long contacts in past centuries of English soldiers and sailors with Hollanders, either as their foes, fighting on Dutch soil, or as their allies. One expression in particular became well known. It was that used by Dutch tavern keepers when the bugler or drummer sounded the nightly call for all to return to their quarters. The tavern keepers said, "*Tap toe*," meaning, "The tap (or bar) is to (or closed)." To the English soldier that sounded like *tattoo*. Hence, from the cause of its utterance, the term was adopted and transferred to the signal itself. (The term *tattoo* as applied to patterns marking the skin, is entirely unconnected with the foregoing word. It was adapted from the Polynesian name for the practice, *tatau*.)

tawdry

The story of this word takes us back to an Anglian princess of the seventh century. In early records her name appears as either Etheldreda or Æthelthreda, but in Norman times it was altered to Audrey. Her father, it is said, had married her to a neighboring king against her wishes, and she fled from him to the Isle of Ely in the river Ouse.

a few miles north of Cambridge, England. Here, after purchasing the
island, she established a religious house, of which she became abbess,
and here, in 679, she died and was buried. Some sixty years later,
the Venerable Bede wrote of her in his *Ecclesiastical History*, and
said that her death had been caused by a growth in her throat, which,
according to the abbess herself, was in punishment for a vain fond-
ness in her youth for wearing golden chains and jewels about her
neck.

The monastery continued to grow after her death, becoming,
many years later, the Cathedral of Ely. A town grew up around it,
and it then became the custom to hold annual fairs upon the day,
October 17, sacred to the memory of St. Audrey. "Trifling objects,"
as they were called in old records, were sold at this fair. Especially
treasured were those that in some way commemorated the foundress
of the establishment. Naturally enough, among the most popular
of the souvenirs was a golden chain or band of lace to be worn by
women about the neck; and this trinket became yet more popular
when, sometime in the sixteenth century, a noted preacher drew
attention to the custom and repeated the story told by the Venerable
Bede of St. Audrey's vanity.

Thereafter, everyone who went to the fair at Ely was beset by
the cry of hucksters: "St. Audrey's lace; St. Audrey's lace!" And as
the quality of the chain or lace began to become less through the
years, so did the cry of the merchants become less distinct. "Saint
Audrey's lace" became "Sin t'Audrey lace," and by the time it had
become "*Tawdry* lace," the necklace might retain its charm no
longer than until its wearer reached home. By association of ideas,
other objects of gaudy ornamentation and inferior quality have
since been described as *tawdry*. (Compare LACE and NECKLACE.)

tea

If it were not for the Dutch, it is not likely that we would have had
tea. Instead we might have had *cha*, which is another name for the
same thing. The leaf was first brought to Europe in the sixteenth
century by the Portuguese, the first to reach China by sea. They
introduced it with the Cantonese name, *cha*. Dutch merchants of
the next century, however, were more successful in selling the chief

ingredient for the beverage, calling it by the name used in Amoy or Formosa, *te* or *thee*, altered by the English to *tea*.

tennis (racket, racquet)

The source of this game and of its name has long been conjectural. Until recent years the most prevalent theory was that the name *tennis* was derived from *tenez*, the imperative of the French *tenir*, to hold. The historical authority on various ball games, Robert W. Henderson, chief of the main reading room of the New York Public Library, did not agree with that theory. The game, in his opinion, was too old to have been known by a French name. He had reached the conclusion that both name and game were of Arabic origin. A letter from Mr. Henderson, which the author is privileged to use, supplies the material for the rest of this article.

The first to suggest an Arabic source was Lady Wentworth who, under the pen name "Antiquarius," in an article in *The Field*, November 10, 1927, wrote: "We find its origin in the Arabic word meaning to leap, and we get further Arabic variants in *t'nazza*, to strive against one for superiority or glory; and to twang string, *t'nazzi*, to make a thing bound, *tenziz*, in constant movement." (Lady Wentworth omitted the main Arabic word, *tanaz*, to leap, bound.)

"In 1932," Mr. Henderson writes, "I collaborated with the late Malcolm D. Whitman in a book *Tennis: Origins and Mysteries*. In previous research on the game of tennis I had learned of a fine fabric, *tissus de tennis*, which was manufactured at Tinnis, an island at the Nile Delta. Tinnis was famous for its fine fabrics, and also as a health resort. It sank into the sea sometime about the eleventh century. Because early tennis balls were sometimes made of rolled fabrics, I considered it possible that a ball made of fine linen, such as the *tissus de tennis*, might have been desired by the best players. Hence it may have given the name to the game. I wrote this up for the book, and Whitman accepted it. But long before publication, because of objections raised by Albert de Luze, tennis historian of Bordeaux, I abandoned the theory as untenable. Whitman, however, clung to it, and insisted that it go in the book."

Mr. Henderson publicly renounced his theory in the March, 1934, issue of *Squash Rackets and Fives*. But in the meantime Mr. Whitman had discussed the theory of light balls made from fabric of

Tinnis with a friend, Philip K. Hitti, professor of Arabic at Princeton University. Professor Hitti accepted the theory, and, perhaps unaware that its author had renounced it, offered it as the true source of the word *tennis* in the Second Edition of *Webster's New International Dictionary*. After the appearance of that dictionary in 1934, Mr. Henderson says that he wrote to Professor Hitti, "asking if he had any evidence that the Tinnis fabric had been used to make tennis balls, but he could produce none."

Mr. Henderson has supplied further historical information of general interest. He says that, far from the word *tennis* having been introduced by crusaders in various places in Europe, "only one early continental reference is known, that in the *Cronica di Firenze* of Donato Velluti, written 1367-70. The form used is *tenes*. The commonly stated derivation of *tennis*, that it comes from the French '*Tenez!*' a cry supposedly used by French players when ready to serve, started with John Minsheu's *Ductor in Linguas*, 1617. But there is absolutely no evidence that such a cry was ever used, in ancient or modern times. The game of tennis undoubtedly had its origin in ancient Egyptian-Arabic religious rites. (See Henderson's *Ball, Bat & Bishop*.) Several of the terms used are of Arabic origin. Racquet, for instance, is from *ruqat* or *raqat*, a patch of cloth tied around the palm of the hand, the earliest form of the racquet."

Mr. Henderson concludes: "The best conjecture to date is that *tennis* is derived from the Arabic *ṭanaz*, on the grounds that the game is from Egyptian-Arabic sources and that the earliest use of the word in English, *tenetz* (about the year 1400), approximated the sound of the Arabic word."

termagant

At a time when legends of the Saracens were popular subjects of poetry and drama in Europe—that is, after the Crusades of the eleventh and twelfth centuries—Mohammedan characters began to be added to some of the mystery plays. But so little did the writers of these plays know about the Mohammedan faith that some of the characters had to be invented. Thus they created two deities whom the Saracens were supposed to have worshiped. The names, Old French *Mahum* and *Tervagan*, may have been taken from the eleventh-century poem *Chanson de Roland*. The name *Mahum*, which became *Mahoun* or *Mahound* in English, is readily identified as *Mohammed*, thought by Christians to have been worshiped as a god. But the identity of *Tervagan*, in the French poem and French mysteries, is still undetermined. In English plays his name was variously written, *Tervagant*, *Termagaunt*, and *Termagant*. He was always represented as a boisterous, blustering swaggerer of outrageous violence and ferocity. In due course the name was thence transferred to any person, man or woman, of similar temperament, although it is now rarely applied to other than a brawling woman.

terminus, term

Numa, the second king of Rome, was traditionally believed to have decreed that every one of his subjects should mark the boundaries of his land by monuments consecrated to the god *Terminus*, and that fitting sacrifices should be made to the god annually. The monument was sometimes merely a post or a stone, garlanded upon the occasion of the annual festival, and with a rude altar, upon which were offered sacrifices of cake, meal, or fruit or, later, of lambs or pigs. Sometimes the monument was a statue of the god, by which he was represented as a human head, sometimes with a torso but without feet or arms, to intimate that he never moved from his place. The annual feast, or *Terminalia* as it was called, was on the 23rd of February. At that time the owners of adjacent lands met for offering their sacrifices. Through the passage of time the monument itself came to be regarded as the *terminus*, which thus acquired, even in Roman times, the meaning, an ending-place. It was contracted in Old French to *terme*, with similar meaning; the English form *term* has acquired various extended meanings.

thug

Among the religious fanatics of India there was one highly organized band which specialized in murder, murder in a particular manner—by strangling. The band is believed to have been wiped out now, because the British hung about four hundred of them in the 1830's and transported or imprisoned for life almost a thousand others. No one knows when the association originated nor how it came about, but it was in existence as far back as A.D. 1290. The correct name of the members was *p'hansigars*, stranglers, although they were more commonly known to the British as *Thugs*, a term of Sanskrit source meaning "cheaters" or "rascals." The Thugs believed that they were divinely delegated to strangle a selected victim and that the deed was wrought in honor of the goddess Kali, wife of Siva. The murder was therefore entirely a religious duty, unaccompanied by any remorse. The victims were invariably of the wealthy class, because plunder, both for the goddess and for the association, was the main object. Three or four selected Thugs might follow an appointed victim for many days or many miles before an opportunity presented itself to slip a noose about his neck. Through practiced skill the sacrifice was usually dead before he struck the ground. The assassins were also bound by their beliefs to bury their victims. For this reason, as well as to escape detection while committing the crime, an unfrequented spot was usually selected for the murder.

Thursday

In Norse mythology, as related in the Icelandic sagas, Thor was the most popular of all the gods. He was the son of Odin and Frigg (see WEDNESDAY and FRIDAY), and was represented as a man of middle age with red hair and beard, and of enormous strength. The chariot in which he rode was drawn by he-goats; the rolling of this chariot caused the thunder. Thor was armed with a terrible magic hammer, Mjölnir, the smasher, which he hurled at his foes and which then returned to his hand, for the gods were always at war with the forces of evil which sought constantly to destroy them. But Thor was the friend of man whom he aided, guarding him against evil spirits and disease. He was looked upon, especially, as the god of agriculture and was most widely worshiped for that reason. Accordingly, although Odin (or Woden) was the god most nearly the counterpart of the Roman Jove (or Jupiter), it was Thor who was selected from among the Norse and early English gods for honor by having his name replace the Roman *dies Jovis* (day of Jove) in naming the fifth day of the week. His name, among the early English, was sometimes given as *Thur* and sometimes as *Thunor*, so the Old English name of the day was sometimes written *Thursdæg* and sometimes *Thunresdæg*. The first was the one that survived, giving us *Thursday*. (See also SATURDAY.)

tinsel

Originally this was a much dressier word, the Old French *estincelle* —modern *étincelle*—and its meaning was also smarter. It denoted "brilliance; sparkle," and the name was applied to a cloth of silk or rich wool in which strands of gold or silver were woven. Such cloth made up into robes or gowns sparkled in the sunshine and attracted the notice of all eyes. And of course, those who could not afford such richness found ways to imitate it. In English speech, the Old French spelling became cropped to *tinsel*. Along with the loss in the elegance of the word, its meaning also lost refinement. Copper threads look not unlike gold; brass and tin spangles sewn upon cloth in plentiful profusion glitter even more brilliantly than gold and silver, and if these threads and spangles be attached to a gown of cheap net, the cost becomes trifling. Silk may be worn beneath. In such fashion, *tinsel* lost its elegance and came to denote cheap but brilliant finery, decorations, or other material showy in appearance but of little value.

toady

The makers of nostrums still loudly proclaim and advertise the remarkable curative powers of their remedies, sometimes claiming that they will cure anything from falling hair to ingrown toenails. The charlatans and quacks of the seventeenth century were no less modest. In fact, they went further. It was sincerely, though mistakenly, believed at that time that anyone so unfortunate as to eat a toad's leg instead of a frog's leg would surely die. Toads were thought to be deadly poison. Charlatans, taking advantage of that superstition, sometimes employed a helper who, under compulsion, would eat (or pretend to eat) a toad, whereupon his master would promptly demonstrate the remarkable properties of the remedy that he sold and, ostensibly, save the life of his helper. Such a helper became referred to as a *toad-eater*. And because anyone who would eat such a repulsive and dread creature would needs be wholly subject to his master, both *toad-eater* and its diminutive form, *toady*, became terms for one who fawns upon or is subservient to another.

Tory

The story of how this word of Irish origin—Englished to *tory* from Irish *toruidhe*, robber—became a political term was told in 1711 by Daniel Defoe in his journal, *The Review*. The events he mentions occurred during his own lifetime. Titus Oates, to whom he refers, had been trained for the Protestant ministry, but spent his time hatching up malicious plots aimed against the Catholics, which cost the lives of thirty-five innocent, but alleged conspirators. Defoe's account, in part, is as follows:

The word *tory* is Irish, and was first used in Ireland at the time of Queen Elizabeth's war, to signify a robber who preyed upon the country. In the Irish massacre (1641), you had them in great numbers, assisting in everything that was bloody and villainous: they were such as chose to butcher brothers and sisters, fathers, the dearest friends and nearest relations. In England, about 1680, a party of men appeared among us, who, though pretended Protestants, yet applied themselves to the ruin of their country. They began with ridiculing the popish plot, and encouraging the Papists to revive it. . . .

These men were those who, as falsely charged by Oates, were plotting the murder of the king, Charles II, in order to set upon the English throne his Catholic brother, James. Also included were all royalists who opposed any act of Parliament that would exclude James from accession to the throne. On account of someone saying, Defoe added, "that he had letters from Ireland, that there were some *tories* to be brought over hither to murder Oates and Bedloe (a colleague of Oates), the doctor (Oates) could never after this hear any man talk against the plot or witnesses but he thought he was one of these *tories*, and called almost every one a *tory* that opposed him in discourse; till at last the word *tory* became popular. . . ." The term as applied to a political faction thus came to include, at first, all the considerable number of men, including many Protestant churchmen, who favored the legitimate right of James, the duke of York, to succeed to the crown. The name came to stand for any adherent to constituted authority of Church and State, and thus eventually superseded the former designations, "Royalist" and "Cavalier," of a political party. The name was dropped about 1830 in favor of "Conservative."

town

In many parts of Europe it is still unusual to find a farmer who lives upon his farm. Generally he lives in a nearby village and walks each day to his fields. The custom is a survival from olden times when, for the sake of mutual protection at night, men slept within call of others. Their group of houses in those days was surrounded by a tight hedge or fence through which no marauding wild animal could gain access. In Old England this hedge was known as *tun* (pronounced "toon"). Later, *tun* indicated any kind of enclosure, especially, a wall; and eventually it referred more specifically to the place enclosed by such a wall, a walled village. Thus a *town*, of early and Medieval England, was distinguished from a hamlet or a village by virtue of the wall that then surrounded it.

tragedy

Like comedy, the original intent of the Greeks in naming this type of play cannot be determined. It is derived from the two words *tragos*, goat, and *ōdē*, song, ode. Thus the Greek *tragodia* was apparently a "goat-song." The reason for the name has been variously conjectured. One thought is that the members of the introductory chorus were clad in goatskins, which may have been symbolical of the serious nature of the play, something like the masks worn by actors to indicate the age or nature of the character to be impersonated (see PERSON). Or the goatskins may have been in honor of *Dionysus*, god of wine, to represent the satyrs who followed him. Another thought is that a goat may have been sacrificed when the play was presented. And another that a goat was offered as a prize to the successful writer of a tragedy. The name for the performance was so old that even the later Greeks could not explain its source.

trapezium, trapezoid

When Euclid wrote his work on geometry, about 300 B.C., he used the word *trapezion*, "little table," as a name for any four-sided figure except the rectangle, rhombus, and rhomboid. The name was later Latinized to *trapezium*. Many centuries later, in the fifth century A.D., the geometer Proclus added certain refinements to Euclid's work which have since become part of the study of geometry. Proclus limited the meaning of *trapezium* to any four-sided figure which had two parallel sides, and introduced a new term, *trapezoeides*, "resembling a table" (our term *trapezoid*), to designate a four-sided figure having no two sides parallel. These remained the standard descriptions of the two names throughout Europe. But in 1795 an English mathematician, Charles Hutton, in his *Mathematical and Philosophical Dictionary*, got the two descriptions just reversed. Hutton's error, unfortunately, was subsequently adopted not only in his own writings, but by other British and American mathematicians. British usage has gradually returned to the original meanings indicated by Proclus, but the usage of the United States still follows that of Hutton.

travail, travel

The nature of the instrument of torture cannot be determined. Possibly it was employed by the Roman soldiery in outposts far from Rome at some period of the Dark Ages, because its name survives in all the Romance languages. It was the torment of the "three poles," or, in Latin, *trepalium*, from *tres*, three, and *palus*, pole. The French term for the verb, to be submitted to such torment, became *travailler*, and, perhaps when the form of torture had fallen into disuse, the sense of the verb became extended into those of harass, vex, weary; hence, to vex or tire oneself, to work hard, or, further, to be in labor. These were the meanings when the French *travailler* followed the Normans into England. In England, however, it acquired a further extended meaning. The notion of wearying oneself became akin to the wearying of oneself by journey. Thus the same term came to mean "to make a journey." All meanings passed through many forms of spelling before we separated them into *travail* and *travel*.

treacle

It used to be called *theriac* or *theriacle*; the Romans called it *theriaca*, and the Greeks knew it as *theriake*. But the substance and its purpose were then quite different from the *treacle* of today. The ancients were, rightly enough, extremely fearful of the bite of wild animals. Unaware of the causes of infection, they assumed that many more creatures were venomous than are now known to be. But from remote antiquity it was believed that every venomous animal carried within itself the antidote to the poison which it transmitted by its bite. Consequently, curative salves for the bite of vipers or other poisonous creatures were thought to contain no virtue unless the flesh of the vipers were employed in preparing the concoction. Such a salve the Greeks called *theriake*, which—from *ther*, a wild animal —meant an antidote against poison from an animal. Hence, though *treacle* was originally a salve, the charlatans of the sixteenth and seventeenth centuries, vying with one another, altered its nature to that of a medicinal compound, which they began to sweeten. Ultimately the sweetening agent itself, usually molasses, became known as *treacle*. The common sixteenth-century interpretation of *treacle* to mean a medicinal salve or lotion brought about one use that is now considered amusing. The word "balm," corrupted from "balsam," was not very well understood at that time. Hence, when translating the Latin Version of the Bible made by St. Jerome into English, the translators were at a loss for a satisfactory term to use in Jeremiah viii, 22, which now reads: "Is there no balm in Gilead; is there no physician there?" John Wyclif and others had used "rosin" or "gumme," but neither of these satisfied the group of bishops who, in 1568, brought out the so-called Bishops' Bible. In this, the word *treacle* was substituted, spelled by them *tryacle*, the passage then reading, "Is there no *tryacle* in Gilead?" For this reason the Bishops' Bible is now humorously referred to as the *Treacle Bible*.

tribulation

For threshing grain and cutting the straw the old-time Roman farmer used a heavy board to which, on the underside, were affixed sharp pieces of flint or iron. The driver added his weight or loaded the board with stones, and it was then dragged over the grain by oxen. The device was called *tribulum*. The Latin term *tribulatio*, accordingly, meant the act of separating grain from the husks by the aid of this crushing and cutting instrument. Some early Christian writer—probably the third-century writer, Tertullian, was the first —saw in this a metaphorical likeness to the kernel of spiritual faith which emerges from the harrowings of grief and hardship. Hence, he took this homely term, *tribulatio,* and applied it to human trials and afflictions. This gave us *tribulation* in its present sense.

trivial

Some of the customs of ancient Greece and Rome were undoubtedly very much like those of today. Among them was the custom of meeting and loafing at street corners in idle conversation. In fact, there was additional justification in olden times, because there was undoubtedly at the junction of the road a statue or other representation of either the god Hermes or the goddess Hecate, which one might worship. Such statues were exceedingly commonplace; so much so that Hecate was known as *Trioditis,* or, in Latin, *Trivia,* signifying "one who is worshiped where three roads meet." The latter term was from the Latin prefix *tri-,* three, and *via,* way. Statues of Hermes were even more numerous. It is not likely, however, that the statues of the gods were more than excuse. Nevertheless, through such meetings and gossip at the street corners, *trivia* came to signify things of little importance, things so commonplace as to be found or heard where three roads meet.

trophy

After a victorious battle it was a custom of the Greeks of early days to take from the field the arms of the enemy and hang them up on the stump of a tree in such manner as to imitate an armed man, the helmet on the top, breastplate about the stump, and shield, sword, and spear attached to branches left for the purpose. Such a monument was named *tropaion,* literally, "a turning point," for it signified the turning point of a battle, the place where the enemy had been put to flight. If the enemy permitted the monument to be erected, it was a confession of defeat. The Greek term became *tropæum* among the Romans, who followed a similar custom, but was later altered to *trophæum,* from which our term *trophy* is derived.

Tuesday

When the Teutonic peoples attempted to render the Latin name for the third day of the week, *dies Martis,* day of Mars, into a name that would honor one of their own gods, they chose *Tyr* as the one who most nearly resembled the warlike Mars. At one time Tyr was probably one of the foremost gods in Teutonic mythology, but little is known of this early prominence. In Norse mythology he appears as a son of Odin, and is the bravest of all the gods. The story is told that a wolf monster, Fenrir, threatened the destruction of all the gods. They sought to bind him, but he broke their chains easily until, on the third attempt, Tyr, who had befriended the creature, put his hand into the wolf's mouth as a pledge of good faith. The third chain was too strong for Fenrir to break, but in his struggles he bit off Tyr's hand. In a later battle among the gods, the one-handed Tyr was slain by Garm, a hound of hell, at the same moment that he killed the dog. Old English mythology gave this god the name *Tiu* or *Tiw*. The day which gave honor to him was *Tiwesdæg*, descending to us as Tuesday. (See also SATURDAY.)

turnpike (pike)

Comparatively few of our roads could now rightly be called turnpikes. The Merritt Parkway in Connecticut; the Skyline Drive in western Virginia; the Pennsylvania Turnpike stretching more than a hundred and fifty miles between Harrisburg and Pittsburgh, and a few other roads in the United States could properly be so termed, but the onetime great National Road, begun in 1835 and running from Maryland some eight hundred miles across Ohio and Indiana and into southern Illinois, although locally still called "turnpike," is one no longer. That is, a *turnpike* is really a road for the use of which a traveler pays a toll; actually a tollroad. But even so, our English ancestors four or five centuries past would have found it difficult to understand how *turnpike* could be construed to mean "road." To them it had a literal meaning; it denoted a series of pointed rods—pikes—so mounted about a beam as to prevent the passage of a foot traveler or mounted man across a bridge or along a path until the array of pikes was rotated or turned aside, a form of chevaux-de-frise. (Compare CHEVAUX-DE-FRISE.) It was probably similar to the mechanism that we now call "turnstile." In a later period, when communities or private persons began to maintain roads and bridges that would accommodate vehicles as well as horsemen and foot travelers, the devices were so placed, with keepers to operate them, as to compel a toll from travelers. Our ancestors properly called such a road a *turnpike road*, a name that con-

tinued when the original device was replaced by a gate or beam or
other barrier that could be opened only by the keeper. Roads and
bridges were maintained and improved through this revenue. The
descriptive term was too long; hence it was commonly shortened
to *turnpike*, to distinguish the improved road from others. In
common speech even this shortened form was then often further
abbreviated to *pike*, and both this and *turnpike* loosely applied to
any road, especially an improved road.

tweed

Sometime about the year 1830 a weaver in the south of Scotland
shipped a quantity of his woolen fabric to a London merchant. The
material was twilled and with a rough surface, but there was nothing
otherwise unusual about the shipment. The merchant who received
it is said to have been James Locke, although in a book by Locke,
Tweed & Don, published in 1860, he did not acknowledge the story
told by others. That story relates that, following the Scottish
custom, the word *twill* was written *tweel*, and the weaver had billed
the merchant for so many yards of *tweel*. Thanks either to careless
handwriting, however, or to a careless clerk, the word was read, not
tweel, but *tweed*. The assumption was, therefore, that the weaver,
who lived near the river Tweed, had used the name of the river as
a trade name for his product.

ultramarine (lapis lazuli)

The pigment that we know by this name was formerly obtained only
by extracting it from the mineral *lapis lazuli*, or "azure stone" (from
Latin *lapis*, stone, and Arabic *lazward*, azure). The pigment was
known in the eleventh century A.D., at least, and may have been used
at an even earlier date. It was then very costly, literally worth its
weight in gold, for only a small amount of pigment was obtainable
from the mineral and the mineral was itself imported, probably
from Persia. It was to the fact that the mineral came from a foreign
country that the pigment received the name *ultramarine*. That is,
for many years after importation was begun, it was simply referred
to by the Latin phrase, *azurrum ultramarinum*. The meaning is
"azure from over the sea." The English translation reduced it to
ultramarine, literally meaning, "over the sea."

urchin

When the Normans invaded England they brought with them their name for the hedgehog, an animal that we do not have in America but which is related to the porcupine. The Norman name was *herichon*, from the popular Latin name, *hericion*. English attempts to master the French name produced forms variously spelled *hurcheon*, *irchin*, and ultimately *urchin*. Popular superstition had it that these creatures were not always what they appeared, but sometimes disguised an elf or goblin who had assumed the form of the innocent animal for concealment. Thus it came about that a mischievous child, likened to an elf by his conduct, has had the name of the hedgehog, *urchin*, applied to him.

utopian

Sir Thomas More was a contemporary of Christopher Columbus and of Amerigo Vespucci and was well informed upon the discoveries of the former and the alleged discoveries of the latter. Accordingly, in a book published in 1516, he represents that the island which furnished the setting for his story was an actual western island, described to him in 1514 by its discoverer, a supposed companion of Vespucci. It was, he said, a place of ideal charm, but especially was inhabited by a people who had perfected an ideal social, political, and economic system. More called this wonderful but nonexistent island, *Utopia*, and Greek scholars had no difficulty in discerning it to mean "no place," from *ou*, not, and *topos*, place. His book, first published in Latin, achieved great popularity and was soon translated into the chief languages of Europe. The name of the fictitious island is now applied to any place where life appears to be ideal, and *utopian* now describes anything regarded as ideal but visionary.

valentine

Legend has it that there were two Christians, each named *Valentine*, and both of whom suffered martyrdom on the same day. The day was February 14, and the martyrdom is supposed to have occurred during the reign of Claudius II, or about A.D. 270. One was a bishop, the other a priest; both were subsequently canonized. The bishop is sometimes said to have been so exceptionally distinguished for love and charity that his friends inaugurated the custom of selecting his day, February 14, upon which to designate one's choice of a sweetheart. Another theory is that the custom was altered and put one day forward from an old practice in the ancient Italian observance of the Lupercalia (see FEBRUARY). This festival occurred on February 15, and it included among its ceremonies the custom of putting the names of young women into a box from which they were drawn out by the young men. Old customs were hard to stamp out after the advent of Christianity, and the priests of the early Church sometimes did no more than to transfer innocent pagan practices to a festival of Christian flavor. Thus the latter theory is probably correct; if so, connection of the customs with either Saint Valentine is accidental, and the practices of the day actually commemorate the Italian pagan festival, the Lupercalia.

vandal

In the fifth century A.D., a remarkable group of Teutonic tribes crossed the Rhine, descended southward through lands occupied by the Franks, fighting their way as they went, crossed the Pyrenees, lived for twenty years in Spain, and then, upon invitation from the Roman count of Africa, Boniface, crossed the Mediterranean into Africa. Eighty thousand persons were said to have made that crossing. The group, although including various tribes, was called *Vandals*. Their leader, at the time of the crossing, was Genseric, a man naturally endowed for war and dominion. In October, 439, he led his forces against Carthage, third largest of the cities of the Roman Empire and the last in Africa to fall before him, and made it thenceforth his own stronghold. In the year 455 he sailed across to Italy and took, without much difficulty, the city of Rome. This city he sacked completely, his ships loaded with plunder when he returned to Carthage. The son of Genseric, Hunneric, who succeeded him in 477, was noted for even greater rapacity than the father, but spent it chiefly in persecution of Christians, extorting from them by cruel torture and death all the treasures and sacred vessels of their Church. The remnants of the Teutonic tribes were finally subdued, captured, or scattered in A.D. 536, and the Vandals disappeared from history. Their name lives as a reminder of willful or ignorant destruction or mutilation of things beautiful, sacred, or historical.

vaudeville

In the early fifteenth century there lived in Normandy a notable fellow, a fuller by trade, who achieved local fame for his satirical, but rollicking drinking songs. His name was Olivier Basselin; his home in the valley of the Vire. The songs that Basselin composed took off the follies of the day and eventually attracted notice far outside his humble valley. *Chansons du Vau de Vire* (or *Vaux de Vire*, for there were two valleys) became popular all over France. Songs of similar nature, always with topical satiric verses and sometimes accompanied with country allusions or sayings, were composed by others and introduced into the music halls. Gradually the name of the valley was forgotten or was corrupted, so that *Vire* became *ville*, town. The change into *vaudeville* was fully effected by the eighteenth century.

vie (envy)

Originally it was a contraction of *envy*, formed by lopping off the first syllable. But *envy*, in the sense in which it was thus employed, was a gambling term in the sixteenth century, meaning to invite, to challenge; the contraction, *vie*, was the more popular word at the gaming table. One *vied* or made a *vie* by putting up a stake on the strength of a hand at cards. Hence, *vie*, meaning to contend or strive against another at cards, later embraced any kind of contest.

volume

Most of the written literature of ancient times was on continuous sheets of parchment or papyrus. For convenience these sheets were wound into fairly tight rolls about sticks, one stick at either end of the roll. In reading, the scroll was thus unwound from one stick and, as the reading proceeded, wound upon the other. The Latin term for the rolling of the scroll was *volvo*, to roll. For that reason the thing which was rolled was anciently known as *volumen*, a derivative of *volvo*. When books were no longer rolled into scrolls, *volume* continued to be used, especially for a book of considerable size. Further, from this notion of a book of considerable size, *volume* then acquired a second meaning, "any large quantity, any considerable amount."

Wednesday

Chief among the gods of the Scandinavian peoples was Odin. It was he, with the aid of his two brothers, who created the world out of chaos and who ruled the heaven and earth. His throne was in Valhalla. There, as the god of war, he received all those who were slain in battle, and there they fought and feasted according to the pleasures they had most enjoyed on earth. Odin was also the god of wisdom and learning, which he had obtained, at the sacrifice of one eye, by drinking from the fountain of Mirmir. His wife was Frigg, goddess of marriage. In the Icelandic sagas, from which most of our knowledge of Scandinavian and Teutonic mythology is derived, Odin is represented as an old man, whose greatest treasures were his spear, known as Gungner, which never failed to hit its mark, his eight-footed steed, Sleipnir, swift as the winds of heaven, and his broad ring of red gold, Draupnir, made in the form of a snake, from whose mouth, every ninth night, a similar ring was dropped. In the early mythology of England, the name of this god was Woden. In naming the days of the week after the Roman system, his name was substituted for the Roman *dies Mercurii* (day of Mercury) as the name of the fourth day. In Old English, accordingly, the name was *Wodensdæg* (day of Woden), which has gradually shifted to our present Wednesday. The pronunciation, "wenzday," is a survival from the fourteenth and fifteenth centuries when the word was variously spelled, *Wensday*, *Wenysday*, *Wonesday*, and *Wanysday*. (See also SATURDAY.)

Whig

All the Presbyterians of Scotland bound themselves by a covenant, in 1638, to resist all attempts to alter their form of worship and to maintain the Presbyterian doctrine as the sole religion of their country. This oath was taken because Charles I, king of England, was then employing every device to bring Scotland into the fold of the Church of England. Hence, it was not difficult to enlist the support of the Scots against him when the English Parliament finally rebelled against the king's autocratic rule. Charles was eventually taken prisoner in 1646. Many throughout England and Scotland, however, had opposed him only to secure better government, not to do harm to the person of their monarch. Hence, in 1648, when it appeared that the English captors under Cromwell might try and condemn the king for treason, a number of those loyal to the British throne and to the House of Stuart resumed arms in an attempt to rescue him. These Royalists included many Scotch Presbyterians, a large force of whom were led into England, under the Duke of Hamilton, in support of the king. There were other Scots, however, who were greatly incensed by this act. It seemed treachery to them, and they banded themselves into an opposing force. They called themselves *whiggamores*, a word of uncertain origin, and marched upon Edinburgh with the insistent demand that their own parliament stand firmly against the king. Cromwell suppressed the attempted rescue, and Charles I was tried and beheaded in 1649. But the term *Whig*, shortened from *whiggamore*, remained in the language in memory of those Scots who had risen up in wrath against the wealthy and powerful Royalists who would support a king whom they could not trust.

yacht

The original craft from which this vessel derived its name was not used for pleasure. Its early Teutonic name, *jaght*, indicates that it was intended as a hunter; its modern German descendant, *jagd*, is "a hunt." Thus, along the shores of the North Sea, the *jaght* of the sixteenth century was a speedy vessel which had undoubtedly been originally designed for piracy. In that and the following century, however, British seamen had learned that vessels of that type were also ideal for pleasure. More and more of them were designed for wealthy British patrons, especially for the royal family. But the spelling of the Teutonic word was as varied as the number of the craft built. That which probably most nearly represented, in English spelling, the sound of the foreign word was *yaught*. The form that finally became standard, *yacht*, probably represented the German pronunciation, even though the average British tongue has been content to call it "yaht."

Yankee

One of the great mysteries, for two hundred years, has been the source of this word. Some have thought that it came from the mispronunciation of the word "English" by the Indians of Massachusetts. Others, that its source was in the name of a Dutch captain whose name was Yanky. And still others, more reasonably, credited it to *Janke*, diminutive of the Dutch name, *Jan*, John. But in 1945, H. L. Mencken, that indefatigable delver in Americanisms, in his *The American Language: Supplement One*, presented some additional findings in substantiation of an earlier theory. His statement,* which he has authorized me to use, follows:

The etymology adopted in *The American Language, Fourth Edition*, to wit, that *Yankee* comes from *Jan* and *kees*, signifying *John Cheese*, is not approved by the DAE (*Dictionary of American English*), but it has the support of Dr. Henri Logeman of the University of Ghent, and it seems likely to stand. In its original form the term was *Jan Kaas*, and in that form it has been a nickname for a Hollander, in Flanders and Germany, for a great many years. In the days of the buccaneers the English sailors began to use it to designate a Dutch freebooter, and in this sense it became familiar in New York. Presently the New York Dutch, apparently seizing upon its opprobrious significance, began to apply it to the English settlers of Connecticut, who were regarded at the time as persons whose commercial enterprise ran far beyond their moral scruples. A little while later it came into general use in the colonies to designate a disliked neighbor to the northward, and there was a time when the Virginians applied it to the Marylanders. In the end the New Englanders saw in it a flattering tribute to their cunning, and so not only adopted it themselves, but converted it into an adjective signifying excellence. The DAE's first printed example of *Yankee*, then spelled *Yankey*, is dated 1683, at which time the term still meant a pirate, and was applied as a proper name to one of the Dutch commanders in the West Indies. By the middle of the Eighteenth Century it had come to mean a New Englander, and by the Revolutionary period the English were using it to designate any American. During the Civil War, as everyone knows, the Southerners used it, usually contemptuously, of all Northerners, and in consequence its widened meaning became restricted again, but in World War I it underwent another change, and since then, though they objected at first, even Southerners have got used to being called *Yankees*, *e.g.*, by the English.

* Reprinted from *The American Language: Supplement One*, by H. L. Mencken, by permission of Alfred A. Knopf, Inc. Copyright 1945 by Alfred A. Knopf, Inc.

INDEX

NOTE: Main entries are presented in alphabetical order throughout the preceding pages. This index is therefore concerned (a) with variant spellings, such as "hoiden, see under *hoyden*"; (b) with words of related origin treated under one entry, such as "bruin, see under *reynard*"; and (c) with persons or places connected with the stories that are told, such as "Rabelais, François, see under *gargantuan*," or "Milan, see under *milliner*." The page reference is an additional finding aid.